ANIMATE PLANET

ANIMA

ANIMATE PLANET

Making Visceral Sense of Living in a High-Tech Ecologically Damaged World

KATH WESTON

Duke University Press   Durham and London   2017

Printed in the United States of America on acid-free paper ∞
Designed by Courtney Leigh Baker
Typeset in Minion Pro by Tseng Information Systems, Inc.
Library of Congress Cataloging-in-Publication Data
Names: Weston, Kath, [date] author.
Title: Animate planet : making visceral sense of living in a high-tech,
ecologically damaged world / Kath Weston. Other titles: ANIMA
(Duke University Press)
Description: Durham : Duke University Press, 2016. | Series: ANIMA |
Includes bibliographical references and index.
Identifiers: LCCN 2016026991 (print)
LCCN 2016028136 (ebook)
ISBN 9780822362104 (hardcover : alk. paper)
ISBN 9780822362326 (pbk. : alk. paper)
ISBN 9780822373827 (e-book)
Subjects: LCSH: Human ecology. | Human geography. |
Climatic changes—Effect of human beings on.
Classification: LCC GF41.W475 2016 (print)
LCC GF41 (ebook)
DDC 304.2/8—dc23
LC record available at https://lccn.loc.gov/2016026991

COVER ART:
Michael Peck, *Untitled*, 2011. 198 cm × 198 cm, oil on linen. Courtesy of the artist.

CONTENTS

ACKNOWLEDGMENTS
Generosity and Nothing But

———

Appreciation and debt: these are the topics of many an acknowledgment. Appreciation, to be sure. Without it, misrecognition ensues, things break apart, and what then is the point? But rather than speak of debts incurred in the making of a book that works hard to avoid reducing a world of cottonwood saplings, RFID tags, bedtime stories, computer modeling, pilgrimages, moose hunts, nuclear ruins, and ever-shifting entanglements to the terms of finance, I dedicate a few pages here to interdependencies. Interdependencies rely on give-and-take, on call-and-respond-and-call-again. Listen carefully, and even if you never consult a footnote, you can hear legacies of conversations past and bids for reciprocity whistle through the passages. Interdependencies thrive on generosity. Without them, nothing happens. Certainly not the writing of a book.

Above all, I am grateful to Geeta Patel, my once and future inspiration, for the many delectable debates, references, meals, and critiques that have underwritten and overwritten this text. With experience I have come to wonder why spouses, especially when they serve as indispensable interlocutors, conventionally come last in acknowledgments, when it seems clearer and clearer that they should come first.

Ken Wissoker took a chance on a volume whose complexities seemed suspiciously unlikely to lend themselves to the marketing magic of an elevator speech. What a titan among editors you have become. Early in the writing process, Kavita Philip made room in an impossibly busy schedule to read a draft of what eventually morphed into the final chapter. At that crucial stage, I benefited from her comments and her encouragement in equal measure. Richard Handler gifted me the reprieve of Sunday afternoon football when the writing dragged on and pushed me in the direction of a "snappier" title. Colleagues in the Department of Anthropology at the University of Virginia amiably accepted my time away during the leaves necessary to accomplish the considerable research required by a book grounded in multiple case studies across three countries. The opportunity to work cooperatively and in interdisciplinary fashion with colleagues from the Climate Histories Network at Cambridge, and the "Food, Fuels and Forests" Program of Distinction at the University of Virginia, was invaluable. I am grateful to Deborah Lawrence for inviting me to participate in the latter. My thanks to Hugh Gusterson, Lisa Messeri, Rosalind Morris, and Andrew Palmer for comments that emerged from deep engagements with the arguments in different chapters. Thanks also go to two anonymous reviewers whose detailed suggestions I hope I have implemented in ways that materially improved the arguments as well as the manner of their exposition.

The concept for the book derived from the invitation to deliver a public lecture series called "The Intimacy of Resources" at the University of Cambridge in 2011–12, while serving as a Wyse Visiting Professor in the Division of Social Anthropology. My thanks to Henrietta Moore, Perveez Mody, and others who were instrumental in bringing me to Cambridge for a year of animated intellectual exchanges through a grant from the Leverhulme Trust. Linda Layne and Cindi Katz showed up with visiting appointments and provided just the sort of inquisitive companionship that spurs a project on.

During my time in the UK, Vick Ryder, Stacy Makishi, Max Carocci, Simona Piantieri, and Yael Navaro provided life support in every sense of the word. Salem Mekuria stopped by en route to Addis to remind me, as she always does, that it's all well and good to reason, but sometimes you just have to laugh. *Ad astra per aspera*, dear friends, no matter what beckons. I was also hosted in fine style by Janet Carsten and Jonathan Spencer in Social Anthropology at the University of Edinburgh, where they graciously engaged with a frightfully preliminary version of chapter 2; by Jeanette Edwards and Penny Harvey on several inspiring occasions at the University of Manchester; and by James Leach and Marysia Zalewski at the University of Aberdeen, who were game enough to stray from the topic of my designated talk to puzzle through some of the topics explored in these pages. I can't say enough about how this book has benefited from the intellectual curiosity that illuminated a series of conversations that same year with Barbara Bodenhorn, Janet Carsten, Sophie Day, Jeanette Edwards, Robert Foster, Sarah Franklin, Kriti Kapila, Cindi Katz, Nayanika Mathur, Henrietta Moore, David Sneath, and the inimitable Marilyn Strathern.

Throughout the research process, the giving/receiving moved in serendipitous directions. The John Simon Guggenheim Memorial Foundation provided the very definition of serendipitous support by granting me a Guggenheim Fellowship for an unrelated project, which in turn led me to the research in the history of science on embodied empiricism that became integral to chapter 4. Administrative staff at the Bhasin Group in New Delhi with no previous experience with a wandering anthropologist kindly provided admission passes to gain entry to the soft launch of the Grand Venice mall described in chapter 3. An invitation from Andrea Muehlebach and Nitzan Shoshan to contribute to the special issue on "Post-Fordist Affect" they were editing for *Anthropological Quarterly* galvanized the writing of "Political Ecologies of the Precarious," which reappears here in a substantively modified incarnation as chapter 5. Yasuhito Abe helped me track down the いってきます image in chapter 2, while Allison Alexy suggested a way to draw on the literature in medical anthropology for the same chapter. An International Studies Research Grant from the Center for International Studies at my home institution funded my way to an Asian studies conference in Tokyo that never happened, but it also located me in Tokyo during the earthquake/tsunami/nuclear meltdown at the heart of that same chapter. Satsuki Takahashi, my partner Geeta Patel, friends too many to name, and participants in the Reuters live blog set up to cover the disaster offered a lifeline of counsel and support while the earth continued to shudder through the nights, the wind threatened to shift, and it wasn't at all clear what would happen next. I'll never forget.

Invitations from colleagues at universities in varied places have allowed me to experiment with early versions of these chapters and to benefit enormously from listeners' feedback, including feedback from audiences of intellectual companions once-met. Venues for these presentations included the Reverberations: Violence across Time and Space conference held in Istanbul in 2015, sponsored by the European Research Council and the Division of Social Anthropology at Cambridge; the Critical Life of Information conference at Yale University in 2014; the 2014 Animal, Mineral, Vegetable preconference to the Forty-Third Annual Conference on South Asia in Madison, Wisconsin; the 2013 Science, Technology, and Society Symposium on Nuclear Power in Asia at the National University of Singapore; the 2013 STS Forum on the 2011 Fukushima/East Japan Disaster at the University of California at Berkeley; panels at the annual meetings of the American Anthropological Association in Chicago (2013) and Montreal (2011); and the Seminar in Experimental Critical Theory VII: Re-Wired: Asian/TechnoScience/Area Studies at the University of Hawaii at Manoa in 2011. Very special thanks to Itty Abraham, Atsushi Akera, Naisargi Dave, David Theo Goldberg, Inderpal Grewal, George Mentore, Yael Navaro, Neni Panourgiá, Kavita Philip, Priti Ramamurthy, Laura Wexler, and their associated departments and planning committees for making participation in these conferences possible. I also delivered papers based on draft sections of the book in 2015 during talks sponsored by the Department of Anthropology at the University of Chicago, the Department of Anthropology at Stanford University, the Department of Anthropology at George Washington University, and the Department of Anthropology and the Center for the Study of Women at the University of California at Los Angeles. Many thanks to Sean Brotherton, Shannon Lee Dawdy, Alex Dent, Paulla Ebron, Akhil Gupta, Rachel Lee, Sharika Thiranagama, Sylvia Yanagisako, and everyone involved in hosting these visits.

Yet these named interdependencies are only the most obvious and gratefully received, a paltry gesture toward acknowledgment. Without Raoul Peck and his prose-poem of a documentary, *Profit and Nothing But!*, this section of the book would have a different title. Without a childhood enlivened by a great-aunt like Elsie, the third chapter would have to open with a different vignette. Without the daily companionship of a "reading cat" like Paco, my restless attention might have been diverted elsewhere. Without what passes in the United States for health care and an income sufficient to support a varied diet, I might not have managed to think clearly enough to make certain connections. Without the Charlottesville T'ai Chi Center run by Hiromi Johnson—a teacher's teacher and maker of worlds—I might not have slowed down enough to make *any* connections. And while we're at it, here's to Henry Bessemer, Sir Alistair Pilkington, and their colleagues, who engineered across two centuries a succession of techniques to form molten glass into cylinders, floating ribbons, and large sheets that could be cut to order. By turning windows into an affordable mass-produced accessory, they gifted a view—with its promise of a beyond—to every room in which I've ever sat down to write. Without their clever interventions, I might be writing still.

INTRODUCTION

Animating Intimacies, Reanimating a World

———

The bedtime story that sings a fitful world to sleep while it hurtles toward ecological destruction goes something like this:

Long ago but not so far away, perhaps in the very place where you lay your head tonight, the creatures of the earth depended on one another, and they knew it. It was the Age of Intimacy, the Era of Connection, an Anthropocene in which Relation had not yet birthed Alienation, its shadowy twin. Even on the hunt—especially on the hunt—the people waited to see which animals might offer themselves, and made sure to handle those gifted bodies properly, with respect. Then came a mighty gale, scouring every field and glade and village in its path, until the winds of Capital had laid the old ways bare.

Some creatures took flight before the relentless advance of the market, finding solace on islands, seeking shelter in hollows, until eventually there was nowhere left to go. Their cousins, too weak to travel or fixed in place by the siren song of More, stayed behind and became something different from what they once were. Many looked down after the gale swept past to find themselves shackled—ankles, wrists, and minds—to desks, furrows, machines. Huddled in shiny new towers, they raised their hands to the sky waiting for the plans or the planes that would seed the clouds with jobs and water the earth with wondrous playthings to light up the nights.

Chained or unchained, chained and unchained, the lords and lieges of Capital had something in common. What the lieges shared with the lords was this: They had come to live a life once, twice, thrice removed from all that sustains it. They piled their glass castles high with plunder or whatever ambitions they could afford, until the castles became so heavy that the turtles upon turtles upon whom the land rested could no longer come up for air.

Everyone knew better than to inquire too deeply into the matter of where the jobs and packages came from, or why during the lean years known as Re-

cession the deliveries stopped. Oh, they asked why, all right, but they stopped expecting answers that would make a difference. When occasionally they visited their plant relatives in the forests that had not yet been turned into charcoal, or their animal relatives near rivers whose sand had not yet fed the cement mixers, they forgot how to signal their approach. They forgot to bring gifts. Eventually they forgot they had forgotten.

Then one day something stirred on the mesas and whispered through the gullies laid bare by Capital. "Do you think there's something missing?" one brave (or was it foolhardy?) soul asked. She gathered comrades to venture out into what was left of the deserts and the tundra and the forests to ask the animals the same questions but found that her human companions could no longer understand the replies of the lizard or the bear. Where water trickled in streambeds below the dams, they thought they heard a lazy gurgling sound but couldn't decide if it was a message. In the sharp crack of ice cliffs tumbling to the sea they thought they heard something ominous, but the ice was on its way before their jerry-rigged prayers could reach it.

So they set about reconstructing, as best they could, what they suspected might once have been. They built temples of commerce to new gods called Sustainability and Resilience (whom they imagined to be old), tried catching rainwater in barrels, rediscovered how their grandmothers had brightened winter days by turning jars crimson with tomatoes. They dusted off ancient technologies to see what they could learn about living "in harmony with Nature." They tasked their scholars with revealing the paths traveled by things, so that every link in that most binding of bonds, the commodity chain, could be laid out for inspection. When the faces of the farmers who had raised their coffee beans appeared on the packages dropped from planes, they felt a bit better, if not quite cured of their malaise. They had a vague sense that something more was required, which they called "Community," although the ways to build it seemed as mystifying as they were varied.

They knew something had to change, so they changed, constantly, too quickly and never enough. They thought they heard something coming, so they looked around and they waited. They prepared for the day when the waiting would end, but they never really prepared for the waiting. Eventually they grew tired, too tired to read a book, much less write one, about things they thought their ancestors had already mastered.

Then suddenly, a sign appeared. It was small at first, a tingling sensation that started in . . . what was that? A foot? One person started to roll over, then another, like sea otters diving back into the dream, but now someone was shouting, shouting, and that tingling sensation was getting harder to ignore . . .

This is modernity's story, not necessarily or always our own, dropped onto pillows in candy-colored foil-wrapped installments, two sustainable steps forward and three steps back, night after night another character lost. Passenger pigeons yesterday, the Kalimantan mango today, pandas tomorrow. Like any dreamwork, this one is a farrago, a mélange of reminders about the proper way to hunt recounted by elders in the pages of *Indian Country Today*, descriptions of New Guinea cargo cults from introductory anthropology textbooks, the uses of a fairy tale in the hands of a theorist like Michel Foucault, *Hindustan Times* exposés of riverbed dredging by the construction industry's "sand mafia," the shifting registers of billboards across three decades and four continents, Christian echoes of exile from any garden worthy of the name, the things my grandfather might have told me if silence had not already claimed him.[1] It is the sort of narrative that can only be pieced together at a time when the travelers who long to range across borders are forced to settle, while people who have just invested two month's wages in their first set of chrome and veneer furniture are chucked out onto the road. As such, and even so, it is a story to take with two lumps of salt.

If Apocalypse had a fifth rider, it would be Foreshadowing. Although the final chapter in modernity's tale has yet to be told, Foreshadowing (as a lead category in an updated morality play) has long insisted that the story's end must coincide with the End of the Planet, or with some respite that only an Age of Miracles can provide. Even though the dreamers think they know what is coming, the pathos these endings evoke keeps them coming back for more, lured not so much by the denouement as by the intermediary spectacle of What Comes Next. When last we tuned in, the new god Resilience had demanded that animacy and intimacy no longer be sacrificed to the old god Development, that humans reimmerse themselves in a world of connections they have yet to recover. Most excellent: a quest! While the earth continues along its trajectory of ecological destruction, this, at least, gives them something to do.

Like the best bedtime stories, modernity's tale directs the sleepy listener's attention to an elsewhere. If worldly intimacies with anyone and anything other than the human belong to some far-ago place before capitalism, before roads, before the advent of an "environment" in need of rescue, why would anyone look for them here? Likewise, if such worldly intimacies become possible only by overcoming a modernity whose distinctive demand is a perpetual progressive overcoming, surely the seekers will only find themselves transported, night after night, to endless vistas of deferral?[2]

Yet there are other stories that could be told—aren't there always?—about a world in which each ravaged ecosystem, each technological triumph, each bold new synthesis of Nature pulls creatures into new forms of connection, as compelling as any that shadowed futures past.[3] New animisms and new intimacies thread their way through these alternate stories, as humans come to terms with both the injury they daily inflict in the name of "advance" and the transformation of their very bodies through biotechnology, industrialized food production, and synthetic chemistry.

Older animisms, in the limited way that European anthropologists such as Edward Tylor (1871) understood them, prompted nineteenth-century debates about the status of cultural beliefs in trees with "souls" and twentieth-century controversies about studies that claimed flowers cry out when plucked on a decorative whim. The new animisms of the twenty-first century (dubbed "animacies" to mark the distinction) are less concerned with whether trees and rocks and cows are sentient or "like us" or even in need of our salvific ministrations (although they occasionally discuss all that as well). Instead they remake the world with the conviction that animacy renders trees and humans and rocks and cows inseparable, not only in the sense that each acts upon the others in ways that may or may not be deliberate but also in the sense that each takes up something lively from the others that contributes to its very form.

Synthetic hormones flow into cows into milk and back into humans, accomplishing life-altering work along the way. Plants need not be genetically modified to ingest more than water from polluted streams and pass it on when creatures turn them into food. Uranium extracted from rocks to power turbines yields hot radioactive particles that lung tissue can incorporate in the event of a nuclear meltdown. In this sense new animisms literally reconceive humans as the products of an "environment" that has itself taken shape through embodied human action, often in pursuit of profit.

These visions of an animated world are as remarkable for the conditions that have produced them as for their distinctive take on how bodies move through industrial and postindustrial landscapes. My purpose here is not to extend the arguments on one side or the other of recent debates on posthumanism, new materialities, or what anthropologists have dubbed "the ontological turn." As any beaver caught up in the more animated versions of these debates can tell you, the discussions have already grown somewhat long in the tooth. My interest, rather, lies in taking the twenty-first-century fascination with ecologically infused animacies and intimacies as a symptom—perhaps a sign—worthy of investigation in its own right.

New animisms may differ in their details, in their materialist versus epistemological emphases and so on, but collectively they represent an intimate, emergent, mutually constitutive vision of a world infused with life, down to the pavement caressed by our feet as we walk down the road and the exiled wildflowers finding a way back to the sun through crevices in the asphalt. What "life" in this extended sense means has, not surprisingly, become the subject of yet more debate.

Many recent accounts of animacy have focused on decentering the human, while others come closer to the approach I favor here, which studies animating and reanimating as an efflorescent, historically located process. But which parts of this process are conceptual, perceptual, or made in practice? What part, if any, is given or, for that matter, *a* given? Marilyn Strathern (2012) has suggested that we set aside the morally laden assumption that proper knowledge-making occurs prior to doing, to events, to action, long enough to reconsider what *actualization* might entail, particularly when it comes to emplacement of a world as we (or you, or they) know it. Even the conundrum of actualizing the virtual appears different then: "For isn't the body—or the part we call mind—always on the edge of description?" (Strathern 2012:404). This is not the world fully formed, springing from the hands or head of a god (not even the secular pantheon of science, society, and modernity). This is not the kind of lifeworld that dutifully offers up a holistic cosmology to the anthropologist. Instead, the pressing matter of what evokes embodied worlds on the edge of description, and how, becomes the very thing.

Animate Planet presents five case studies of the animacies and intimacies involved in particular reworlding projects that have emerged as people in rather different places have begun to wake up from the dream of modernity that opens these pages. Of course, they do not always manage it. Sometimes they stir, then drift off again. Occasionally they marshal enough clarity for lucid dreaming, knowing they are sleeping as they sleep, understanding themselves to be guests or prisoners or authors of the dreamwork, depending. What happens along the way, as they try to make sense of incongruities between modernity's vaunted technological prowess, its ecological harms, its claims on life, and its still glistening yet wavering promises? What sorts of visceral sensory engagements are embedded in these bids to *make* sense?

In the pages that follow I draw on ethnography, STS (science and technology studies), social critique, and political theory to flesh out the cases I take up. There is even a bit of memoir. Instead of quest narratives in which the hero sets out to regain a lost paradise of ecological balance and interspecies connection, readers will find themselves dropped into scenarios in which the characters have already arrived, living however they are living, in ways that matter for understanding their simultaneous attraction to and disillusionment with technology's siren song. And wherever the characters are living, Chicago or New Delhi or Tokyo, "the environment" is already there, not off in some faraway place that requires saving.

Although cultural theorist Lauren Berlant (2012) might not have been thinking about relentlessly rising greenhouse gas emissions when she described how the dissociative life can be lived in intimate relation to (and through) a world, her observation that this can be so is right on the mark for understanding the things that ecologically ail us. People do not leave their bodies behind when they feel detached, or even when mysterious manufacturing processes stand between them and the food in a box. For every moment in which urban dwellers confess to having no idea where their water comes from, there is another moment when they use their bodies to connect viscerally with whatever materials capitalism sells back to them in a bottle. And for every coal seam, aquifer, energy drink, and chicken nugget that late industrialism produces as alienated "resources" destined for consumption, there are people who have to engage—intimately, creatively, sometimes eagerly, sometimes reluctantly—with the land dispossession that new factories entail, the arsenic poisoning as borewells sink ever deeper, the sweet scent of the latest chemical concoctions, the unreliability of electrons dispatched on overstretched grids, the taste of hydroponically grown vegetables, the fish ladders that salmon disdain, the monsoons that fail to come, the monsoons that fall in a day, the advertisements for "green solutions," the too-familiar warnings about where such a world is headed. Technology mediates it all, in ways that the literature on intimacy and animacy has scarcely begun to explore.

"To call something a resource is to make certain claims about it," Elizabeth Emma Ferry and Mandana Limbert (2006:4) remind us: claims that are "imbued with affects of time, such as nostalgia, hope, dread, and spontaneity." The chapters in this book take up classic environmental resource categories—food, energy, climate, water—to search for intimacies embedded in them. There is the techno-intimacy threaded through North American surveillance regimes that tag and track animals destined for stir fries or sandwiches. There is the bio-intimacy spawned by the 2011 nuclear meltdowns in Japan, which ensured that radioactive isotopes would become part of the walking, crawling, and swimming creatures they encountered, as well as the trees and mountains culturally charged with protection.

There are corporeal intimacies that suffuse the highly politicized North American debate over climate change, in which some climate skeptics argue they should be able to sense these changes with their bodies if they are really happening. There are playful intimacies that water spectacles stage in the north Indian desert, where players may not know how the water gets there but capitalism throws up new possibilities for becoming viscerally acquainted with water nonetheless. There are the affective intimacies fostered by synthetic chemistry, whose sensuous qualities tempt even people who want to "heal the planet" to act in ways that seem at odds with their politics.

Why introduce a term like *intimacy*, already applied rather loosely by scholars, into a discussion of animation and political ecology? Why not simply use *closeness, proximity, entanglement, incorporation,* or *suffusion* instead?[4] For several reasons: First, because although any one of these terms might substitute for *intimacy* in any given instance, *intimacy* is capacious enough to carry all these meanings and more. It is this conjuncture of meanings and the way they play off one another, the slip-and-slide between the spatial contiguity of *proximity* and the permeability of *suffusion* that accounts for some of the appeal of a term like *intimacy* for our times. The particular range of meanings that the concept carries also serves as a reminder that situated modes of intimacy do not automatically lead to empathy or identification. As Veena Das (1995:3) has pointed out with regard to knowledge production in anthropology, the "intimacy and experience" of immersive fieldwork can equally well produce the kind of alterity that transforms acquaintances into exotic Others. Last but not least, the generative imprecision of a term like *intimacy* allows interesting and fruitful things to happen when analysts extend that concept into arenas that have no well-worn historical associations with it.

When most people think about intimacy, ecology is not the first thing that comes to mind. Intimacy dwells in the realms of family, friendship, sexuality, and romance—or so the latest scholarship and the latest cinema releases, from Hollywood to Bollywood, tell us.[5] Those established kingdoms for intimacy, staked out through world-traveling calls for modernization, constitute, by and large, a human preserve, with occasional exceptions made for pets or other creatures granted companion status by those self-same humans.

In this book I use the cultural category *intimacy* not as some universal free-floating descriptor, not as an ontological claim, but as a heuristic that can be helpful for getting at some of the ways in which people try to make creative sense of tensions between all that technology promises and the way they keep looking over their shoulders at an ecological deterioration, if not devastation, that seems to be gaining ground. My focus throughout is on scenarios in which people (but not always only people) throw their bodies into the mix by *viscerally* engaging with a socially manufactured, recursively constituted "environment" that is also, crucially, them. For Gimi villagers in Papua New Guinea, people and the forest have been one as long as the elders can remember, with the life force (*kore*) of humans who die returning to and animating the wildness (*kore*) of the forest (West 2006: 80). But even heirs to the Euro-American conception of a Nature held at arm's length and reserved for aesthetic contemplation are having trouble maintaining their distance, as they imagine polluted rivers infiltrating their bodies and call upon those same bodies to register changes in abstractions like climate.[6]

Industrial capitalism still packages trees, oceans, air, uranium into "resources" that it relegates to a sector called Nature, located at a remove where it waits for humans to utilize, exploit, manage, destroy, or even sustain it (see N. Smith 1990). This way of apprehending the world is evident, for instance, in the parlance of international mining corporations, which transforms topsoil, rock, and their associated ecosystems into "overburden" notable only for its part in obstructing machine access to underlying minerals. After World War II a flurry of projects initiated under the sign of development melded notions of progress via modernization to narratives about a Nature that would supply the necessary matériel for capitalist expansion (Sachs 1999). Awareness about environmental harms inflicted in the name of development might have grown since, but the basic stance of separation from a world of insensate resources forever bonded into human service persists (Sullivan 2009). When today's conservation initiatives portray Nature as a provider of essential ecological services (water filtration, landslide prevention, and the like), they traffic in what Jim Igoe (2013: 38) has called "eco-functional nature," a way of approaching the world "as though it can be calibrated to optimize ecosystem health and economic growth" simultaneously. Calibrated by humans, that is: everything else is still consigned to its place as impassive matériel for a more enlightened, less ecologically damaging form of growth. But it was not, is not, always and everywhere thus.

As Tim Ingold (2000:243) points out, this neat division between humans and, well, everything else "bears the imprint of a certain way of imagining the human subject—namely, as a seat of awareness, bounded by the skin, and set over against the world." It is entirely possible to inhabit a world in which things work differently, as senior Cree hunters in Canada tried to explain to Fikret Berkes (2012:106), an ecologist, when he interviewed them. It was quite clear to them that animals, not people or high-powered rifles, controlled the success of a hunt. Bear, beaver, and elk would not offer themselves to someone who treated them disrespectfully or failed to distribute their meat in the proper manner. Where plants and animals are the ones who determine whether people will find them, rather than vice versa, human management of "the environment" becomes more than hubris: it is impossible.[7]

Resource management discourse replicates nature/culture dualism through the very act of divvying up the world into managers and managed, with the experts and activists who argue for environmental policy on one side, and the resources crying out for benevolent administration on the other. Philippe Descola (2013:32), whose writing, like Ingold's, has been part of a move in anthropology to decenter the human, puts it this way:

> Distinguishing among the objects of the world those that are a matter of human intentionality and those that stem from the universal laws of matter and of life is an ontological operation, a hypothesis and a choice with regard to the relations that beings maintain with one another as a result of the qualities which are ascribed to them. Neither physics, nor chemistry, nor biology can provide proof of this, and it is furthermore extremely rare that the practitioners of these sciences, in their everyday use, actually refer to the abstraction that is nature as their domain of investigation.

But for every elder and every scholar who recognizes this nature/culture divide for what it is—a somewhat strange, somewhat arbitrary, sociohistorically particular way of parsing the world—there is another who perpetuates that divide, sometimes unwittingly. Descola (2013:66), for one, contends that Ingold's ontological critique smuggles nature/culture back in through an inversion that elevates "the animism of archaic peoples" into the position of "the true objectification of reality" previously claimed by the Moderns, leaving the divide between the two firmly in place.

In the absence of any presupposed distinction between culture and nature—between humans and the watersheds they terraform as they drink to replenish the liquid that makes up most of what they are in any material sense—things look rather different. Intimacy then does not confine itself to set activities such as flirtation or fixed categories of relationship such as friendship. Intimacies emerge once animated in practice. Practice fosters the intimate sensory knowledge of plants acquired in the course of raising them, that intimate longing for manufactured products whose ingredients may be killing you, the visceral delights of close encounters with meals whose ingredients are becoming harder to find. Practice also occupies the gap between constituting something as a source and reconstituting (re-sourcing) it into a product (see Ferry and Limbert 2006:6). These days a capitalist economy dedicated to resource extraction and management con-figures life at the molecular level, intimately insinuating itself into the ar-chitecture of organisms through genetic manipulation, chemical synthesis, and the like. None of this can happen without bodies *and* technologies, working their alchemy.

If you attend carefully to the layout of this book, you will notice an attempt to begin to describe a range of ecological intimacies through which people have co-constituted a world in which their finest technologi-cal achievements are implicated in habitat destruction. These intimacies emerge not least from attempts to make sense of the pleasures and the suf-fering that late capitalism affords, in which they are viscerally implicated. So it is that the chapters speak of intimacies lost and intimacies unwanted, as well as empiricist intimacies, affective intimacies, and the topsy-turvy intimacies of the carnivalesque. This is not meant to be an exhaustive list but a suggestive one, composed with appreciation for how often the way we imagine things to be could just as easily be otherwise.

These days, organisms live in and through scientifically reconstituted ecosystems that include their own bodies, which are subject to constant technological amendment. We are not just talking about strontium from aboveground nuclear testing making its way into mammalian teeth, or the industrially modified mix of gases that now cycles through plant and ani-mal respiration. When it becomes possible to swallow a vitamin pill that "remembers" your online passwords and uses them to unlock accounts while it feeds your body vital nutrients, all bets as to where "nature" begins and "culture" ends are off (see Gates 2013). The resolutely corporeal crea-tures you will meet in the following pages assume the forms they do with a technological assist from power plants, engineered foods, water pumps, do-it-yourself Geiger counters, mass-produced combustion engines, even the humble radio frequency tags attached to the ear of a cow. In the chap-ter on the relationship of empiricism to climate change skepticism, bodies even double as scientific instruments, every taste bud a sensor, every skin fold a measuring device. In the process, technologies draw people into new forms of embodied intimacy with themselves and with others, with air in its feathered cloak of newly industrialized colors, with water that falls from the skies or evaporates from the fountains in a shopping mall, as the case may be.

But prepare yourselves: what follows are not bedtime stories, suitable for just any sort of dreaming. They are analytic stories, where the narratives that *look* like stories illustrate the text and the analytic passages tell a tale of their own. If the analytic passages, too, are the stuff of dreams, they are dreams meant to be spoken, passed from hand to hand, reworked, each one finding in them what they can. They are stories to wake up by, best encountered in the morning when the mind is fresh enough to see the sandy shorelines of the world in those gray blocks of apartments rising everywhere around you, glistening.

Swish, Crackle, Fizz

Although you can still hear strains of the old twentieth-century alienation song whenever modernity lulls a child to sleep, lately there are other sounds vying for attention, sounds that have something to do with the swish, crackle, fizz a boundary makes when it dissolves. It is, if you will, the sound of intimacy as it works upon a material world, though not perhaps intimacy as conventionally conceived. It is the sound of people trying to make visceral and political sense of the damaged ecologies that late capitalism has bequeathed them, in the shadow of the promise and the peril that high technology represents.

The ecological challenges of the twenty-first century do not turn on morality tales about the conquest of nature or exile from some self-contained paradise. They have more to do with the gritty, messy, often intricate, inevitably intimate matters of infiltration and interdependence. What might making visceral sense of a less boundary-inflected world look like, feel like, in the course of a day? Perhaps something like this:

- The cancer that was once someone else's malady has now become yours, or not yours exactly, but you, or as much you as any other cells in those skeins of tissue that come together as a body. There is no history of cancer in the family, so you wonder: Could it be pesticide residues in your food? Something in the carpet they laid down at work that you breathed in, tens of thousands of times per day? A rather less satisfying explanation called randomness? Kismet with a materials technology twist?

- You come across an article in which Marijn Dekkers, CEO of the drug maker Bayer, extols the virtues of the fully industrialized body that renders manufactured goods and cellular "machinery" indistinguishable. "Once we move on with material science," he explains, "every product we make ends up in the cell of a living species and regulates their processes" (Vasagar 2014:17).
- The you who sips morning chai while reading that article in a Tier II city in India puts on yesterday's sweaty clothes, gingerly. And why are they still sweaty? Because the municipal authority never sent water through the pipes yesterday, and when some finally arrived today, it was too oily for washing laundry. But the water came!
- By afternoon this same you, or perhaps it is another, discovers that your eco-minded boss at corporate headquarters in North America has not been able to sleep since his hybrid-powered car hit one of the deer that seem to be everywhere on the roads. He understands that when humans banished top predators like the wolves from eastern forests, deer populations exploded. He knows that the shrubs and forbs deer love to eat are getting harder to find in the forest. It is just that the eyes of that tawny doe keep trying to meet his, whenever his mind wanders.
- Come dusk you skim a hard copy of the day's news by solar lantern, your evenings miraculously extended once the kerosene runs out. Unpaid utility bills or a desire to live off the grid, in this respect it does not matter: The sunlight is free and makes you feel rather virtuous. Yet the plastic in the lantern's base, and the photovoltaic technology that lights up its diminutive panel, come at a cost. That you know, because you read a lot, and when you first found out, your eyes stung. Mine tailings, oil wells, plastic pellets clogging the innards of sea birds who mistake them for fish eggs, nights without electricity: it seems impossible to "go back."
- As you read, you watch the journalist watch a young man in Alaska hunt his first moose. No romantic about-face there: the setting is a suicide prevention camp for Native American teenagers. When the moose charges one of the organizers, the young man fires his rifle. Killing becomes inseparable from taking care of the animal, as the hunter pours water from his mouth into the mouth of the moose. When the animal breathes

his last, "the young man felt it go through him. It was a blessing" (Woodard 2013:34).

Swish, crackle, fizz. As nation-states took measures to fortify their borders with walls, fences, and capital controls at the turn of the twenty-first century, social theorists increasingly marked the ways in which boundaries between received categories would not hold. Gloria Anzaldúa (2012) directed attention away from the fences and the walls toward the borderlands on either side, divided by fiat but united by history and culture. Homi Bhabha, Paul Gilroy, Stuart Hall, and Françoise Lionnet displaced oversimplified assumptions about group membership with inquiries into the hybrid affiliations and complex allegiances forged in the long shadow of colonialism and the slave trade (see Prabhu 2007). Donna Haraway (1991) and Lucy Suchman (2006) reframed debates about human–machine interaction, which had previously taken the distinction between the two for granted, using the figure of a cyborg who melded them into a single form.[8] In the wake of decades of such interventions, from Bruno Latour (1988, 2010) to and through Philippe Descola (2013), the old "nature versus culture" dualism in which structuralism trafficked gave way, transformed in some quarters into a "natureculture" that echoed Einstein's amalgamation of Kantian categories of space and time into "spacetime."

In the growing field of political ecology, conceptual and material boundaries also seemed more permeable than before, for reasons that exceeded the preoccupations of theorists. Fieldwork-based studies such as Arun Agrawal's (2005) *Environmentality* and Paige West's *Conservation Is Our Government Now* (2006) explored how politically and culturally negotiated conceptions of "nature" and "development" make a difference for what happens to land and livelihood. Analysts stopped positioning technologies over or against landscapes. Harris Solomon (2016), an anthropologist with a focus on biomedicine, introduced the concepts of "absorption" and "metabolic living" in order to grasp how people in Mumbai associated the rise of diabetes and obesity with bodily infusions of substances from the city where they lived: everything from "stress" to packaged snacks. As glass-fronted shopping districts crept from town to town, circling the planet like some carbon dioxide–enhanced jungle vine, "nature" had become inseparable from its cultivation, synthesis, and reincarnation in the form of commodities, available for those with resources of a rather different sort to buy.

Before you could say "save the rain forest," it seemed you did not have to have a day job as a scholar to question the relevance of a host of entrenched dualisms: not only nature/culture, but also derivatives such as technology/nature, animal/human, and human/ecology. With no place untouched by human in(ter)vention, and with ecologies ever more broadly conceived to incorporate the industrial byproducts on which they now feed, anyone could see that such cut-and-dried oppositions obscured as much as they revealed. Everywhere they looked, it seemed that someone was attempting to bridge, integrate, or at least tack between bits of a world once imagined to be marooned on one or another side of an ecological divide.

As one might suspect, this conceptual reorientation entailed much more than the way people thought about the world, which is to say, the organization of knowledge. To illustrate the far-ranging implications, consider just three examples of the visceral shift toward a more intimate engagement with all that surrounds us and all that *is* us, as the lines between technology, bodies, and their surroundings smudged. The first comes from the rise of the environmental justice movement in North America, the second from developments in bioscience, and the third from an Indian eco-magazine for children.

The environmental justice movement emerged in the 1980s from predominantly African American and Latino/a communities in metropolitan areas of the United States. Under its banner, grassroots organizations worked to raise awareness about the inequitable ways in which ecological damage is distributed. People who had never thought of themselves as environmentalists began to mobilize against the targeting of poorer neighborhoods—*their* neighborhoods—for projects such as chemical factories and trash incinerators. To these newly minted activists, racism and classism seemed obviously, achingly central to understanding ecological harm. They launched their own studies to demonstrate how asthma rates skyrocketed in the vicinity of bus depots, which never seemed to be located where wealthier people lived. They started growing vegetables in abandoned lots as a creative response to "food deserts" that made it impossible to get the ingredients for healthy meals in neighborhoods where retailers refused to invest. A push for conservation might serve the needs of well-off white families who took their vacations in the national parks, since they were less likely to experience environmental violence at home, but for activists in the environmental justice movement, environmentalism had to hook up with a much broader struggle for social equality. Their rallying cry of justice, carried forward from the civil rights movement, targeted power differentials, not simply conservation or protection as such (see Bullard 2005; Corburn 2005; Nayak 2009; Steady 2009; Stein 2004).

One of the consequences of introducing justice into an already established environmentalist discourse was to foster a new and deep-seated conviction that "the environment" is located wherever you live, not in some unlogged remnant of a far-off nature preserve—brownfields, special export zones, and skyscrapers included. After critiquing the "sadistic admiration" embedded in an environmentalism that places Nature on a pedestal, the philosopher Timothy Morton (2007) argued for an "ecology without nature." Environmental justice advocates addressed the same problem by calling for more expansive, inclusive notions of "nature" and "environment." In his essay "Healing Ecology," David Loy, a Buddhist scholar and activist, offers an insight into one of the principal ways in which the environmental justice movement broke with the back-to-the-land movement of the 1960s, when middle-class white youth attempted to build low-cost ecologically viable lives in the North American countryside. "The solution does not lie in 'returning to nature,'" Loy (2010:262) writes. "We cannot return to nature, because we have never left it." While offering diametrically opposed prescriptions for what should become of "nature," Morton and Loy met on the common ground of intimate engagement: no elsewhere, no divide.

As one century gave way to another, that swish, crackle, fizz sound could also be heard emanating from the bodies that roamed through these high-tech ecologically pressured landscapes, if you knew how to listen. It was no longer just ecologists like Paul Shepard (1996:72) who urged humans to come to terms with themselves as "edge animals," lest, "by disdaining the beast in us, we grow away from the world instead of into it." The isolated, armored body described by Emily Martin (1995) in her review of an earlier generation of medical textbooks had begun to disappear. Once biomedicine recognized the important part that viruses and bacteria played in keeping bodies healthy, it no longer seemed to make sense to stage an all-out war against "germs." Doctors advised parents to protect their children from allergies by letting them play in the dirt, instead of treating all microorganisms as potential invaders from a dangerous exterior world that must be kept at bay. Popular articles featured headlines such as "Our Germs, Ourselves" (Herper 2009), "Microbes Maketh Man" (2012), and "Some of My Best Friends Are Germs" (Pollan 2013).[9] In the latter essay Michael Pollan (2013) explains how he "began to think of myself in the first-person plural—as a superorganism, that is, rather than a plain old individual human being." Humans acquired a "microbiome" and a "virome" made up of tiny creatures that turned out to influence everything from immunity to metabolism. The science and technology editors at the *Economist* encouraged readers to "think of the microbiome . . . as an additional human organ, albeit a rather peculiar one."[10] As Elizabeth Pennisi (2010:1619) noted in a review published in the journal *Science*, although these "intimately intertwined" denizens of the body had been there all along, "the ideas of a microbiome and a virome didn't even exist a decade ago."[11]

Like most emergent phenomena, this one did not sweep away everything that had gone before. The old melodrama that treated germs as villains persisted in the adversarial language of "friendly" and "unfriendly" bacteria, which pits bacteria that help keep organisms running smoothly against bacteria that tend to make humans sick. The legacies of imperial politics lived on in accounts that portrayed microorganisms as "colonizing" the gut. A tattered nature/culture divide resurfaced in the notion that eating, as Pollan (2006:11) puts it, "turns nature into culture, transforming the body of the world into our bodies and minds." There is a meaningful difference between a microbiome conceived as some contained diversity *inside us* and a microbiome made up of bacteria that are *as much us* as lymph or blood cells or a stomach, so integral to gene transport and digestion that we need them to live. Be that as it may, both views describe a "without within," a bodily "ecosystem" where old separations no longer obtain and the skin no longer functions as a purely defensive boundary. In both versions, intimacy edges over into animacy: people are not just *in* the world, but *of* it.

The world: that would be the place where, when the big organism called a human opens its mouth, the microorganisms in residence eat from the same pot. The world: that would also be the place where ecological injustice prevails, where the happy commensality in which microphages and "their" humans dine together coexists with diminished lifespan for those whose diet lacks vital nutrients or whose water comes from polluted aquifers. Only an analysis that links knowledge production to power can explain how people make visceral sense of scenarios that sanitized terms like *chronic exposure* and *ecological disaster* cannot possibly begin to cover.

When a British Petroleum (BP) well blew out in the Gulf of Mexico in April 2010, creating one of the worst oil spills in history, Gary Smith (2010) set out to interview some of the area's boat pilots, rig workers, restaurant operators, fisherfolk, realtors, even monks at a Buddhist temple. The aftermath of the Deepwater Horizon spill had affected each of them profoundly. Smith found that the way they expressed their distress linked economic survival to both the loss of everyday pleasures and what was happening to their bodies:

People from every part of the earth had been carried here by the world's loop current: Cajuns, Croats, Cambodians, Canary Islanders, Cubans, Serbs, Africans, Vietnamese, Native Americans, Filipinos, Greeks, Italians, Germans, and Lebanese. They couldn't watch TV anymore, they said. The marsh was their workplace, their playground, their grocery store. *They smelled oil at night, they said, and couldn't sleep, wondering how they'd pay off the big loans they'd taken to rebuild after Hurricane Katrina. . . . They sensed the oil had begun seeping inside them.*" (G. Smith 2010:70, my emphasis)

The kind of damage that the Deepwater Horizon survivors literally embodied lent a sensory dimension to protests outside BP offices, demands for corporate responsibility and compensation, as well as the ongoing struggle to consider what might be at stake before laying a pipeline or drilling a well. If, as Kim Fortun (2012) has argued, ecological disasters are only going to become more common due to aging infrastructure and profit-driven constraints, then it becomes that much more important to understand how visceral entanglements with the "resources" that guarantee loans, health, and breath will play into what lies around the corner.

Given an outside that is always already inside (inside bodies, that is), it becomes possible to link visceral apprehension to "nature's" synthesis, in everyday as well as corporatized forms. There is not a reader of this book who does not rely on synthetic chemistry, which inhabits the ink that renders these words fleetingly indelible, the glue that holds the pages together, and (in the case of a digital edition) the transistors and diodes that render the products of algorithms accessible to the eye. For better or worse—for better *and* worse—synthetic chemistry has altered the very composition of the earth. Those "friendly germs" that medicine now seeks to understand, the toxic ecologies that investigators now look for in human bodies as well as contaminated ponds, derive their characteristics in part from industrialized processes. It takes political economy as well as political ecology to explain why the microbiome of someone whose staple diet relies on fast food restaurants in one of Phoenix's food deserts will vary in some not so salutary ways from the microbiome of someone who eats regularly from a rooftop garden in Caracas.

Synthesis of the material world involves more than the stuff cooked up by food processors and materials scientists in laboratories. It includes, of course, attempts to reverse-engineer plants into "essences" that allow manufacturers to serve up methylated theophyline (manufactured caffeine) in lieu of more expensive coffee beans. But a certain synthesis of the material world also occurs whenever human labor is involved. What begins as a *daikon* (white radish) seed becomes food not just because it grows into a root vegetable that stores well, adds a bit of zest to a meal, and helps a farmer aerate a field by pushing its way deep into the soil. That seed becomes synthesized into food only in the course of activities such as planting, cooking, sharing, and harvesting.

It may sound obvious, but a focus on the transformative power of labor underscores the extent to which eco-intimacies involve what people do as well as how they think about what they do. Feminist environmentalism has long emphasized how divisions of labor can give people who perform certain sorts of tasks a more intimate knowledge than others of the resources with which they work (see Agarwal 1992). Water is the classic example. Where women (and children) spend hours every day securing water for their households, they are likely to know more about its quality, where to find it, the timing of its comings and goings (by the season or at fitful municipal taps), and how to negotiate the claims that neighbors make upon it. If a man who has not lugged water home since he was eight years old speaks in the local river parliament about how to "manage" upstream/downstream disputes, his recommendations might be expected to differ from those of his female colleagues. That is, unless those colleagues are themselves wealthy enough to employ someone else to fetch water, in which case being women without performing "women's work" would afford them no special insight into the condition of the river at all.

The intimacies embedded in any attempt to work a change upon the material world are as integral to ecological restoration projects as they are to running a household, protesting a waste incinerator, or living in an environmental "sacrifice zone." And so we come to our third illustration of the eco-intimacies that have emerged as boundaries drawn in an earlier age waver and diffuse (if not thoroughly dissolve). This one comes from a magazine aimed at primary school students in India called *Gobar Times*. Each issue contains a sidebar framed with the question that may be preoccupying you right now: "Why *Gobar Times*?" In northern India, even city kids enrolled in English medium schools know that *gobar* means cow dung. What is not so clear is why a word for the stuff that emanates from the business end of a cow should grace the cover of the country's leading eco-publication for kids.

"So why such a 'yuck' and 'tacky' name when we could have a more cool or sophisticated one? Well, because it captures our eco-philosophy and tradition of generating wealth from waste. How? Because the apparently waste gobar serves as an anti-bug and water-proof coat for walls, an energy source for non-LPG India, and a natural manure for farmers' crops" ("Why *Gobar Times?*" 2013:61). Like the humble daikon seed, gobar is what you make it, and what you make *of* it.

Gobar can mean cow dung molded into patties, sticking first to the hands, then to the sides of buildings where people leave them to dry in the sun. Gobar means grasses, bits of Styrofoam, old *chapatis* traveling through the innards of a cow until the unused bits of that particular "outside within" emerge in a bid for a new life as stucco or fertilizer. But that new life can ensue only when hands are willing to touch it, when minds see something of benefit to life rather than a nasty mess to step over in the road. The conceptual and practical transformations go together.

Swish, crackle, fizz: There went the parceling of the world into resources that drop from the sky into the hands of those who can pay. There went the reification of "the environment" into a damsel in distress who exists out there somewhere, immobilized, waiting for rescuers to appear. As the lines between nature and culture, habitats and organisms, power and knowledge dissolved, scholarship on new materialisms emerged that treated plants, water, even plastics as agents or actants in their own right. These new materialisms, however controversial, had much to say to people who were trying to make sense of how their bodies kept changing in tandem with the "environmental conditions" produced by a high-octane brew of capitalist finance and new technologies. How were they to live in a world that seemed newly invigorated, if not enchanted, through some of the very processes that had damaged it? But first, a word about the structure of this book.

The Varieties of Eco-Intimacy

The chapters that follow present more than a series of essays that thematically link ecology to the topics of intimacy and animacy, although they do that as well. Certainly each chapter can stand on its own. Read in sequence, however, they invite readers to join a *yatra*, a pilgrimage that may double as a protest march of sorts, through some of the questions that people in otherwise culturally disparate places are asking as they notice the harm that many projects undertaken in the name of modernization have inflicted on the ecosystems that sustain them. Should they "look back" toward older, healthier ways of growing food, or "forward" to technologically innovative means of coming up with the nutrients that animals need to thrive? Can people "get along" with radioactive cesium in the aftermath of a nuclear meltdown? Should they even try? Does hostility to science really undergird the skepticism that has provided political cover for those who wish to block climate change treaties? Is there more to water politics than disputes over distribution, supply, and demand? Might there be better ways to pose these questions after taking eco-intimacies into account?

Each chapter departs from the premise that intimacies must be animated and so may emerge anywhere under the right conditions, rather than springing forth in pregiven sites such as marriage that may be culturally designated as "intimate relationships." The animating factors in a town filled with refugees from a massive hydro project are likely to differ from the animating factors in a village where second-generation bonded laborers fire bricks in a kiln or in a village engulfed by an expanding metropolis. What forms those differences take is the kind of empirical question that ethnography excels at addressing. The case studies taken up here draw their ethnographic and archival material from three countries—the United States, Japan, and India—with rather different histories when it comes to technological modernization drives and their associated ecological impacts.

Chapter 1, "Surveillance in the Food Chain," examines the deployment of surveillance technologies during the attempt to establish a National Animal Identification System in the United States. The use of electronic devices to tag and track millions of animals bred for human consumption has come to symbolize the loss of an intimacy that ostensibly once prevailed between animals and the farmers who raised them during an earlier, less mechanized era of food production. In the United States, people often contrast face-to-face animal–human relations on small farms with the alienated relations they attribute to the "modern" bureaucratic oversight that prevails on factory farms. Yet even the most high-tech surveillance schemes can generate their own forms of intimacy: techno-intimacies that produce "close" knowledge of animals from a technologically mediated distance.

Rather than trying to get reacquainted with the food we eat by settling for high-tech traceback schemes and/or searching for connection on the artisanal side of a premodern/modern divide, this chapter argues that there are compelling reasons to foster more intimate engagements with the *conditions* of food production, regardless of the abstracted or face-to-face relations involved. For it is the conditions under which animals mature that have the most to say about the increasingly industrialized, often impover-

ished fabrication of their bodies, not the intimacies generated through surveillance or even some nodding acquaintance with a harried farmer.

Chapter 2, "The Unwanted Intimacy of Radiation Exposure in Japan," reminds readers that not all forms of intimate entanglements with "resources"
are desirable, or desired. Even people who aspire to own the latest electronic gadgets are not so enamored of unregulated exposure to the radioactive isotopes that help the world meet its energy needs. After the March
2011 earthquake/tsunami led to triple meltdowns at the Fukushima Daiichi
nuclear plant, many Japanese residents who found official government data
unreliable decided to take their own radiation measurements. Because the
body's senses cannot detect radiation directly, they had to *seize the means
of perception* by acquiring equipment such as Geiger counters and dosimeters. In order to make meaningful use of the equipment, they then began to
familiarize themselves with aspects of nuclear science, including processes
of radioactive decay and various configurations of nuclear technology.
Some used crowdsourced maps of radioactive hot spots and other digital
technologies to disseminate the results of their studies. Citizen science–
based initiatives like these can be considered a form of *technostruggle* in
which ordinary people avail themselves of technology to produce knowledge about their visceral engagements with potentially lethal derivatives of
the "resources" upon which they rely. Technostruggle can foster a politics
of popular sovereignty when used to challenge government and corporate
reassurances about safety. Alternatively, technostruggle can end up foster-
ing other culturally resonant forms of political engagement, which in the
case of Japan took the form of a *politics of protection*. Technostruggle also
generates new forms of bio-intimacy, as people come to experience "the environment" not as something separate that surrounds them but rather as
a constitutive part of the very fabric of their bodies, which take up radioactive strontium and cesium right along with vital nutrients. This chapter
concludes with a look at the post-3.11 phenomenon of the "radiation divorce" in order to consider how bio-intimacies can affect intimacies more
conventionally conceived, such as those entailed in kinship.

Chapter 3, "Climate Change, Slippery on the Skin," asks what it would
mean to take North American climate change skepticism seriously when
that skepticism takes the form of the adamant assertion that global warming cannot be happening because it's not particularly hot out and the observer has hardly broken a sweat. The idea here is not to marshal evidence
to refute such claims but rather to stage an earnest inquiry into why *some*

climate change skeptics wield the body as an instrument they judge capable of registering conditions that enliven or imperil it.

Although many have characterized the conclusion that "there's no such thing as climate change" as anti-science, intimate appeals to the evidence that bodies can provide are not necessarily strangers to scientific inquiry. Researchers have utilized their bodies as testing, measuring, and tracking devices since the very birth of empiricism. In the early days of the Scientific Revolution in Europe, the body's senses doubled as a sensory *apparatus* when investigations were underway. The eye seemed every bit as integral to generating knowledge about the movements of comets or planets as that revelatory upstart the telescope. By the time climate change entered North America's vocabulary in the twentieth century, the telescope's precision had long relegated the eye to the status of unreliable informant, yet scientists continued to irradiate themselves, ingest poisons, and expose themselves to strange concoctions of gases, in an effort to use their bodies to better understand the properties of substances and the effects of atmospheric conditions. These corporeal forms of investigation, sometimes called embodied empiricism, treat the human body as a technology at once intimately connected to and set against objects of scientific inquiry through the very act of training the senses upon them.

To an embodied empiricist, "I'm (not) sweating" looks more like evidence than resistance. Without for a moment disputing the gravity of the changes now upon us, my goal here is to sketch an alternative sociohistorical genealogy for climate contrarianism in the United States in which certain strands of contrarianism run through the reasoned history of science rather than through theistic forms such as creationism. This approach opens a space for dialogue by extricating discussions of climate change skepticism from simplistic dichotomies that oppose science to religion, facticity to denial, and evidence to belief.

Chapter 4, "The Greatest Show on Parched Earth," focuses on some of the ways in which a visceral approach that attends to intimate, playful, yet spectacular engagements with a critical "resource" like water can have nontrivial implications. The ethnographic focus here is on the Grand Venice, a water-themed multiuse shopping and business complex located in the semiarid scrublands outside New Delhi, which promised investors gondola rides, a mermaid show, and India's first aquarium. Tucked into the confection of a building façade meant to conjure the Doge's Palace, these enticements raise the question of whether there might be room for embodiment, play, and aesthetics in a sea of utilitarian treatments of water, and if so, whether it would matter for anything more than an elite's passing entertainment. As the world rightly turns its attention to the mounting problems associated with overuse, contamination, and inequitable distribution of water, a casual observer could be forgiven for concluding that water politics must concern itself solely with a logic of scarcity and need. Human beings are *made* of water, the pundits explain, anywhere from 45 to 75 percent, while a mere 3 percent of the world's water supply is freshwater, and much of that inaccessible. Odes to the profits to be made from declining supplies, dire predictions about water wars, and jeremiads about an increasingly illiquid future all share this framing device. Critics depict waterworks that seek to escape this logic, including elaborate displays of fountains in the desert, as simple acts of hubris. Yet the appeal of such spectacles cannot be denied, as well as the social struggles embedded in them. This is not the bio-intimacy discussed in previous chapters in which food, water, bacteria, and radioactive isotopes become integral to organisms at a cellular level but an equally embodied intimacy of connection through contact, in this case with sparkling displays of a life-giving substance in locations where clean water is already scarce. Might the carnivalesque intimacies staged in places like the Grand Venice have the potential to reanimate relationships with neglected or exploited surroundings that critics assume to be evacuated of care and meaning, even as developers of such spectacles put added pressures on workers and ecologies?

Chapter 5, "Political Ecologies of the Precarious," raises the mother of all questions when it comes to the paradoxical coupling of technological prowess with ecological harm: Why do diverse societies with such varied histories and relationships to capitalist markets seem stuck in a downward spiral of resource exploitation, even as evidence mounts that if things carry on like this, the future of life on earth for complex organisms may be in doubt? Any answer would have to take politics and economics into account, as well as the many critiques of modernity. But the notion of affective intimacies suggests there is also a rather specific materiality involved: a viscerally fueled romance with synthetic chemistry embedded in current modes of production and consumption. As Geeta Patel (2016:2) points out, innovative technologies can serve as "incitements to closeness of various kinds." In this chapter a series of ethnographic *stopgaps* set in Chicago, New Delhi, and Venice (the "real" Venice this time) examines the part that one key technology, the automobile, has played in cultivating this affective stance by bringing people into an intimate, visceral engagement with newly created chemicals. What is it about such an affective stance that allows people to live with apparent contradictions, reassuring them that they can poison the world without limit even as they recognize that a limit must be out there somewhere, and suturing them to ecological damage even as they work against it?

The interactive ending to this just-so story of how humanity acquired its industrial spots will be either a reanimation of affective intimacies that organizes the world into something other than a collection of dead resources waiting to be managed, or a cataclysmic one, in which ecological precariousness bleeds into the economic precarity that has already robbed a generation of steady work under livable conditions. The apocalyptic finale is all too familiar. What would, what could, a reanimation of distanced abstractions such as "the environment" and "natural resources" for our (still) modern times look like?

The Last Animist

In an essay that isn't much read these days, but ought to be—"'What I'm Talking about When I'm Talking about My Baskets'"—Greg Sarris (1992: 24) describes the perplexity that greeted Mabel McKay when he invited her to speak to a class at Stanford University. Mabel was a renowned basket weaver, a fellow Pomo tribal member, the focal point of Sarris's research, and by most accounts a mischievous if not downright cantankerous woman. On this particular day, after two hundred students file into the classroom and the professor finishes his introduction, Mabel puts out her cigarette, unties a bundle of sedge roots, and starts weaving. And weaving. And weaving.

Sarris, who is not above indulging in a bit of wicked humor of his own when he implies that the professor decked himself out with a turquoise ring in Mabel's honor, seems truly mortified when he realizes that the speaker he has escorted to class may very well never say a word. Perhaps this is her way of showing her determination not to become another exhibit of the vanishing, but then again, with Mabel, who knows?

Much to Sarris's relief, Mabel finally has words for her audience. "Traditional weavers," she explains, "only weave the designs the spirit tells you," whereas "some modern weavers and the white people" court danger because "they just weaves whatever they like." A person "could get trouble that way," she cautions, holding up a basket: "These things . . . is living, is living." After a pause, she asks, "Now who can tell me what I mean 'is living'?"

"Does it breathe?" ventures a student. Mabel bursts out laughing. "That's cute," she says, "'Does it breathe?'" Another student asks if the basket talks. "Depend what kind of basket, what it's talking to," Mabel responds. "You got to hear it, but how *you* going to hear it?"

Anthropological studies of what animates our surroundings, even now, often find themselves in the position of that first student: earnestly and respectfully inquiring into phenomena so beyond their ken, materially-cum-ideologically, that they attempt to grasp those phenomena by replicating the very habituated ways of thinking they hope to transcend. To be fair, it is not easy to convey to people heavily invested in Euro-American conceptions of dead matter what it means to live in a world where trees ruminate, baskets talk, ancestral spirits inhabit palisade fortifications, elk decide whether to offer themselves to the hunter, and so forth, much less a world in which radioactive isotopes and polyamide resin pellets have their way with people. This business of tethering things newly apprehended to more culturally and historically familiar notions, the better to comprehend otherwise inexplicable differences, is anthropology's forte as well as anthropology's predicament. But it is one thing to recognize the difficulties inherent in the project and quite another to believe that you have moved on, moved up, or otherwise achieved some kind of clear-eyed understanding at the very moment you insistently relate everything back to the categories already in your bag. That last move is the one likely to provoke giggles.

When posthumanist anthropology opened one possible avenue for re-animating the world by taking steps to decenter the human, it seemed a radical step for a discipline once known as the study of man. This controversial anthropost-ology, as it were, beckons practitioners to investigate the lives of baskets and bacteria, to engage in an enterprise called multispecies ethnography, and to bring it all back to bear on the little matter of what it means to be human in the first place. In these endeavors ethnographers have had plenty of company of late. Their work coincides with (and draws upon) research by a contingent of philosophers, ecologists, and political theorists who have also stopped treating humans as the consummately sentient beings who dominate a fundamentally inert universe where everything else serves at their pleasure.[12] That lively company would include Jane Bennett's (2010) work on vibrant matter, Mel Chen's (2012) use of Silverstein's linguistic animacy hierarchies to "trouble the binary of life and non-life," and Noortje Marres's (2012) technologically infused concept of "material participation" in which "things" engage in a transformative politics with the capacity to mobilize publics. Even the sociologists have gotten in on the act, treating plastic as a substance with work to do in the world, as well as a life and a death that may or may not be metaphorical (see Gabrys, Hawkins, and Michael 2013).

As scholars continue to debate the vitality and even volitionality of matter broadly conceived, one development stands out: everybody wants to rethink animacy, but almost no one wants to be an animist.[13] I am not referring, of course, to people who weigh in on blogs like *The New Animist* or *The Allergic Pagan*. I'm talking about intellectuals with degrees and reputations to protect. A basket may act as an agent or enter into social relations with other things, in scholarship as in life, no problem there, but in a Deleuzian or Latourian world of assemblages there is not much room for animist visions that are more than material.[14] That remains true even for theorists who have flirted with the concept of animism while remaining wary of its broader connotations. In an interview with *Eurozine*, Jane Bennett, who seemed to shy away from the term *animism* immediately following the publication of her book *Vibrant Matter*, alluded to "what could playfully be called my neo-animist views," but with a critically distancing emphasis on the playful (Bennett and Loenhart 2011). Timothy Morton (2013b:101), another philosopher interested in rethinking "objects," concurs with Bennett that "a little bit of animism" might be of some use if carefully deployed, but that "it would be better if we had some term that suited neither vitalism nor mechanism." Sian Sullivan (2013:50) hedges by proposing the temporally qualified "becoming-animist" (not yet! not quite!) to describe the impasse at which social theory finds itself with the emergence of "new techno-configurations of nature."[15] Morton (2013b:101) suggests creating an alternative to animism by "appending some kind of negation to life and death, so that objects become *undead*." But in a cinematically infused world, it seems that would simply force theorists to grapple with the living legacies of another culturally charged form: the zombie (see McNally 2012).

It's quite striking, really, the breadth of this qualification and disavowal. Why in the world, in these times of renewed interest in the animacy of everything from puppies to rocks, would analysts take such pains to distance themselves from animism as such? Why would they insist on working out the intricate details of everyday life and sociocultural difference in a way that melds subject to object without a close reading of the classic debates about animism that preoccupied Edward Tylor (1871) and his interlocutors in the nineteenth-century? Why would they dismiss out of hand the possibility that a concept such as spirit (if not spirits) in the way that Mabel McKay used it could convey something important theoretically, while coming down so resolutely on the hard ground of a materialism that too often conceals its own debts to history?[16] These days a biologist such as Colin Tudge (2006:359–60) might describe how mopane trees in Africa release pheromones to promote tannin production in neighboring trees by depicting a forest in which "the air is abuzz with their conversations . . . conducted in vaporous chemistry." It is an interesting development that he should explain things just this way, in an account filled with plants that can "warn" one another about threats or even "summon help" from insects. Still, the conversation Tudge has in mind denotes a strictly material exchange of fragrances.

Now you might say to yourself, "My goodness, all these folks must be taking a long detour around animism for a reason." And you'd be right, but perhaps not for the reasons you originally conceived. It can't simply be because animism is oh-so-nineteenth-century. After all, the twenty-first century began with steampunk fiction and steampunk fashion, bringing Victoriana back into vogue. How hard would it be to imagine the emergence of a steampunk anthropology in which theoretical fashions such as animism could be revived with a bit of polish on the brass and a nod to latter-day critique? Alternatively, and to their credit, perhaps contemporary writers have no taste for the contempt that Tylor occasionally visited upon those he consigned to the animist stage of social evolution.

It might also be, however, that when today's new materialists and speculative realists hold relations momentarily constant by using "the assemblage" as a marker in order to focus on the intrigues of immanence, they intend to give a wide secular berth to anything that smacks of anthropomorphism or the kind of *indwelling* immanence that many versions of Christianity fostered. Lo these many years on, surely "we" know better than to project a soul or a spirit into a palm tree. Don't we? So long as that remains the case, Mabel's interlocutors can take her seriously, but only up to a point. That point arrives when she talks about weaving "the designs the spirit tells you."

It is not that Mabel necessarily understood herself to be in communication with a subjective presence that inhabited the "mere matter" of the basket's willow, feathers, and sedge; indeed, her laughter seemed directed at the very notion of such a subject/object split. It is rather that the commitment to matter which underwrites the new materialisms already presupposes a certain ontology that precludes the possibility of others, an ontology bound up with the voyages of discovery undertaken by European science. In this respect new materialisms find themselves at odds with the so-called ontological turn in anthropology, since the ontological turn, from Eduardo Viveiros de Castro (1998) onward, committed ethnographers to taking people (especially indigenous people) at their word as a starting point for inquiry.[17]

Let me hazard a rather different sort of guess as to the reasons for this adamant, almost embarrassed, backpedaling from animism, one that does not necessarily preclude explanations such as these: The disavowal of animism in accounts that position themselves as beyond humanism constitutes what the con man or the poker player would recognize as a tell. A tell reminds those who care to look that all is not as it appears. But what can this particular tell tell us?

Performatively speaking, the move to distance an argument from animism marks the moment in which the posthumanist puts paid to humanism. When it comes to animism, soul and spirit are the headliners for people who have not read many nineteenth-century texts. At best most scholars command a potted history of ethnological research on the subject, populated by soul-filled baskets that breathe. And nothing spells humanism like subscribing to the notion of a soul.

For Pico della Mirandola (2012), who left his imprint on Renaissance humanism as much as any philosopher, it was the thoroughly Christianized immortal soul that allowed shape-shifting humans to leapfrog right over Seraphim and Cherubim in the Great Chain of Being and assume a place beyond this world in the presence of God. Whatever else it might be, then, the flight from animism is a credentialing move. If you reject the attribution of soul/spirit to objects, even objects newly resignified as subjects, you must have put the problematic assumptions embedded in humanism behind you. Except, as the tell reminds us, all may not be as it appears.

Take the piece of lifesaving advice Eduardo Kohn (2013) received when he bedded down for the night during fieldwork in the Amazonian forests of Ecuador. Lie face up, his Runa companion Juanicu instructed him. Going to sleep face down encourages a jaguar to attack. Kohn has good reason to place this vignette at the opening to his eloquent multispecies inquiry, *How Forests Think*. By pondering what it would mean to greet a jaguar eye to eye in the wee hours of the night, the sacred cord that binds representation too tightly to language loosens, leaving room for a being of another sort who parses the world without words, in this case a world divided into fellow creatures versus dead meat. The jaguar pursues an intimacy of incorporation: eat or be eaten, unless some perceived kinship counsels forbearance.

In this imagined encounter, conventional understandings of representation become more capacious. But the implications do not end with a
rethinking of what the jaguar sees or what the anthropologist knows. By
returning the jaguar's gaze, Kohn (2013:2) contends that humans—his
"we"—*become* something new, "aligned somehow with that predator."

That last bit of Kohn's argument implicitly responds to the critique that
charges the ontological turn, in its execution, with having gotten mired
in the quicksand of worldview instead of adequately addressing the more
properly ontological matters of being or becoming. It is not that there isn't
something important about urging people to take seriously Mabel McKay's
"view" that a basket lives. If you treat her declaration as a testament to
the way the world *is* (at least if you are Pomo), rather than merely some
folkloric *belief*, different possibilities for inquiry as well as living open up.
But—leaving aside the matter of relativism—a focus on *testimonio* and
truth claims still does not get at how the world is, full stop, which is to say
never stopping at all.

For an anthropologist such as Tim Ingold (2000), seeing is never a matter of view and never confined to the eyes. Sensation becomes a whole-body
activity for humans and presumably jaguars as well, involving the kind of
participatory movement that led William James to write, from within his
thoroughly Euro-American context, that "the first time we see light . . . we
are it rather than see it" (Ingold 2000:269). Kohn, for his part, goes directly
for negotiations over is-ness. Even when he enters the mind of the jaguar,
one could argue that he does no more (albeit sans language) than cognitive
linguists do with their theory of mind when they attempt to explain how it
is that one human can speak in any meaningful way to whatever is going on
in the ostensibly separate and unknown mind of another. The profoundly
visceral realignment Kohn describes at the moment when two sorts of animal eyes meet in the dark matters hugely for the earth's hard-pressed ecosystems. But there is still in this lullaby for people and for jaguars the scent
of something not only human but humanist, and that whiff of humanism
emanates from the gaze.

In many posthumanist studies, if humans no longer monopolize the
picture, they are at least left holding the frame. Inside that frame, as in any
self-respecting Renaissance painting, perspectivalism rules: points of view,
lines of sight, vanishing point and all. (Note that here I am not speaking
of perspectivism, the Nietzschean animal that has prowled the jungle of
ethnographic ruminations on ontology since Viveiros de Castro delivered
his famous lectures at Cambridge, but of perspectivalism, its playful artis-

tic ancestor, more comfortable in the hill country outside Florence.)[18] A perspectival gaze emanates linearly from a viewer who occupies a distinctive vantage point. Face up is not face down, after all. And it is hard to have emanation without something immanent, be it ever so simply conceived, perhaps as a starting point or a source. The looking-back emanates from someone at least covertly imagined as immanently present, a being with an inside and an outside, albeit these days with leaky boundaries: in other words, a classically, suspiciously humanist subject, however much the disavowal of animism might seem to indicate otherwise.

The perspectivalism embedded in this gaze exemplifies Ingold's earlier point about "the imprint of a certain way of imagining the human subject — namely, as a seat of awareness, bounded by the skin, and set over against the world" (2000:243). This was the human subject who could "look off" into the distance in a Renaissance painting by Masolino or Raphael, watching buildings and floor tiles recede along then newly invented "lines of sight" into a mathematically generated distance. Or, in another part of the world, on another day entirely, the one who can open startled eyes to "look out" onto a predator who looks back, then makes its/her/his own fine-grained distinctions before deciding whether to dine.

And here is where it gets interesting. Instead of dissolving the humanist subjectivity of the human, the tactical device of perspectivalism begins to constitute the jaguar as a humanist subject, too, complete with his own "point of view" and his own gaze looking down or out. This is no garden-variety anthropomorphism that attributes humanized traits, habits, or sensations to an emphatically nonhuman creature. Quite the contrary: perspectivalism becomes the very ground that opens up representation to allow some not fully fathomable communication to take place, as the predator pads away from an alert fellow traveler or sticks around for a meal.

To any jaguar who knows her Renaissance history, the retention of a bit of humanist perspectivalism in posthuman inquiry offers more than additional evidence of human duplicity. (As though any creature sizzling away in rainforest temperatures jacked up by greenhouse gas emissions needs evidence of *that*.) It is an indication that much of posthumanism has not quite yet come to terms with the subtleties of its humanist legacies in an era when "post-" is all the rage and everyone reaches for a beyond. Whether humanist legacies like perspectivalism can be of value to a project that sets out to jettison human exceptionalism is, of course, another matter entirely.

Perspectivalism is not integral to the way that Gujars living in the Sariska tiger reserve in India approach tigers, for example. They have devised a protocol—an etiquette, if you will—for how to meet and greet a tiger, complete with specific vocalizations, that has proved remarkably successful in terms of minimizing human casualties. Paul Greenough (2012:337) calls this "interspecies accommodation," no projection into the imputed mind or gaze of another creature necessary to carry it off.

Neither is perspectivalism integral to Ingold's analysis. If, as he argues, perception arises as a whole-body experience produced by moving through the environment, then eyes, ears, mouths no longer figure as single-point origins of sensation. Seeing, hearing, and tasting holistically effectively banish the interiority assumed by discussions of animism when they picture spirit or soul as something that inhabits a thing and persists as an indwelling presence. Yet some sort of divide remains, insofar as Ingold's creatures remain on the side of life, neatly distinguished from this nebulous thing called an "environment" that activates perception as they pass through.

Animate Planet adopts another approach by attending to the shifting eco-political context that has given rise to posthumanism in the first place. Rather than trying to explain the living baskets and discriminating jaguars of the world, the case studies in this book ask what happens to people's visceral understanding of what it means to be human when damage to ecosystems has muddied any interior/exterior divide.[19] This is a move that sidesteps the arguments for and against attributing personhood to plants, rocks, or animals (see Hoeppe 2007:123), in favor of inquiring into the circumstances that made it seem important to stage such debates in the first place. The goal is to learn from the new animacies and to identify the intimacies embedded in them, but at the same time to read them as symptom.

If "materialism by itself is like honey on a razor's edge," as rapper Born I Music has it (qtd. in Sperry 2013:63), then a creatively *historical* materialism that asks "why this, now?" swaps the razor for the cutting edge of bittersweet insight from a time when modernity's story no longer suffices. Objections to the use of surveillance technologies to track livestock in the United States enlist nostalgia for what Leo Marx (2000) called "the machine in the garden," the historical yet fantastical production of a pastoral world of face-to-face relationships through an engineered landscape.[20] The rush to buy Geiger counters following the 2011 nuclear meltdowns in Japan addressed practical concerns but also historical memories of how radioactivity had insinuated itself into people's bodies through wartime bombing. Allusions to the body as a measuring instrument in North American debates on climate change make more sense with a grasp of the history of empiricism in European science. The attraction to spectacles staged with water in the arid lands around New Delhi signifies differently than the attraction to similar spectacles staged in Las Vegas, provided the historical ecology of the Yamuna River watershed is taken into account. All of these cases have arisen at a moment in which the ecological impacts of several centuries of industrialization have become so inescapable that they frame even the most triumphalist versions of the tale of how we got here.

In late industrial societies people increasingly depict themselves as capable of intimacies with matter that they have trouble describing because they have inherited a language of relationship and connection after-the-(individuated)-fact. Of late, they seem to be feeling their way toward something less fragmented. As they wake up to an ecologically compromised world, they have started to imagine it less as a setting for binding discrete entities into some sort of relationship and more as a place where beings permeate and co-constitute one another from the start. In the process, living versus nonliving, biological versus technological, creature versus environment, cease to be hard-and-fast dichotomies. The world becomes a place in which human beings are and are not separate, a place in which people begin to perceive themselves as integral to ecologies that they acknowledge, however begrudgingly, they need.

Though born from ecological decay, even catastrophe, this latest turn of the wheel refuses to place "resources" or an "environment" over, above, or against the lives they sustain. More is at stake than some "disintegration of our notion of the natural world," as Descola (2013:83) puts it, although his phrase describes as well as any an important aspect of the shift. Without a circumscribed natural world, the enchantments that travel in modernity's wake do not, cannot, spring from naïve calls for return to some ethnologically enhanced realm of totems and animal spirits, unless those animal spirits happen to include the Keynesian ones said to haunt the financial markets upon which industrialized edifices rest.

If the plot of modernity's story advanced through *techne*, then the reanimation of the world that modernity has gifted us emerges from attempts to grapple with the knock-on effects of a certain technological intensification. It is the sort of reanimation that becomes possible only once industrialized prowess has transformed the earth into a glorified makerspace of inequitably distributed ecological harms and marvels. It is the sort of reanimation that arises with the contention that the supposedly "dead matter" upon which the Industrial Revolution fixed its sights (and altered) appears to have had its way with the earth's inhabitants in the process. What people in different parts of the world make of their newfound eco-intimacies—

whether they long for them, evade them, embrace them, or propose to re-configure them in some more deliberate and deliberated manner—is the open question that animates this book.

The entanglement of animacies with intimacies under investigation here is not the same as the one sketched out in posthumanist briefs for the equal standing or ontological equivalence of all creatures. These twenty-first-century eco-intimacies are not about separate-but-equal. Neither are they the products of relations between entities, be they rice seedlings, farmers, waterways, puppies, or robots. Rather, these eco-intimacies are *compositional*. They inhabit the growing conviction that creatures co-constitute other creatures, infiltrating one another's very substance, materially and otherwise, with "creatures" broadly conceived to include the products of industrial technologies.

How do people come to terms with such a world, even as they constantly rework it? How do the enchantments that travel in modernity's wake diverge from those that have gone before? At stake is the difference between ingesting probiotics to help an ostensibly bounded immune system survive a daily chemical assault and taking probiotics to nurture gut bacteria that are also in some sense me. It is also the difference between a relationally conceived "exposure to" radiation after the meltdown at Fukushima Daiichi and a historical moment in which Mochizuki Iori can speak of a generation of people in Japan becoming nuclear fuel rods.[21] The forms of ecological damage that environmental justice movements target, in which some bodies are compelled to take up more heavy metals or Cesium-137 or E. coli 0157:H7 than others, make these political as well as perceptual observations. This is not your great-great-grandmother's animism.

FOOD

Biosecurity and Surveillance in the Food Chain

At first it seemed like just another school day in Sutter, California. Groggy eight-year-olds stumbled out of bed while family terriers yipped and working parents raced to get their children out the door. But this morning in January 2005 was different in one crucial respect. As the children donned their T-shirts, sweatshirts, and jeans, they topped off their outfits with a school board–mandated identification badge that contained a tiny radio frequency transponder. Readers installed in doorways at the school and handheld devices issued to teachers could instantly register the information encoded on the badge and track wearers' movements on campus. Students who refused to wear the new tags on lanyards around their necks became subject to disciplinary action. Radio frequency identification (RFID) tags had already begun appearing in consumer goods — clothing, packaged food, even automobile tires — as well as the ankle bracelets used to track prisoners. But this was one of the first times public officials had used the technology systematically to monitor children.[1]

At the time, the Sutter County episode generated intense debate. InCom, the company that installed the RFID system, praised the technology for making it easier for teachers to take attendance. An American Civil Liberties Union lawyer characterized the program as an egregious instance of "kids walking around with little homing beacons." Administrators contended that the tags enhanced campus security; one alarmed parent countered that the lanyard attached to the badge introduced new "risks" such as strangulation. The school district superintendent, for his part, called the technology "exciting . . . cutting edge . . . kind of Star Trekkie" (Lucas 2005b, 2005a). Techno-lust notwithstanding, this particular voyage to new frontiers, noted a columnist for the *Sacramento Bee*, had brought the district "a whole galaxy of trouble" (Lundstrom 2005).

The controversy that dogged the Sutter County initiative sounded well-worn, if important, themes familiar to scholars who study surveillance: privacy concerns, the mandate's allegedly Orwellian and dehumanizing aspects, claims for improved safety and efficiency, fascination with the wonders of technology, apocalyptic fears of becoming inscribed with the Mark of the Beast, and critiques of the profit motive involved in the sale of tracking devices (see Haggerty and Ericson 2006; Lyon 2001, 2006; O'Harrow 2005; Parenti 2003; Whitaker 1999). Responding to parental opposition and threats of legal action, the Sutter County school board provisionally shut down its RFID monitors, vowing to reintroduce a better-designed system in the future.

As time passed, the Sutter County Schools initiative no longer appeared to be an isolated incident. One year later, a Cincinnati-based company called CityWatcher.com, which conducted video surveillance for police and other clients, gave employees the "option" of using an electronic key to access the room where sensitive records were kept or having an RFID chip implanted in their arms to trigger the room's electronic lock (Sieberg 2006). In Mexico the attorney general's office had already chipped high-ranking officials in order to allow them to access restricted areas (Weissert 2004). Before long, a private school in Tokyo would make international news by affixing wireless transmitters to students' backpacks ("Overcoming Hang-Ups" 2007:8). In 2013 a Texas school district introduced RFID-chipped badges in order to secure extra state funding by proving that students were on campus. When one of the students tried to contest her suspension for refusing to wear the badge, a federal judge ruled against her (DesMarais 2013). Organic metaphors that had framed discussions of a body politic for centuries acquired new salience as surveillance technologies conferred unexpectedly material meanings upon the so-called long arm of the state.

As the Sutter County Schools experiment unfolded, the *San Francisco Chronicle* noted a less well-developed angle to the story: in previous deployments, RFID technology had primarily been used to track animals ("Chipped Kids" 2005; Lucas 2005b). Microchip implants in pets generated a spate of feel-good stories about caretakers reunited with little wandering Nigels, Cocos, and Fluffies. Cartoonists added radio transponders to the accessories worn by cows, sheep, and pigs in the comics. Before RFID tags ever found their way into the public schools of California or the government offices of Mexico's capital city, the most extensive state-sponsored programs for electronic tracking of vertebrates in North America involved livestock, that is, creatures destined for the dinner table. Indeed, what made the Sutter County story news at all was the application of these technologies to a youthful class of animals known as humans.

Considered in this context, the way that one of the children involved in the Sutter County experiment described her experience of wearing the tag appears prescient. "Look at this," she told her mother when she came home from school brandishing the badge. "I'm a grocery item. I'm a piece of meat. I'm an orange" (Lucas 2005b). Her description presumes a system of industrialized food distribution in which the constituents of meals appear on store shelves divorced from the sociality of the plant or animal to which they were once integral, always and already rendered piecemeal for sale. Surveillance technologies render the edible bits and bobs of that body accountable, much as the rendering plant transforms the body into marketable parts.

The back story here is a tale of face-to-face relations and lost intimacies, the eclipse by modernity of a fabulous era in which farmer-artisans grew their own food, kids raised sheep to enter into county fair competitions, and milk came from a named cow like Bessie.[2] Only once Bessie has been reduced to a picture on the dairy carton at the grocery store can a child express *alienation* by identifying with an orange or a shrink-wrapped cut of beef. Perhaps, then, it is not the tried-and-true topic of privacy—at the heart of the Sutter County controversy—that raises the most suggestive questions about the relationship between technology, intimacy, and food repackaged into "resources" but rather the appeal to technology to supply the intimate knowledge about whereabouts and well-being that people have long derived from conversation, observation, and labor.

In this regard, the defense of the RFID experiment formulated by Patti Draper, a Sutter County School employee, is telling. "We only have your children's best interests at heart. We're trying not to lose them," she explained to reporters (Lucas 2005a). Which, of course, only begs the question: Why should these children have seemed in imminent danger of becoming lost? Because they disappeared on a daily basis into the bowels of a modern bureaucracy known as the educational system? People who live in settings where the organization of labor allows adults to keep children in sight know where a child is in a way that the techno-intimacy of the RFID tag promises but can never fully deliver, since tags can be exchanged, mislaid, destroyed, reprogrammed, or even surgically removed. At the same time, any fetishized characterization of face-to-face relations as intimate by definition loses sight of the fact that intimacies do not automatically spring forth from relationships unless they are animated, not least by relations of production.

One of the earliest usages of the term *techno-intimacy* appeared in a talk on diasporic subjects' Internet use delivered by Geeta Patel (2002), in which she described "a curious form of intimacy—techno-intimacy—remote, and at once familiar (a familiarity through remoteness, a familiar remoteness) to those whose intimacies are produced across distance."[3] In her work on Japan, Anne Allison (2006) has used *techno-intimacy* to describe the affective, often sentimental, attachments produced through virtual interactions with aspects of high-tech devices such as characters in a computer game. Here I extend the concept to encompass intimacies generated by relations of production that deploy technology to reconfigure the world as an alienated (and therefore distanced) collection of resources, the better to extract them for profit, whether those resources take the shape of nuclear energy, water, or pigs on their way to becoming pork.

To know where your food comes from, in a calculus of face-to-face relations, is to have previously encountered the plants and animals that end up on your table, or at least the fields in which they grew and the people who raised them. To know where your food comes from, in the calculus of techno-intimacy, is to have the ability to link a store-bought product by bar code or lot number to a particular location. One way techno-intimacies abjure anonymity is by producing what Michael Pollan (2006:135) calls "storied food." For example, codes supplied with filets allowed consumers to pull up stories on Canada's "This Fish" website (thisfish.info) about the geographic origins of the particular fish they were about to cook, along with biographical snippets about the fisherfolk involved. The website developed a rather heroic character for its "harvesters" (and for the moral economy of traceability more generally), with little attention given to the many other crew members, processors, shippers, and retailers involved in the food chain. This sort of traceability is, by definition, highly selective about which faces a consumer sees, as well as what sorts of cultural narratives coalesce around them on the screen.

Over at MeineKleineFarm.org ("My Little Farm"), based in Germany, the motto was "Wir geben Fleisch ein Gesicht" (We give meat a face). From the very first click a visitor found herself nose to snout with the magnified visage of a pig that had been rooting around for something tasty. "Glück-licken Schweinen" (happy pigs), "relaxende Rinder" (cattle taking it easy), and a remarkably limber "Aerobic-Schaf" (aerobic sheep) garnered their fifteen minutes of fame on the home page in close proximity to photos of organic hamburger rolls and lamb sausages. While the animated counte-nances of these frolicking animals presented themselves in already existing realist fashion, the better for consumers to get to "know" their food, it was no accident that the company's slogan spoke of *giving* meat a face. Indeed, the proprietor, Dennis Buchmann, had thought carefully and philosophi-cally about the move to pair photographs of individual animals with meat products from those same animals. But without the technological media-tion of photography and the Internet, the website's call for customers to renounce anonymous mass-produced meat ("auf anonymes Massenfleisch verzichtet") would not have made sense. After all, most of them could not meet their meat "in person," as it were, until it arrived in a container with the animal's "portrait" on the lid. Some found this pairing upsetting, but the whole point, according to Buchmann, was to encourage meat eaters to face the fact that animals died for their dinners. These animals, too, had had lives. In this way Meine Kleine Farm sought to undercut any sentimentality associated with nostalgia for the lost intimacies of small-scale agriculture.

Note, however, that the scale of operations in mediated encounters with "storied food" has little bearing on their techno-intimate effects. Industrial agriculture might not (yet) be set up to bottle particular pigs into their very own jars of wurst, but enterprises of all sizes can and have used animal por-traiture, scanning devices, web links, and so on to foster the sense of inti-macy that sells products. Although the politics of small-scale and industrial agriculture might seem miles apart, the intimate knowledge of "where food comes from" that each promises to generate, with face-to-face relations on the one hand and machine-forged techno-intimacies on the other, is com-patible in both instances with the "digestive turn" in political thought de-scribed by Chad Lavin (2013). Where intimacy and animacy are concerned, the ongoing controversy over the application of surveillance technologies to living bodies stages a Gemeinschaft/Gesellschaft drama for our times.

The opposition between Gemeinschaft, with its idealized community of personal connections forged through kinship or religion, and Gesellschaft, with its equally idealized depiction of the rationalization and attenuation of ties in modern bureaucratic settings, shadows a number of contempo-rary social debates about the effects of capitalist finance on the provision of resources such as food or shelter.[4] During the Great Financial Crisis that engulfed the world in 2008, for instance, commentators in English-language business publications mourned the loss of face-to-face relations in banking, arguing that if bankers had maintained personal ties with their clients, à la Jimmy Stewart's character in the film *It's a Wonderful Life*, instead of repackaging shady loans and selling them off to the highest bidder in some faraway land, the ripple effects from mortgage defaults would not have been so damaging and millions of people would still be living in their houses. A new breed of cross-border lenders, critics argued, had ignored at their peril "old industry axioms of 'know-your-customer' and 'lend locally to long-standing corporate and individual clients'" (Guerrera 2009:10). Never mind that the plot of *It's a Wonderful Life* turned on the threatened demise of the family-owned Bailey Building and Loan Association, which survived a bank run only to nearly succumb to the forgetfulness of Uncle Billy, who misplaced a deposit that constituted the bulk of the Building and Loan's reserves.[5]

Critiques of agribusiness, in theory and in practice, have applied a similarly romanticized Gemeinschaft/Gesellschaft dichotomy to the food chain. They often associate intimacy with face-to-face relations per se, whether it be an intimate acquaintance with grass-fed cattle on a particular farm or the intimate knowledge of animal habits acquired in the course of caring for them personally. It is an association that threads its way through sources as diverse as environmental journalism, the reasons students give for leaving college to become apprentice organic farmers, and the accounts rendered by anthropologists who are busy studying foodways in this place or that (see Counihan 1999; Counihan and van Esterik 2007; Sutton 2001).

Why do I call this association of intimacy with community and face-to-face relations romanticized? Because on the Gesellschaft side — the "modern," industrial, bureaucratic side — of the equation, the worker stationed with a scanner at the entrance to an industrial-scale feedlot, like the teacher with a scanner stationed in the school hallway, uses the latest technology to enter into a face-to-face relationship, however fleeting, with each passing RFID accessorized cow. In Japan technologically traceable food is sometimes called "food with a visible face" (顔が見える食品, *kao ga mieru shokuhin*), with a nod to the capacity of tracking regimes to link retail food packages to narratives of origins, fisheries, growers, and farms (Hall 2010:827).[6] Meanwhile, over on the Gemeinschaft side of the equation, you might have a daydreaming organic farmer, whose inattention to a disease- or drought-stricken raspberry bush that is "staring her in the face" leads not to an intimate understanding of the plant's predicament but to its demise. No one better understood the perils of treating the Gemeinschaft/Gesellschaft dichotomy as anything more than an ideal type than its inventor, Ferdinand Tönnies, whose father's business merged cattle breeding with merchant banking in ways that straddled the divide.

Sponsors of the surveillance systems that have introduced techno-intimacy into the food chain usually don't think of themselves as trafficking in *any* kind of intimacy. Instead, they have legitimated their efforts by keeping a social evolutionary version of the Gemeinschaft/Gesellschaft drama alive. The ostensibly lost intimacy of the family farm must be replaced, they argue, with more practical and efficient, albeit faceless, modes of accounting for what happens to bodies in the course of being eaten or fed. In their eyes, intimate relations with animals belong to an outmoded agricultural world that cannot survive today's market pressures. Rather than accept this story at face value, as it were, I would argue that if you want to understand what ails the food chain, you cannot consign intimacy to the past, or even to a present-day revival of artisanal farming. It makes more sense to inquire into the *kind* of intimacies (techno or otherwise) that different modes of producing food generate.

Securing the Animal Body with Big Data

In the years after 9/11, the United States Department of Agriculture (USDA) laid the groundwork for a National Animal Identification System, the NAIS, in the name of enhancing the nation's biosecurity and bolstering its "agricultural infrastructure" (USDA APHIS 2004b). NAIS literature initially described its goal as tagging every domesticated animal within the borders of the United States with a "unique individual identifier" that would render that creature, in all of its parts, traceable, even once the animal's body was cut up and distributed for food. My goal in this chapter is thankfully somewhat less ambitious. I merely take up the NAIS as an instance of the phantasmagorical ways in which surveillance technologies consign the face-to-face intimacies created between people and animals in the course of food production to an imaginary past and call them lost, while using techno-intimacy to reconstitute animals as resources that industries can process into food. After describing NAIS protocols and contrasting them to those of earlier livestock protection campaigns, I examine some of the claims about animal citizenship and the rhetoric of uniqueness incorporated into its comprehensive tracking scheme. Rather than taking the uniqueness conferred by NAIS tracking markers as a given, I discuss how USDA concerns about animal "commingling" drew attention away from the conditions in which animals were raised. Finally, I look at an alternative way of organizing food production that leaves the Gemeinschaft/Gesellschaft opposition behind, a kind of production that does not rely on either technological enchantment *or* nostalgia for a simpler past when humans and the animals they proposed to eat lived together in places like North America.

When the agribusiness-oriented USDA began to invoke biosecurity after 9/11, its main concern was the identification and interdiction of anything that could endanger the nation's food supply. "Agroterrorism" had emerged as a newly constituted threat in a country where the principal cause of disruption to the food chain actually involved parents whose lack of access to a living wage forced them to send one in five children to school hungry each day. There was no evidence that anyone in recent times had tried to wreak economic havoc by destroying crops or livestock, but that did not stop governments from worrying about the prospect. In the United States, the USDA had already ceded agriculture inspection duties at the country's borders to the Department of Homeland Security. In 2003 the agency duly consulted with the Pentagon on a military exercise dubbed Silent Prairie, a simulation in which foot and mouth disease introduced by "terrorists" ended up infecting a third of the nation's cattle herds (Dupont 2003). Whatever else such cooperative ventures with security services might have achieved, they certainly played to what Brian Massumi (1993) has called the politics of everyday fear.[7]

While the concept of agroterrorism capitalized on post-9/11 angst, it never captured people's imaginations in the United States in the same way as the specter of terrorism more conventionally conceived. The kind of food scares that *did* command public attention had more to do with food adulteration, infection, and contamination, old-fashioned concerns augmented by scandals and elongated supply chains that made it hard to judge quality. Secular interest in private certification schemes—organic, kosher, halal—testified to a loss of public confidence in the oversight capabilities of scaled-down government agencies (see Lytton 2013).

As budget cuts reduced the number of USDA inspections, the agency attempted to bridge the gap between its mission and its diminished resources with technology. In workaday practice, it focused less on the potential for deliberate sabotage and more on preventing the unintentional spread of afflictions such as avian flu or porcine epidemic diarrhea virus (PEDV), maladies the agency would have monitored in any case but which, with the National Animal Identification System, it proposed to control in a new way. USDA literature described the NAIS as consisting of three components whose correlation would enhance food safety: premises registration, animal identification, and animal tracking (USDA APHIS Veterinary Services 2006). What distinguished the implementation of the NAIS from earlier efforts to track animals—the use of radio collars in studies by field biologists, for example—was both its overarching reach and its proposed deployment of surveillance technologies to follow livestock "from the farm to the fork" and "from pasture to plate."[8]

The clever use of alliteration in these slogans obscures the fact that relatively small numbers of domesticated animals ever graze in a pasture in an era of factory farming and feedlot pens. Under the nostalgic sign of the pastoral, supporters of the NAIS argued that only science and software engineering could provide the intimate, up-to-date knowledge of an animal's movements required by a country whose meat consumption in 2010 totaled a remarkable 34,156,000 metric tons (U.S. Census Bureau 2012). It was the picture of Bessie the cow on the milk carton all over again.

Animals, especially predatory animals, have appeared for years in commercial advertising in North America as representations of the hypothetical threats to safety that consumer products offer to assuage. In an advertisement for a software package designed to eradicate spybots from computers, for instance, the big cat lurking in the grass signifies the danger posed when malicious bits of code infiltrate a hard drive. Once security becomes the watchword, alleviation becomes integral to technology's promise. Publicity for USDA campaigns has tended to invert this relationship of spy to spied upon. In a surveillance society, animals take up their places as remedy as well as threat. The telescope-wielding chicken on the logo of the USDA's "Biosecurity for the Birds" initiative, introduced in 2004, is a self-policing agent, the type of subject that helpfully assists the government by searching out creatures of its own kind who need to be reported and culled.

Nor have more scholarly representations proved immune to the commercialized allure of animal tagging and tracking schemes. The fancifully bar-coded drawings of goat, wolf, and tiger on the cover of the December 4, 2004, issue of *Science News* pointed readers to an article on the search for "a unique bar code" for each species on earth that would target a short string of nucleotides in an agreed-upon gene. "We're looking at distinguishing the major product lines of life, if you will," commented Paul Hebert, a geneticist involved in the project (Brownlee 2004:360). Indeed, the DNA barcoding system that Hebert and his colleagues developed modeled itself on the

Universal Product Code (UPC) manufacturers had introduced in the late twentieth century to track retail goods. A DNA segment common to all animal species corresponded to the manufacturing code, with variations along that segment corresponding to the product identifiers. Only plants seemed capable of eluding this scheme, since they sported no obviously standardized DNA segment (Gambino 2009).

The so-called product lines of life that the NAIS proposed to secure through industry–government cooperation were more than metaphorically linked to trade. It was only following the discovery of a case of bovine spongiform encephalopathy (BSE or "mad cow disease") within U.S. territorial borders in 2003 that implementation of a comprehensive animal tracking scheme rapidly gathered momentum (USDA APHIS Veterinary Services 2005). Millions of dollars in beef-related investments were at stake. When fifty-two of the sick animal's "herd mates" could not be located using paper records, *Scientific American* concluded that "the problem lies with the antiquated method of keeping tabs on animals" (Grossman 2004). Yet there was also something curious about the emphasis and allocation of funds in the government's response to the mad cow scare. Calls to improve monitoring of the food supply coincided with *cuts* in the funding available for USDA inspections at meatpacking plants (see Rampton and Stauber 2003). Instead of augmenting the budget for site visits and laboratory tests, the state borrowed from popularized discourses of risk utilized by social workers, insurance companies, and public health officials to create a classificatory scheme for cattle.

In order to detect BSE, government officials advised ranchers to keep a close eye on older animals and "downer cows" (i.e., cows that could not stand or walk). By treating age and limited locomotion as classificatory "risk factors" that increased the chances of an animal contracting BSE, the USDA drew attention away from the growing suspicion that animals acquired BSE from what they ate, and that, in any case, BSE need not manifest in visible symptoms. Apparently little had been learned from earlier public health campaigns to combat HIV in human communities, where the strategy of dividing populations into risk groups was roundly discredited as ineffective for combating infections that spread through specific forms of contact rather than through group affiliation.

While the USDA focused on less costly risk assessment strategies, the European Union and Japan conducted intensive, routine testing of the animals themselves (Ansell and Vogel 2006). Under public pressure, the USDA's Animal and Plant Health Inspection Service (APHIS) finally inaugurated a ramped-up testing program in 2004 but described it as "a one-time effort" designed to take a "snapshot" of domestic cattle to help determine the presence or absence of BSE. Significantly, only cattle from the so-called high-risk population were scheduled for tests. Cattle in the random sample portion of the study came from a pool of "apparently normal, aged animals," thereby tacitly incorporating a variable, age, that the USDA elsewhere had identified as a risk factor for BSE (USDA APHIS 2004c).

Nowhere did officials demonstrate any critical purchase on the concept of risk of the sort that Geeta Patel (2007:104) develops in "Imagining Risk, Care, and Security," where she explores how the risk mitigation strategies employed by insurance companies incorporate fantasies that "stage the possibility of holding at bay something that may or may not happen." The enchantments of risk identification, like the enchantment associated with the idea of tracking technologies that can keep tabs on all bodies at all times, issue from a pledge to order and secure the future, rather than from, say, any demonstrated impact on disease eradication.

In the decades before the introduction of the NAIS, state-sponsored disease control efforts had stressed education about the *means of transmission* rather than risk assessment or tracking devices. Wash your boots with bleach, went this sort of homely advice, before leaving any pen containing sick animals. After scientists identified animal byproducts in processed feed as a vector for BSE transmission, the USDA did work with the industry to publicize this information in pamphlets with scintillating titles such as "Biosecurity of Dairy Farm Feedstuffs." It placed a hold on air-injection stunning, which can force brain tissue into a carcass during slaughter, thus exposing meat destined for market to infection. The government also tightened record-keeping procedures and modified the regulations that govern production of animal feed. Yet USDA fact sheets on BSE had surprisingly little to say about prions, the proteins linked to the onset of mad cow disease, much less studies that suggested that prions can bind to soil, where ruminants might ingest them as they grazed for up to three years (Raloff 2006).

A 2004 Food and Drug Administration (FDA) proposal to ban poultry blood, litter, and restaurant waste from cattle feed faltered after industry lobbyists objected to its cost. By 2006 the FDA was still trying to broker agreement on a diluted (and not incidentally much less expensive) proposal to ban the practice of feeding cattle parts to chickens and to prohibit the use of brains and spinal cords from older cattle. Although the new rule aimed at "reducing the risk" of cross-contamination between species, livestock

Figure 1.1. The telescope-wielding chicken from the USDA's "Biosecurity for the Birds" campaign [Credit: U.S. Department of Agriculture, Animal and Plant Health Inspection Service]

continued to consume the brains of younger cattle (D. G. McNeil 2006; Zhang 2005). In the eyes of critics and international trade partners, such half measures failed to address the larger problem of creating so-called cannibal animals in the first place. Even the fast-food giant McDonald's Corporation called upon the U.S. government to "take further action to reduce this risk" after suffering heavy losses in its European division (Lindsey 2001; Quaid 2006).

Mad cow politics might not have prompted the USDA to root out contagion in the food chain, eliminate loopholes in meat processing regulations, address overcrowding in livestock pens, or systematically screen livestock, but for advocates of the NAIS, the emergence of BSE was a godsend. When "the nation's third case" of BSE appeared on a farm in Alabama in 2006, government veterinarians focused their efforts not on testing but on tracing the cow to its birthplace and locating other members of its "birth herd." (Indeed, the rate of testing for BSE in the United States remained relatively low at approximately one in every ninety animals [D. G. McNeil 2006].) By worrying a bit less about *vectors of transmission* (prions, farming methods, animal feed) and quite a bit more about *routes of transmission*, in the sense of the routes traveled by animals in whole and in part, the NAIS in its very conception argued for a switch in the investments of governmental oversight.

The technologies utilized by the NAIS ranged from the simplicity of RFID-chipped ear tags, to databases of places that housed meat and livestock over the course of the journey to market, to satellite transponders sheltered within the bodies of ruminants themselves. Ideally the correlation of geographic sites, unique individual identifiers (assigned to tags or transponders), and tracking (efforts to map one onto the other) would establish the ability to trace what happens to an animal's constituent parts, at least retrospectively if not in real time. According to promoters (although of course they did not use this language), techno-intimacies established through the NAIS would allow officials to keep close tabs on meat and livestock from the remotest of locations. Exaggerated claims made for animal tracking in terms of biosecurity and enhanced safety of the food supply also fostered the impression of a state intimately concerned with the public's well-being.

Once agricultural ventures began to utilize tracking technologies under the auspices of the NAIS, they entered the business of *warranting*. Warranting, in Allucquère Stone's (1995) formulation, involves a demand to produce the body. Stone employs the concept of warranting to describe attempts to tether multiple personalities and variable online personae to a single materially present body that appears in a courtroom or sits in front of a computer. Like the written warrant issued by a judge, this less tangible warrant stages a reductive demand to tie breakaway social formations, with all their creative multiplicity, to someone who is visibly and materially embodied, and in some cases, to surrender that materiality to the state.

When the state attempts (even as a voluntary measure) to comprehensively warrant animals destined for the food supply, it asks farmers, ranchers, and processors to produce them for the purposes of tagging and tracking. Note that the object of warranting in this case is not the potentially infected food that an animal eats, not the creature's blood for the purposes of running diagnostic tests, not the blueprints for twenty-first-

Figure 1.2.
Electronically
unenhanced ear tags
for cattle, on sale
in Virginia [Credit:
Author photo]

century feedlots, but the animal's body. And not just the animal's body, but the animal's body with reference to its location at any given point in time, a location pinpointed by technologies directed at and/or embedded in the body itself. Bar codes, RFID tags, real time location systems (RTLS), retinal scanning, electronic boluses that lodge in a ruminant's reticulum: all these surveillance technologies participate in the work of creating a *trace* of the animal at its most material.[9]

Because many of the machines that can read the signals emitted by these devices work only at short range, effort initially went into establishing stations where handheld or chute-mounted readers could generate what Identec Solutions, an RFID and RTLS manufacturer, calls "localization of assets." (The company's website, www.identecsolutions.com, has also gestured toward human applications with the phrase "localization of personnel.") As in real estate, the value of a promise to secure the animal body through surveillance depends on location, location, location. In order to track animals through and beyond the process of slaughter, Identec went on to develop its patented Intelligent Long Range (ILR) technology to keep tabs on livestock in the "transportation, logistics, and manufacturing environments."

To be of value, readings from such devices need schemes such as the NAIS to link them to multiple and shifting accounts of the premises where an animal resides, *premises* serving as a term of art that, at any given moment in the progress from farm to fork, could mean a barn, feedlot, corral, meatpacking assembly line, freighter, truck, restaurant, waste disposal vehicle, or supermarket. The animal's body may be long gone, but it can be virtually produced and reproduced by consulting electronic records of its passage. Its various constituents can be followed to the ends of the earth, or wherever global trade may have taken them. With this overarching tracking system in place, both investments and public health will be protected. That, at least, was the promise.

Animal Citizenship and the Unique Individual Identifier

It is one thing to attempt to restore, through the use of surveillance technology, the intimate knowledge of animal well-being that lets human carnivores know whether meat is safe to eat. That, in itself, is a dubious proposition, because traceback always occurs after the fact, once well-being has come into question. It is quite another to warrant the nation, in this case as a disease-free space in which people can munch their way through anything that makes it to market without a worry about their health. Yet the attempts to bio-secure a category called "U.S. meat" through techno-intimacy have ventured precisely that, rhetorically producing the body of a safe nation by vaunting the ability to track the bodies of every cow, pig, or ostrich destined for the dinner table.

When veterinarians detected the first case of mad cow disease "on U.S. soil" — to use the nationalist trope repeated in media coverage of the 2003 incident — the U.S. government went to great lengths to assign a Canadian identity to the cow in question. After painstakingly assembling a record of the animal's movements, the administration concluded with obvious relief that this particular ruminant had journeyed south to rural Washington from a ranch in Alberta. In this ersatz citizenship story, the ill-fated Holstein was born in Canada and only later crossed the border to take up residence in the States (Kershaw and Simon 2004; D. G. McNeil 2006; Zhang 2005).

Geographic location at birth, rather than migration, nurture, or parentage, established the nationality that the NAIS promised to confer upon domesticated animals. Cows, it seems, cannot be naturalized. For the U.S. government, establishing the site where the animal ingested contaminated feed was never at issue when it used tracking to assign nationality to the body and territoriality to the infection. Once again, routes of transmission had superseded vectors of transmission. Canadians, on the other hand, tended to regard their cows as "indistinguishable from American cows because they cross the border so often," the New York Times reported in an article on tensions in the wake of trade disputes over transnational shipments of beef (Krauss 2004). Some of the Canadians the reporter interviewed pointed out that regulations for animal feed were similar in both countries at the time. What's more, in the absence of systematic testing, how could the U.S. government assert that the food supply was safe? With the border closed to trade in beef, Canadian livestock producers lost billions and ended up suing their own government for losses ("In Court: Mad Cow Blame" 2005).

The context for official declarations of animals' nationality exceeds the nation, of course. Meat production, like the manufacture of surveillance equipment, has become an increasingly lucrative and globalized industry. Agribusiness processes its sentient "raw materials" in huge batches and moves them from place to place at different stages of growth and disassembly. Due to the transnational character of twenty-first-century meat marketing, the discovery of mad cow disease in the United States quickly translated into layoffs for hundreds of thousands of food service workers in places such as South Korea and Taiwan (Johnson 2004). Apparently the sick cow's "Canadian" identity provided little reassurance to the Asian governments that suspended imports of "U.S. beef." Throughout these disputes, fragile hopes of assigning a convincing nationality to meat relied on the ability to trace the movements of animals that succumbed to contagious diseases.

More refined regulation of imports in turn required more refined databases. When Singapore once again began accepting beef from the United States in 2006, for example, it continued to deny entry to ribs and bones (determinable by inspection) as well as meat from cows over thirty months old (determinable only through records that warranted cuts of meat to individual cows) (see "US Beef Ban Lifted" 2006). Likewise for Japan, which

アメリカ、カナダへ
ご旅行される皆様へ

BEEF JERKY

加工製品

アメリカ（ハワイ、グアム、サイパンを含む）、カナダで販売されている
ビーフ・ジャーキーなどの牛肉加工製品については、牛肉輸入再開後も
引き続き輸入停止となっています。

このような日本語記載がある製品
も、持ち込み出来ません！

（日本到着後、税関検査の前にこのビーフジャーキーを
動物検疫カウンターまでおもちになり、検査をお受けく
ださい。このシールをはがしたり包装を開封しますと、
輸入できなくなりますのでご注意下さい）

農林水産省 動物検疫所

Figure 1.3.
Border control:
A sign at Narita
airport outside Tokyo
in 2013 instructs
travelers not to bring
meat into the United
States or Canada
[Credit: Author photo]

ended its two-year ban on "American beef" in 2005, but only for cattle less than twenty-one months old, presumably too young to have developed BSE (Fackler 2005). But even the knowledge of an animal's age and whereabouts produced through techno-intimacy could not guarantee enforcement. In 2006 Japan placed a new embargo on beef products imported from the United States after it discovered cattle backbone, a prohibited cut, in a shipment from Atlantic Veal & Lamb Inc. (Tabuchi 2006).

The United States was not alone in its bid to secure trade and investment through the introduction of tracking schemes. Both Australia and the European Union introduced electronic animal monitoring programs in the form of a National Livestock Identification Scheme (NLIS) and the Identification Electronique des Animaux (IDEA) project, respectively. When Poland sought to join the EU, the country could not qualify for farm subsidies until it set up livestock registration systems (Young 2004). While governments might disagree about how to interpret animal tracking data, especially in light of the desire to assign strategically profitable nationalities to cuts of meat, a country that wishes to ship its animals in whole or in part to buyers in major markets will soon have no option but to institute a tracking system of its own.

So what form does techno-intimacy take when a state or other polity uses surveillance technology to assign individual identifiers for the purpose of producing each animal body? How is the fetishization of uniqueness tied up in this quest? It is perhaps worth noting that the push to create comprehensive national registries for animal bodies as a prerequisite for border crossings now occupies a place in a growing roster of such schemes, including one advanced by the Financial Stability Board to create a global database of "legal entity identifiers" (LEIs) that would assign every company that engages in financial transactions its own unique code (Masters 2012).[10]

In a technical sense, NAIS registration never depended on numbering alone. Electronically registered tags increasingly encode identifiers of the sort used in serial numbers, which are not really numbers at all, but chains of letters *plus* numbers. This is a critical distinction, because it indicates that the markers are not designed for tallying or time sequencing in any intuitive sense. Rather, they are designed to register uniqueness, and with it, reassurance.

Strings of letters interspersed with numbers cannot be added or subtracted, divided or multiplied, which means that technologies such as alphanumeric bar codes lend themselves to a different sort of inventory accounting. These strings of letter-numbers map onto entities that can only afterward be categorized and counted, in a second-order operation, be it as bodies, herds, lots, shirts, or copies of your latest book. Alphanumeric sequences transform the process of taking inventory into a precursor of tabulation. Chronology cannot immediately be inferred from the letter-numbers encoded in the tag, as it can be when managers enter numbers into ledgers in sequence, one after another, with 101 listed after 100. That means, when it comes time to take inventory, alphanumeric codes require extra steps to arrive at figures more easily produced by classical modes of reckoning. In that sense, the type of markers adopted by surveillance technologies seem at odds with the increased efficiency that modernity promises, unless one considers what the trackers have in their electromagnetic sights. In her work on cinematic depictions of contagion, Kirsten Ostherr (2005:20) observes, "The search for carriers of plague [read: mad cow disease] . . . becomes a search for external markers of internal conditions." Markers can be produced as such, all the better to discover them, whether they take the form of high-tech alphanumeric codes or low-tech categorizations of "risky" cows.

The alphanumeric identification markers incorporated into animal tracking schemes help confer an impression of uniqueness by supplying a "strong" index for identification: strong in the sense of the type of digit sequences sought for electronic passwords, where strength indicates a resistance to unauthorized appropriation or alteration. This password-like sequence can double as a passport of a sort, once linked to the assurance that only "safe" meat will clear a country's borders. Significantly, the measure of safety here is not the verified absence of contaminants or the misshapen prions characteristic of BSE but instead the ability in a crisis to locate bits of the body that the unique individual identifier is said to secure.

An identification marker may be one-of-a-kind, but it cannot confer uniqueness except in its relationship to the body it indexes. The uniqueness of the individual identifier depends upon the correspondences that a tracking scheme establishes between body and marker, between marker and identifying letter-number sequence, between sequence and location. When industry can profitably assign a marker to a new body without altering the coded sequence after the old body is distributed and consumed, those correspondences may not be one-to-one. After a farmer shoots a tracker bolus into a cow's belly using a balling gun, the bolus stays inside the animal but can later be removed and recycled. Put more bluntly and minus the green recycling language, the transponder contained in a bolus can send electronic signals through muscle and integument during one animal's lifetime, wait for retrieval by meatpackers at the point of slaughter, then take up a new life inside the body of another ruminant destined for market. In that case, the alphanumeric sequence associated with a single bolus would eventually correspond with more than one body for the purposes of tracking.

Indeed, most cattle, pigs, and sheep in North America can expect to bear more than one alphanumeric sequence in their short lifetimes. A cow in the United States might have as many as five different identification codes associated with it, each keyed to a different program (herd improvement, disease eradication, and so on). Rather than inaugurating a "one number–one animal system," the NAIS in its first stage of implementation mandated assignment of a thirteen-character lot ID to each body raised as part of a herd, in addition to a fifteen-character body-specific animal identification number (AIN) (USDA APHIS Veterinary Services 2005a). One variant of the fifteen-character marker showcased the nation-state by opening with the letters "USA," followed by a randomly assigned unique number sequence. A decade after the roll-out of the NAIS, the fantasy of a unique identification marker technologically warranted to each animal body still seemed far from realization, not least because many meat producers resisted the scheme, for reasons as various as they were variously positioned.

Small farmers argued that the NAIS favored large meat operations, which could better afford the equipment as well as the time required to keep additional records. A few objected that the NAIS unfairly subsidized the businesses that manufacture tracking gear. Others cited the NAIS premises registry as an instance of unnecessary government intrusion on privately held lands. Amish farmers registered religious objections to a scheme that enlisted the power of the state to get them to adopt particular technologies. Although the NAIS was a voluntary scheme from its inception, farmers of all sorts worried that nonparticipation would affect their access to distribution channels (Emery 2006). When Bill Hawks, Under Secretary for Marketing and Regulatory Programs, remarked at a press briefing that the Animal Health Protection Act had given the USDA authority to "address the animal ID system in a mandatory fashion if we so chose," they were hardly reassured (USDA 2004).

There were other historical legacies besides religious persecution that the NAIS had to negotiate. Plans to inscribe bodies with state-monitored identity markers remain haunted by the history of numbered tattoos that the Nazi state forcibly etched into the skin of prisoners in its *Konzentrationslager* during World War II. As the proprietors of the Boggy Creek Farm in Texas wrote on their website, "The mountain of paperwork and the fees and fines threaten all small animal farmers, but will be minimal for the corporate concentration camp 'farms,' whose thousands of animals and birds will be identified with only one number, as they are treated as 'lots.' (Or, 'widgets.')."[11] For small operators like these, the language of "collection of animal movements at concentration points (markets, feedlots, etc.)" contained in the NAIS Draft Strategic Plan (USDA APHIS 2005) hardly seemed neutral. On the contrary: The abstractions embedded in such phrases denied the animacy of the animals while echoing the use of bureaucratic language to disguise wartime atrocities.

After the magazine *Mother Earth* published an article that was highly critical of the claims made for the public health benefits of traceability (Kittredge 2007), an owner of thirty-two free-ranging chickens in Wisconsin wrote to protest his state's decision to make the NAIS mandatory. In his reckoning, the new law would subject even children to state surveillance because county fair committees had received instructions to "keep track of the kids whose premises are registered, and whose are not" (Schubert 2007). What's more, he argued, his refusal to register his premises had effectively criminalized him. When other states passed legislation that prohibited forced participation in the NAIS, it placed farmers in a kind of legal limbo ("No Mandatory NAIS in Arizona" 2007).

At outdoor markets like the ones I have patronized in Virginia, growers with small flocks and herds sometimes contrasted the insistence on traceback built into schemes like the NAIS with the federal government's disinterest in tracking or even labeling genetically modified organisms (GMOs) in food for fear of damaging sales. "Tracklessness" can be every bit as much of a social creation as tracking. In *The Omnivore's Dilemma* Michael Pollan (2006:59–60) discusses an innovation he calls "trackless corn," which debuted in the United States in the mid-nineteenth century with the advent of grain elevators and railroad cars in which cobs and kernels from hundreds, even thousands, of producers mixed. To reassure buyers who could no longer source products by consulting the farm label on a burlap sack, the Chicago Board of Trade created a grading system that established Number 2 corn from one farm as the equivalent of Number 2 corn from any other. The coexistence of such refusals to track with the insistence on tracking that the NAIS represented made it easy to conclude that the public health concerns voiced by architects of the NAIS simply veiled another push to advantage "big agriculture."

Resistance to the surveillance built into new schemes like the NAIS need not always confine itself to genteel (if often heated) discussions in media, state legislatures, and farmers' markets. For all the talk of biosecurity associated with surveillance technologies, tracking devices themselves can be hacked (Thornton 2007). Even before the widespread deployment of RFID tags, security consultants worried about the potential for thieves who understood the technology to "fool merchants by changing the identity of goods" (Lemos 2004). Changing identity here refers not, of course, to modification of the goods themselves but rather to changes in the information encoded on a tag, which would disrupt correspondences between electronic marker, product, and geographic location. It is precisely this slippage that renders surveillance schemes such as the NAIS less than fully reassuring even to their backers. Promises, promises.

To make matters even more difficult for anyone hoping to establish unique correspondences between organisms and letter-number sequences, animal bodies rendered into meat through industrial farming generate avatars whose numbers threaten to become unmanageable at the point of slaughter, when workers transform "the" body into steaks, chops, chitterlings, wings, ground meat, and those tainted scraps dignified with the term *byproducts*. The result is a kind of accounting allometry in which the parts to be tracked grow at a rate disproportionate to the body as a whole. If the state is going to promise to produce the animal body under these conditions, whether it be for routine surveillance purposes or to stem outbreaks of disease, it has to warrant that body's bits.

Warranting in whole *and* in part creates new problems. At a USDA-sponsored listening session on the NAIS in North Carolina, David Ridlin, president of GlobalTrac, a manufacturer of "animal identity technologies," described his company's perception of the limitations of RFID and satellite technologies:

> We don't want us to go out there and do the quick and easy thing for a rancher and stick an ear tag in this ear and that be the end of it. We feel like if you're gonna design a system and we're gonna start to implement a system for National Animal ID, let's implement a system that has the technology and the ability to continue down that retail chain to the end consumer. We can't do that with an ear tag, because once that animal's head's cut off at the slaughter plant, it's over.

Perhaps, Ridlin suggested, a truly effective NAIS would need to trace animals using their DNA (USDA APHIS 2004d:7). For many backers of animal surveillance schemes, as for many evolutionary biologists, DNA remains an *Ur*-marker, the once and future mother of all bodily identity, rather than another tag whose reading will introduce new complications.[12]

It is not just some technical incapacity to establish unique correspondences that prevents schemes such as the NAIS from delivering the comprehensive techno-intimacy with animal bodies they seek. To arrive at the godlike knowledge of animal movements to which they aspire, these technologies would have to cope with infinity. As carcasses move through an industrialized food chain, the practice of butchering in quantity and grinding in mass batches creates an almost infinite density of objects to be tracked, many not even so discrete as to be properly termed items for sale or disposal. It is no small feat to warrant innumerable scraps of mutton, not to mention the wayward flecks of spinal cord that can spread BSE. Like infinity, such a task can be approached but never accomplished.

The point, then, is not that surveillance technology has a long way to go to make good on its ambitions. While civil servants were still busy dreaming up the NAIS, there were already arrangements in place that allowed officials to pinpoint with good success affected livestock during disease outbreaks, without ever reaching for shibboleths such as electronic tracking devices or genetic testing. Before goats in the United States were ever microchipped, they received "unique tattoos" on the inside of their hind legs. Hot iron branding, a technology that dates to ancient Egypt, still constitutes a legally permissible animal identification marker in many jurisdictions (based on rulings that prompted animal rights advocates to rally to the defense of RFID tags).

After a 2002 outbreak of Exotic Newcastle Disease, the USDA initiated a campaign called "Look, Practice, Report" that placed rather old-fashioned surveillance techniques into the service of newly fashioned biosecurity concerns. Campaign graphics featured an anthropomorphized chicken that wielded a magnifying glass in order to get a better look at the condition of a smaller bird ("Look"). The big chicken, concerned by what it sees, dons boots and brushes on disinfectant to ward off disease ("Practice"). Finally, our hero picks up a corded telephone—a vanishing species if ever there was one—to convey the suspicious results of its investigations to the USDA's veterinary service ("Report"). Mission accomplished, with nary an ear tag nor a satellite transponder in sight.

Five years later the Biosecurity for the Birds campaign was still underway, with the same graphics but a significant change in the captions. "Look, Practice, Report" had morphed first into "Look, Report, Practice" and then into "Look, Report, Protect," with the injunction to "report sick birds" taking precedence over practical measures to control disease. Protection now emanated from the act of reporting itself, rather than from a pail of disinfectant. Concerned citizens already steeped in years of antiterrorist security rhetoric could e-mail the Animal and Plant Health Inspection Service to receive a "Free How-to Guide on Biosecurity" that piggybacked, as it were, on the vaunted American enthusiasm for do-it-yourself projects.

"Backyard biosecurity" campaigns like this one featured some of the same elements as Operation TIPS, the Terrorism Information and Protection System legislation proposed in 2002 under the Bush administration, which would have required letter carriers and tradespeople to report "suspicious" activity at homes they visited in the course of their work. The NAIS, for its part, borrowed from a 1998 white paper circulated by the United States Department of Health and Human Services that would have created

Figure 1.4. "Look, Report, Practice" graphic from the cover of the 2006 edition of the USDA's "Biosecurity Guide for Poultry and Bird Owners" [Credit: U.S. Department of Agriculture, Animal and Plant Health Inspection Service]

a "unique health identifier for [human] individuals" to use whenever they received medical care. Operation TIPS eventually went down to legislative defeat. Plumbers and carpenters made their rounds without any obligation to inform on their clients, but the act of picking up the phone to denounce a neighbor's chickens remained perfectly legal, if not patriotic.

Techno-intimacies that legislators had rejected as too invasive when applied to people continue to bid for public acceptance through their application to animals. In the process, biosecurity schemes such as the NAIS have promoted a kind of virtual hygiene in which the pledge of traceability appears more integral to health and safety than any kind of care that creatures themselves receive. The guarantor of safety becomes the system itself: not the quality of animal feed, not the folding of prions into proper shapes, not steps taken to respond to the emergence of a virulent strain of *E. coli*, not any day-to-day acquaintance with the bodies in question.

When Cattle Commingle

The most reliable outcome of the techno-intimacies that biosecurity initiatives generate may not be safety, health, or security but the reproduction of nostalgia for a time when face-to-face relations still organized production. In the United States, that nostalgia can claim a long lineage. Early in the twentieth century, a moral critique emerged of agricultural practices that took industrial production as their model. Upton Sinclair's novel *The Jungle* ([1906] 2004), a stomach-churning account of conditions in the meatpacking industry that became compulsory reading for schoolchildren, portrayed workers falling into vats, their bones retrieved only after their flesh had dissolved to mingle with animal fat in tins labeled Durham's Pure Leaf Lard (see Olsson 2006). Carey McWilliams's bestseller, *Factories in the Field* ([1939] 1999), documented the unjust treatment meted out to migrant farm workers as California agriculture became increasingly mechanized.[13] Nostalgia already inhabits these muckraking chronicles, shaped as they are by a Gemeinschaft/Gesellschaft split in their depictions of sweeping changes in food production.

For all its critical edge, the twentieth-century opposition between the intimate Gemeinschaft cultivated on family farms and the faceless cruelties perpetrated by the factory farm's bureaucratic Gesellschaft organization betrays a yearning for a golden era before capitalists applied the techniques of mass production to meat. This was the time when ranchers could recognize each animal on a spread of land by sight, a time when to be Romani or Dakota was to know how to identify horses in a herd according to spirit, mannerisms, and markings, without recourse to radio transponders. Representatives of agribusiness perpetuate this oversimplified opposition when they characterize foraging chickens and range-fed beef as the last denizens of an antiquated system of farming that could never feed the world. But so do their erstwhile antagonists when they characterize themselves as reviving artisanal practices associated with family farming or resuscitating a kind of intimacy with the land that has (almost) been lost.

This static opposition between family farms and factory farms elides a series of historic changes in production processes that have blurred the Gemeinschaft/Gesellschaft divide. In the 1980s, for instance, meat producers inaugurated a new era of agro-industrialization when they set about "refashioning the interior geography of the pig for profit" in response to demand for leaner, "healthier" meat (Ufkes 1995:683). As a result, nominally independent, family-run farms began to make ends meet through production contracting, in which small farmers raised animals to corporate specifications while companies retained ownership of the animals. Gemeinschaft or Gesellschaft? Neither and both.

The happy pigs, meandering turkeys, and violin-playing cows that grace popular depictions of life on family farms only reinforce the impression that families and small-town rural communities are the place for face-to-face relations, in agriculture as elsewhere. In contrast, a grim, gray, anonymous destiny awaits animals with the misfortune to encounter industrialized agriculture. The dystopian setting of Steve Striffler's (2005) ethnography of meatpacking, *Chicken*, is not so different, in some respects, from the depiction of the surveillance-enhancing technologies of barbed wire and searchlights that set the scene for the feature film *Chicken Run*, in which animated animals unite to defeat the chicken pot pie (pasty) machine installed by the evil money-grubbing farmer's wife, Mrs. Tweedy.

Like all oppositions, the one between face-to-face intimacy on the farm and alienated techno-intimacy in the feedlot works best as the scaffolding for a story. Beyond the event horizon of an incident such as 9/11 or the latest bird flu panic, it becomes difficult to gauge the effects of the techno-intimacies produced by biosecurity schemes such as the NAIS on the lives they target. How do the techno-intimacies produced by a state-sponsored identification system, for instance, differ from the ones produced on a ranch that uses the "Ear-A-Round," a solar-powered headset for cows invented by a USDA researcher that not only pinpoints an animal's location but also allows a "cowboy" in front of a computer to talk to it? In the latter case, the emphasis is as much on herding as tracking. The keyboard cowpuncher moves cattle around by training lead cows to follow verbal cues such as "Come on, girls, let's go," with the promise of an electrical shock administered by the headsets in the face of bovine resistance ("Heard around the West" 2008:32).

When small farmers kit out their cattle with novelties like solar headsets, or burp scanners and gas backpacks to minimize the methane emissions that contribute to climate change, will they use this gear in ways that differ from farms that operate on an industrial scale (see Jopson 2014)? Questions like these cannot be answered without ethnographic attention to the ways that animals and people interact with specific technologies, technologies that researchers too often lump together under the umbrella of "surveillance." It says something about nostalgia, cultural histories, *and* the creative uses of technology that keyboard cowboys have ended up singing "Git Along Little Dogies" and other time-honored cattle drive ditties into the mike.

When events defined as threats to the United States as a nation have occurred in recent years, the most common response has been to highlight the quantitative: calls for more oversight, more cameras, more tracking, more controls. What becomes difficult to discern in the black hole that is "biosecurity" are the qualitatively distinctive effects of various forms of surveillance initiatives, such as the quest for a unique individual identifier, on bodies that still breathe. The assurance of a comprehensive monitoring system—every body letter-numbered, the better to be uniquely and actively surveyed—tends to mitigate observation of the conditions to which those bodies are subjected. Thus NAIS documents contain few references to the extremely high rates of bacterial infection in the meat coming out of North America's processing plants, whereas they have a lot to say about the specter of animals commingling.[14]

You might think commingling would occur whenever chickens, cows, or sheep get together, but the USDA does not see it that way. In a notice about the NAIS published in the *Federal Register*, livestock destined for the food chain "commingled" only in the process of relocating to places where they met new animals, with "a sale barn" given as an example. Fraternizing with other animals in the "birth herds" where they were raised before beginning the journey to market did not count as commingling. The ideal time to assign an animal a unique individual identifier would accordingly be "prior to entering commerce or being commingled with animals from other premises" (USDA APHIS 2005:23962). Animals like turkeys that "normally move through the production chain in large groups" shared a lot number assigned to the entire flock. But leaving the group to commingle elsewhere ("to go to a fair, for example") would trigger assignment of an individual identifier (USDA APHIS 2004d:6).

In USDA parlance, then, *commingling* required one part body-to-body contact and one part geographic removal, with a dash of commodification thrown in to leaven the mix. It is an interesting usage of a term that has strong historical associations in the United States with relations more conventionally treated under the sign of intimacy, including the "commingling of the races" that the Supreme Court sought to forestall with its 1896 ruling in favor of separate but equal accommodation in *Plessy v. Ferguson*, and the illicit commingling of funds that breaches a client's trust by mixing the client's financial assets with one's own.[15]

Regardless of the particular technologies deployed, the tracker's goal is to produce a body in relationship to time and space. All the unique identifiers and transponders in the world are useless unless overseers can map them onto an animal's travels. Documentation of departures and arrivals at a registered premises can supply geotemporal coordinates, but only once an animal is in the system. What the idea of commingling provides is a before and an after that determines when and where animals are authorized to associate. In this vision, the dangerous moment comes when an animal separates from its birth herd and commingles with stranger animals. Like children on their first day of school, farm animals are not supposed to venture forth without suitable identification pinned to their bodies. The result is a morality play, staged in terms of animal intercourse and—with the references to "birth herds"—even a kind of animal kinship.

As Michael Pollan (2006:73) points out, this is also a story about migration from scattered homesteads to the "animal cities" known as Concentrated Animal Feeding Operations (CAFOs), which he fancies resemble European medieval cities in terms of crowding, anonymity, unsanitary conditions, and general squalor. According to Pollan, in an eerie reversal of the Great Transformation, when enclosure acts removed people from the land and herded them into urban areas, animals now make their way under duress to pens in the countryside that hold tens of thousands, while fences disappear from the rural landscape because they are no longer needed to control foragers.[16] When cattle (or pigs, or sheep) commingle in a drama that dates to Elizabethan England, it is not surprising that their passage from the farm to the fork revivifies tired old notions of urbanization as a process that destroys intimacies rather than a process that generates new sorts of intimacies, including techno-intimacies, along the way, however unsavory some denizens of the twenty-first century might find them.[17]

A Tale of Two Farms

Of course, production—of bodies, herds, security, or justice—does not have to be organized this way. For years the Oneida Indian Nation in eastern North America triple-tagged its Black Angus herd, not so much for identification as to deter theft. Although the Nation ran a profitable business as an important regional supplier of meat and grain, it saw no need to warrant each bit of the cattle it sold to restaurants like the ones at its Turning Stone Resort. Those cattle had grown up in pastures the herders knew well; barley and corn grown on Oneida land supplemented what the animals uncovered as they grazed. "The beauty of that," explained Michael West, director of the Nation's agriculture division, "is we don't have to worry about the Mad Cow disease. We don't have to worry about hormones or steroids or pesticides. We know exactly what's going into the animals" (Jim Adams 2004).[18]

In this case, intimate knowledge of land and animals did not require nostalgic reinvention. According to Clint Hill, a Turtle Clan representative on the Oneida Nation Council, the Nation had long banned chemical fertilizers and hormones "because of traditional cultural beliefs" (Ackerman 2010). At the same time, running a three-thousand-acre agricultural operation with one of the biggest Black Angus herds in the northeast required "modern" technologies of various sorts, from cattle trucks to software databases, which generated a *combination* of faceless and face-to-face encounters. These agricultural operations could not be described as either a factory farm or a family farm. Whatever intimacies they produced were neither lost nor found, and they did not rely on surveillance regimes to substantiate claims about food quality. Cattle commingled with enthusiasm on Oneida land, moving from site to site from the beginning to the end of their short lives. There would be no reason for the creators of this type of food chain to embrace, in the name of safety, the kind of lurking problems that traceback allows to fester until the emergence of the next "outbreak" or "crisis."

Lest you go away thinking, despite all caveats, that cattle raised on Oneida land graze timelessly so that scholars and activists can immortalize them with an ode to the pastoral, consider this: Relatively small-scale agricultural projects, even when organized as businesses, conduct their affairs in a context dominated by large corporate players, which can make it challenging for them to survive. By 2004 many tribal governments, like state governments, had accepted USDA funding to begin implementation of the NAIS, this time on Native American land (Staff Reports 2004).

In 2010 the Oneida Indian Nation in New York made a decision to sell its herd, along with its farm machinery, while vowing that "the land will continue to be taken care of in a way that is friendly to the environment and consistent with the Oneidas' longstanding efforts to protect Mother Earth" (Ackerman 2010). The same year that Oneida living on their historical lands in the east auctioned their farm equipment, the Oneida Tribe of Indians of Wisconsin received an Honoring Nations governance award from Harvard University for its agricultural initiative, which featured a bison herd, acres of high-protein Oneida white corn, and a cannery that preserved "traditional foods" for the benefit of the community, including dehydrated kernels for the soup served at ceremonies.

These tribal enterprises nourished more than bodies, as Vickie Cornelius, manager of the tribal cannery, explained. By planting the old varieties of corn, gathering together for the annual harvesting and husking bee, and cooking the corn into mush for schoolchildren, "even though we've been removed from New York, we're still connected" (Herzog 2009). The

Nation used the award money to make a video that explains how its Community Integrated Systems approach to farming draws upon the Oneida philosophy of *tsyunhehkw^*, or "life sustenance," with a little help from the nonprofit Intertribal Bison Cooperative.[19]

Devon Peña (2013), writing about the wider movement in North and South America to grow ancestral crops and restore "indigenous ecosystems," would consider the Oneida Nation's corn and bison operations an example of "deep food." Deep food may be locally grown, with methods that ignore the agribusiness orientation to speed and profit. Yet deep food also differs from local food and slow food in important ways. Its healing effects on bodies cannot be distinguished from its potential to heal communities and ecologies marked by the historical violence of genocide, land grabs, abrogated treaty rights, and disrupted livelihoods.

In 2013, after a lengthy comment period, the USDA issued a Final Rule that enshrined the principle of traceability as key to the agency's mission while backtracking on many of the Big Data provisions of the NAIS as originally conceived.[20] Gone was the centralized database for premises registration, the mandatory adoption of electronic identification, and the commitment to tracking every movement of the animals. Transportation of animals to markets across state lines still had to be documented, but decidedly low-tech devices such as certificates of veterinary inspection, ear tags without electronics, and brands on the rump were deemed adequate for the job. "Commingling" remained a concern, but the new rules allowed fraternization among animals from different "farms of origin" to occur prior to tagging, as handlers reorganized animals into "commuter herds." Animal Identification Numbers, however, remained integral to the scheme. Requirements for document maintenance were now tied to average lifespan (longer for cattle, shorter for chickens) rather than perceived threat levels for disease. The ruling remained silent on the contexts in which animals lived: their diet and surroundings, the quality of relationships formed along the way to traceability.

There is always more than one way to accomplish the needful, however it be defined. Any surveillance scheme that generates techno-intimacies will enlist different means of production than methods that foster intimate engagements with the *conditions* under which crops grow and livestock prosper. In that sense, surveillance will always be a rather different sort of animal than care, guardianship, or the kind of responsibility toward White Corn that Oneida say cannot be explained without reference to their creation story. As Jamie Betters, one of the cannery workers, put it, "Our creation story talks about taking care of the corn and the corn saying it won't stay if you don't take care of it" (Herzog 2009:8). To understand the lure of the unfulfilled promises that people have too often looked to surveillance to perform, it is best to begin with an inspection of the premises. And not the ones compiled in a national registry.

ENERGY

2

The Unwanted Intimacy of Radiation Exposure in Japan

She's twenty-two if she's a day, hair pulled off the shoulder into the kind of windswept look that only styling can create. She looks deep into my eyes, searching for something, as she reaches out to take my hand. I have never met the girl before, but I gaze back, totally absorbed. Totally absorbed. Somehow we have ended up arm in arm. She won't let go and I don't want her to. Time stops. Isn't that what they say, time stops?

It might be a scene from any one of a number of movies until the camera pans out. There we are, three of us, huddled in the doorway of adjacent hotel rooms in Tokyo's Shinjuku district, waiting for the building to decide whether or not it will succumb to a 9.0 temblor soon to be named the Great Tōhoku Earthquake.[1] "*Kowai!*" the girl screams. Scary! It's all I can do to echo her cry before the building lurches to one side. "*Kowaiiiii!!*" Her boyfriend grabs her from behind, one hand clutching the edge of the molding, the other around her waist. Without his quick reflexes, we would have tumbled to the floor.

Through the open door, through the computer I have abandoned next to the window, my partner back in the United States receives a live feed of the earthquake on a Skype connection that miraculously has not gone down. As the shaking intensifies, all I can think to tell my wife is "I love you," an incantation I repeat over and over again, reduced to a cliché that has never been so heartfelt. The skyscraper where we are trying to ride things out twists and moans. The young woman keeps gripping my arm but stops looking my way for a minute to try to get some news on her *keitai* (mobile phone). A grammar of silence descends in which only the building speaks.

Then suddenly the building roars as it shifts on its foundations. The girl looks up from her phone to meet my eyes, and although it is impossible to know for sure, I could swear she is thinking what I'm thinking: This is not just another earthquake. This is bad. We could die right here, right now, together. It strikes me, then, that there are worse ways to die, and I feel strangely peaceful. All those evening meditations in which I have tried to visualize equanimity—a compassion that does not discriminate between stranger, enemy, or friend—and here it is. The moment passes. Our hotel merely sways violently now, which seems like nothing after the last series of jolts. We let go of one another and set out to find a stairway that is not locked. Up and down the hallway the cleaning ladies remain at their posts, despite our efforts to get them to come with us. Jobs are scarce and there are many sorts of fear, as well as responsibility.

In thirty years of going back and forth to Japan since I trained to do ethnography there in the 1980s, I have never seen two strangers reach out to hold one another as we did and remain there, arm in arm, much less hold one another's gaze for such a length of time. Culturally it is just not done. Even if you want to be transgressive, as many Japanese youth, especially, do, your transgressions are likely to take a different form.

People who study disasters say they can bring out the best and the worst in people, from murderous stampedes to selfless rescues. Disasters do so because they profoundly disrupt life as usual, which, when it comes to intimacy, creates the social space to animate a deep if often fleeting sense of connection of the sort more conventionally and gradually conceived under such signs as friendship, love, kinship, neighborliness, or companionship. For someone raised on wordcraft, it is the stuff of poetry, where eyes open to become that proverbial window to a soul.

But not all disasters are alike. The three of us raced to escape down twelve flights of plaster-strewn steps before the first 7.9 aftershock helpfully allowed us to relive the trauma from the outside. We headed to a park. Just when we thought we might be safer, if not safe, a rather different sort of intimate engagement was headed our way, unknown to any of us at the time.

Not long after the earthquake, reports began to circulate that something was amiss at the Fukushima Daiichi nuclear power plant run by Tokyo Denryoku, known in English as the Tokyo Electric Power Company (TEPCO). Trains had stopped running and mobile phone service was out across the city, but FM radio signals still reached mobiles equipped to receive them. Commuters gathered in the street, some wearing the hard hats distributed to office workers as part of the disaster preparedness gear that is ubiquitous throughout Japan.[2] When I joined one of these worried clusters, we learned that a "gas facility" in Chiba had caught fire and that a massive wall of water had slammed into the northeast coast where the Daiichi plant was located.[3] Initial reassurances in the media that all was well at the plant gave way to concerns that the tsunami might have wreaked havoc on the six reactors on site. Months later, investigations would reveal that the earthquake itself had critically damaged reactor components. Utility company executives resisted this narrative of events, since it called the seismic safety of many nuclear plants around the world into question.[4]

Immediately following the quake, attention focused on survivors of the tsunami and pictures of the devastation along Japan's northeast coast: the black wall of water that turned towns into rubble in endless replay, fleets of cars bobbing in the sea, families heating water for tea over open fires with bits of wood that had once belonged to houses, muddy photographs washed up by the waves, a dog that led its baffled owner to higher ground in the nick of time, a grandmother and grandson who managed to live buried for days because their home had collapsed around them while they were next to the refrigerator. But efforts to cool the wounded reactors by the squad of workers dubbed the Fukushima Fifty did not go unnoticed, and when cameras recorded a series of explosions at the Fukushima Daiichi plant, the footage could not be ignored.

A parade of "nuclear experts" on the government-sponsored NHK network were quick to emphasize that these were not nuclear explosions, just "steam" that had built up when the electric power supply needed to cool the fuel rods failed.[5] Others were not so sure. The explosion at Reactor 3 on March 14, by far the most dramatic, sent a plume of "steam" or "smoke" skyward, prompting speculation that nuclear materials had gone critical as they burned their way through the bottom of the containment vessel. What happened next remains a matter for debate. TEPCO either evacuated most of its personnel from the site or workers fled. The company claimed the

Figure 2.1. *Itte kimasu*: TEPCO "abandons" the
Fukushima Daiichi nuclear reactors [Credit: Haru]

evacuation was for the workers' safety; TEPCO's critics styled it dereliction
of duty and "abandonment."

A bit more context is needed to understand the political commentary
embedded in figure 2.1, an image that circulated on the Internet following
this incident. The caption, いってきます (*itte kimasu*), is a commonplace,
the sort of thing children call out when they leave the house for a bit. Literally the phrase means "to go, then come": "I'm going out, but I'll be back."
Most viewers in Japan would also have recognized the image as a parody of
an announcement from a public service campaign designed to teach children manners. Here, as TEPCO steps out for a breath of nonirradiated air,
stricken workers in hand, the steaming plant in the background makes the
prospect of return seem dubious. During the actual event, the prime minister had to order the company to resume cooling operations at the plant to
try to prevent a meltdown.[6]

Despite the high drama at Fukushima Daiichi, to many Japanese at the
time the needs of people in tsunami-stricken areas of Tōhoku seemed para-
mount. The date the earthquake struck, March 11, 2011, acquired a new
name: "3.11," a rubric that echoed the before/after structure of 9/11, an event
accorded world-historic status in which many people claimed that "everything changed." Immediately following the quake, articles in the press directed criticism at foreigners—some of them longtime residents—who fled

the country due to fears of radiation. Local wits coined the term *flyjin*, a play on the word for foreigner (*gaijin*), to describe an exodus portrayed as irrational and self-centered, if not cowardly. A month or two later, however, people began to remark on how the situation had reversed: global attention to deteriorating conditions at the plant had diminished, while worries about radiation in Japan appeared to be increasing by the day (see Lochbaum et al. 2014).

Every morning brought news of fresh radioactive releases. Most of these reports featured astronomical numbers that seemed alarming to nonspecialists in and of themselves, due to their sheer magnitude. The precise bodily impact at a distance of the 1.5 billion becquerels TEPCO announced it had released when it opened the double door to one of the reactors might have been unclear, but it did not sound good. Neither did the 170,000 becquerels of Cesium-137 detected in incinerator ash as far away as Tokyo, the "unsafe levels" discovered in green tea grown in the shadow of Mount Fuji, or the national distribution of radioactive beef from cattle that officials had originally declared safe on the basis of surface scans. Within a few short years estimates for radioactive cesium, strontium, and tritium released from the damaged plant routinely reached (in becquerels) the trillions and even quadrillions ("1.1 Trillion Becquerels" 2014; Casacuberta et al. 2013; Fackler 2005; Tabuchi 2013; and "Huge Leak of Tritium" 2013).[7] Taken together, such colossal numbers raised the specter of a radioactive contamination that was not only severe but also not as localized as wind dispersal maps had suggested. Wind dispersal maps, after all, did not take garbage incineration, commodity chains, or the flow of water into sewage treatment plants into account.

The Japanese state responded to worries about radiation exposure after 3.11 largely by downplaying any possible effects. Officials routinely condemned the practice of spreading harmful rumors about the "accident." Passage of a state secrecy act bolstered informal censorship (see Repeta 2014). Such measures reframed the issue as a matter of careless speech, leaving little room for in-depth investigation of potential health threats. Besides, pundits argued, hadn't human beings lived comfortably for millennia with "natural background radiation" that predated the era of nuclear power?

The question about "natural background radiation" was meant to remain a rhetorical one. But as Itty Abraham (2012) has pointed out, even ambient radiation can occur at levels high enough to damage health and transform residents into biopolitical subjects. Abraham studied the displacement of people from seaside communities in India in areas where the state had decided to mine beaches for radioactive thorium in the name of geopolitical security. "By affirming the long-standing presence of human habitation in the radiation zone, the state seeks to reinforce the idea that ill-health from radiation is neither recent nor man-made, but a natural phenomenon for which no one (read, the state) can be held responsible" (Abraham 2012:113). Some studies of the health of villagers in these areas were inconclusive, but at least one with a robust design documented chromosomal aberrations with multigenerational effects.

In a chapter titled "Suffering, Legitimacy, and Healing," from her book *Critical Events*, Veena Das (1995) notes how, following the toxic gas disaster in Bhopal, the Indian courts demanded that survivors transform their suffering into the language of scientific certainty in order to make their case. Yet the science of epidemiology enlists patterns and probabilities precisely because a measure of uncertainty will always prevail as to the cause of any individual case of lung damage or heart disease or thyroid cancer. Once certainty becomes the standard, proving claims of injury, much less impending harm, from industrially produced substances such as methyl isocyanate and Cesium-137 becomes a Sisyphean task.

Back in Japan, MEXT, the ministry in charge of nuclear emergency response, tried to regularize the phenomenon of radiation by disseminating graphics with titles like "Radiation in Daily-life."[8] The idea was to establish benchmarks to allow comparisons between exposures received as the result of, say, an unmentionable nuclear accident, and exposures that occur under everyday conditions. While a meltdown scenario might not compare favorably to the background radiation received while playing the game of tennis pictured in the MEXT graphic, the heftier 6,900 microsieverts administered during a CAT scan made official statistics on releases from Fukushima Dai-ichi seem less scary. Since people do not, however, participate in activities like a CAT scan on a daily basis, a more accurate title for the chart would be "Radiation in Situations That Are Familiar to You."

A careful observer might note that without regard for context these sorts of comparisons are disingenuous. What makes a *meaningful* difference for living organisms is not some absolute figure beyond which danger lurks but rather the rate of exposure, accumulated exposure, biomagnification effects tied to a creature's position in the food chain, and the specific radioisotopes absorbed, since radioactive iodine, cesium, and strontium target different organs in the body.

To drive home the message that worries about radiation were groundless, politicians and talk show hosts sought to demonstrate food safety by eating Fukushima-grown tomatoes in front of the cameras while discussing the very real plight of Fukushima farmers. (A strategy that backfired somewhat when social media picked up reports of some of those same celebrities falling ill for unspecified reasons.) Legal bans on the sale of foodstuffs immediately following the accident took effect by prefecture (県, *ken*), which devastated farmers in relatively unaffected areas of Fukushima while allowing free distribution of crops from severely contaminated lands in adjoining ken. As with the attempts to establish animal citizenship discussed in chapter 1, people created elaborate strategies to negotiate a favorable origin for the goods they sought to sell. Rather than land fish in Fukushima ports, for instance, some fishermen sailed up or down the coast, where their catch could receive an origin label from another ken. Bans by prefecture had the effect of reinforcing discrimination against people from northeast Honshu, especially residents of Fukushima and Ibaraki (see Takahashi 2011a; Wallace 2011). Landlords in other areas became hesitant to rent to them and classmates bullied refugee children in their new schools, developments reminiscent of the prejudicial treatment meted out to *hibakusha* (被爆者, survivors of the bombings of Nagasaki and Hiroshima).

Disaster compensation schemes developed by the government featured a new category called "damage by rumor" (風評被害, *fūhyōhigai*), listed right alongside claims for destruction of crops and businesses in tsunami-stricken areas.[9] Meanwhile, an animation called *Genpatsu-kun* (原発くん, "Nuclear Power Boy"), which tried to explain what was happening at Fukushima Daiichi in simple visual terms, had gone viral on the Internet (Jeffrey 2011). In the video, Genpatsu-kun, who represents the power plant, gets a stomachache, but then he has a little poo and feels much better. This lighthearted treatment provided much-needed comic relief in a country where scatological humor is par for the course. Yet it was not at all obvious how to read the happy ending to an unfinished disaster for a character reminiscent of *Pluto-kun*, a nuclear industry mascot who reassured the public back in the 1990s that fears about plutonium were groundless.[10]

For every graphic that TEPCO or the government sponsored, activists associated with the small but growing antinuclear movement in Japan created one of their own. When nation-states around the world raised their permissible limits for radioactive isotopes in food—Japan more so than most—a leaflet appeared that illustrated how infants born in Japan could legally ingest much higher levels of radioactivity than their peers in other countries. The red dots used to portray radiation levels in the drawing resonated eerily with lesions that sometimes appear on the skin as a manifestation of radiation sickness. Against the backdrop of the official mantra of "no immediate threat" attached to any and all reports of emissions from the nuclear plant, it began to dawn on people that low-level radiation seldom poses an immediate threat. Whatever dangers it holds surface later.[11]

Following the meltdowns, people in Japan became fiercely divided on the subject of radiation and the response to the crisis staged by the government and TEPCO. Relatively few followed events at Fukushima Daiichi closely or took consistent measures to monitor their exposure to radiation. Most simply went about living their daily lives, out of necessity as much as anything. But as the fraction of the population concerned about radiation grew and became increasingly organized during the first year after 3.11, its members helped inaugurate a new chapter in a long history of Japanese technological innovation.

This time, people with no particular technical training would decide to take technology into their own hands in order to detect ionizing radiation. As they responded to the perceived ineptitude of TEPCO and the Japanese state in handling the nuclear accident at Fukushima Daiichi, they would enlist a creative fascination with electronic machinery that in many ways was historically specific to Japan. Yet their reasons for doing so also drew upon a globalized preoccupation with hazards incorporated into the attenuated supply chains that people in a postindustrial age depend upon to eat, breathe, and survive.

In her book *Inescapable Ecologies: A History of Environment, Disease, and Knowledge*, Linda Nash explores another instance of the "emergence of a landscape that produced disease because of its modernization" (2006: 150–51). Nash studied changes in bodies and land use in California's Central Valley, the heart of industrial food production in the United States, where workers were "literally drenched in pesticides" from the mid-twentieth century onward and public health officials debated how to handle the resulting medical problems. At that time, in that place, most people assumed that bodies and environment were fundamentally distinct. Humans might shape the landscape and find themselves influenced by the landscape in turn, but the two appeared to be separate entities that encountered one another only after they were constituted as such. In this quasi-nationalist imagination, skin supplied a boundary or frontier that protected bodies from environmental threats like the germs and chemicals imagined to be lurking outside, waiting to spot some unguarded port of entry. Not surprisingly, public health officials recommended measures to fortify the boundary: supplying masks and gloves to farm workers, for instance, to ward off chemicals. Call this the interaction model of body and environment.

A rather different perception of body/environment has emerged in the early twenty-first century: one that highlights *bio-intimacy*. In this version, bodies and ecologies are not distinct. Far from it: in a certain sense, bodies *are* their environments, and vice versa. As Brett Walker (2010:70) points out in his study of industrial toxicity in Japan, repeated applications of the pesticide parathion "inscribed their history on the bodies—on the very genetic predispositions" of insects and other creatures. That means the history of political-economic negotiations over matters like the location of a chemical plant or the marketing of a pesticide inhabits ecologies as well.[12]

This strong version of bio-intimacy goes beyond interdependence, since there is nothing "inter" about it. In the older *inter*action model, bodies were said to pollute a river with "their" waste. In contrast, viewed in terms of bio-intimacy, a sewage-polluted river *is* a "river of human waste" (among other things), not just some site where water and humans prove interdependent.

When it comes to radiation, an interaction model pictures radioactive isotopes as bounded entities unleashed upon a body that preserves its integrity, however compromised. Hot particles or beta and gamma rays bombard an immune system conceived as separate from the source of radiation. From a bio-intimacy perspective, however, irradiated bodies are made up of radioactive isotopes (among many other things), lending poignancy to Mochizuki Iori's lament in his blog, *Fukushima Diary*, that "we are becoming nuclear fuel rods."[13]

The 3.11 disaster in Japan illustrates how bio-intimacy can double as a form of techno-intimacy when bodies incorporate products such as radioactive isotopes into their cellular fabric. This is not the pastoral blurring of the human offered by so many posthumanist accounts, where Cree hunters in Canada approach animals as kin and Gimi villagers in Papua New Guinea describe themselves as part of the forest that incarnates their ancestors. It is bio-intimacy as techno-intimacy, where bodies are fully industrialized products of a highly industrialized world.

Where bio-intimacy prevails, bodies and ecologies do not so much *inter*-act as *co*-constitute. Care of one is never separate from care of the other. Treating the body as something to be protected from an environment imaged as "out there" and potentially hostile makes no sense. In the case of industrial disasters like the one at Fukushima Daiichi, relocation, food monitoring, and so on offer mitigation strategies, not escape, and then only just. Rather than calling for more masks and better nuclear waste solutions, policies based on an understanding of bio-intimacy would need to address the ways that nuclear power and pesticides have reconfigured bodies in the course of reconfiguring ecologies. They would have to ask the question: Are these the bodies and ecologies we want?

The turn of the twenty-first century saw the publication of a raft of books about poisonous substances that had crept into domestic settings, volumes with titles like *Exposed: The Toxic Chemistry of Everyday Products* (Schapiro 2007) and *What's Gotten into Us? Staying Healthy in a Toxic World* (Jenkins 2011). Food scandals about transnational shipments of tainted milk, deadly pet food, and lead-painted toys exacerbated fears, revitalized safety discourse, and undermined trust in government regulation. But the new emphasis was on toxic exposures that had become regularized, not the occasional scandal: hormone-disrupting plasticizers in the liners of cereal boxes, mutagenic flame retardant in mattresses. As the authors of *Slow Death by Rubber Duck: The Secret Danger of Everyday Things* pointed out, the pollution that menaced twenty-first-century lives had changed, not least with respect to its invisibility (R. Smith and Lourie 2009). It took laboratory studies by specialists to reveal that large numbers of synthetic chemicals had traveled great distances to insinuate their way into living organisms, from the PCBs discovered in hapless polar bears in the Arctic to the dioxin that now laced human breast milk (see Landrigan et al. 2002). Few people understood what went into most household products, and even those who knew were often sworn to treat the ingredients and their potentially deleterious effects as proprietary secrets. This was also the time when concepts such as "body burden" and "chemical load" entered the lexicon of popular science, and with those concepts, the notion of a cumulative, cell-altering exposure to chemicals that could equally well be applied to radiation.

In Japan since 3.11, many people have treated irradiation of their bodies with industrially produced ions such as Cesium-137 or Iodine-131 as a form of unwanted intimacy with invisible matter. Unlike irradiation of the body under specialized circumstances, such as medical treatment for cancer, no one requested the uncontrolled releases from Fukushima Daiichi. Radioactive isotopes moved into bodies like an uninvited guest who takes up residence, refuses to leave, and throws the entire household into disarray.[14] Unlike other forms of intimacy that seem desirable, this one had the potential to slowly and secretly alter bodies in ways that could lead to their untimely destruction. I should emphasize here that "unwanted intimacy" is my analytic category, not a category in circulation in Japan. Yet the phrase captures something that many parents, workers, farmers, and ruined shopkeepers have worked hard to articulate, as they questioned platitudes about "safe levels" issued by a state that lost a great deal of credibility for withholding computer trajectories of the radiation plume that would have allowed people to take basic preventive actions like staying indoors.[15]

One way to characterize the unwanted intimacy of irradiation is as a byproduct of living in what Joseph Masco (2006) calls mutant ecologies. When radioactive particles lodge in living tissue, they alter physiology unknowingly. Organisms transmute into something other than what they once were. The key word is unknowingly: as an invisible force, radiation reworks bodies in ways that human beings might suspect but cannot sense. They can only confirm its presence with the aid of technology, which is why X-ray diffraction machines and canisters of "hot" materials carry warning symbols. But when the keepers of the equipment with the power to detect radioactivity refuse to use it, misuse it, and deny access to the results, radioactive embodiment reveals itself as a political consequence. To be radioactively embodied after Fukushima Daiichi is to imagine radiation suffusing you, but also to wonder whether your imagination has gotten the better of you, and to contemplate how in the world you are going to get the better of this thing that you and your loved ones have become.

Seizing the Means of Perception

In the beginning, the tools were in the hands of the authorities. When equipment that could detect radioactivity made an appearance in the period immediately after the earthquake, the figure wielding it was usually stationed at a checkpoint, control room, or refugee center, garbed in a uniform, hazmat suit, or white coat. High radiation readings led to segregation, quarantine, a handful of iodine tablets, or denial of entry. In cities spared by the tsunami, people had little time to worry about radiation as they took up an urbanized version of hunting and gathering, scouring the rapidly diminishing supplies on store shelves for that last cabbage, yogurt carton, or *nigiri* sushi. They left their offices early, when they could get to them, and turned off lights to save energy per government instructions, but most left the Internet and television switched on.

For all the detailed diagrams broadcast of the innards of the reactors at Fukushima Daiichi, news reports offered little to anyone inquiring into the dangers of radiation. On the contrary: the steady stream of contradictions, redactions, and retractions in official announcements hollowed out a big space of doubt for rumors to blow through. Everything began to appear unsubstantiated. For those who followed the headlines, the "10 million times higher than normal" levels of radiation emitted by Reactor 2 would turn out to be a "mistake." While the absence of a radiation spike constituted good news, "TEPCO gave wrong numbers" was the takeaway message tweeted by observers ("Japan Nuclear Crisis" 2011). The "gas facility" that caught fire in Chiba on the day of the earthquake, posing "no danger" to the public, turned out to store depleted uranium, but none of the uranium had burned. Then on July 9: "Depleted Uranium Storage Facility Also Burned When Cosmo Oil's Gas Tank Exploded."[16] Apparently 765 kilos of uranium had gone up in smoke.

During this time radiation traveled through Japan as what Bruno Latour (2010) would call a "factish," something that mediates between the fact and the fetish, the fabricated and the real. A writer who worked undercover at the Fukushima Daiichi plant revealed that the "heroes" risking their lives to keep things cool subsisted on two rice balls per day and had not even received dosimeters to gauge their exposure. While the press later reported TEPCO had rectified the situation, workers said some supervisors pressured them not to use the dosimeters, so they turned the badges around or covered them with lead (J. Sato et al. 2012).[17] After TEPCO detected plutonium in the area around the plant, the utility hastened to add that the density was "equivalent to the fallout observed in Japan when the atmospheric nuclear test was conducted in the past" (a statement intended to reassure, until people reflected that plutonium was plutonium, and perhaps there was a reason for relocating atomic testing underground) (TEPCO 2011). Signs that recast TEPCO as the "Truth Expanding Power Company" appeared in street protests.

Some local governments sampled radiation, but only in a few places. Ambient air measurements taken from the tops of buildings tended to yield much lower figures than samples collected at street level where radioactive particles settled. In one case, a decontamination worker employed by a government subcontractor told journalists that his company had instructed him to clean up only the areas around the radiation measurement equipment (Aoki, Kihara, and Tada 2013). Citizen groups deemed government radiation figures suspect, just like TEPCO's, and demanded better monitoring, but they had no way to monitor the situation themselves.[18]

Meanwhile what was the status of the plant? A manageable situation, with cooling operations calmly directed from a "control room," or a topsy-turvy world in which the interior of the building housing Reactor 3 had become an exterior, with its yellow containment vessel exposed to the open air? Even the engineers called in to stabilize the site found themselves mystified as they discovered a bricolage of pipes, tunnels, and cables that did not correspond to the original architectural drawings ("Fukushima Plant 'Set to Collapse'" 2013).

Predictably, guesswork began to fill the gaps in corporate and government accounting. After Nakagawa Shoko, a media personality or タレント, posted photographs of mysterious bruising on her thighs, others followed with shots of their own bruises, thinning hair, and detached fingernails. Tweets ostensibly from nurses mentioned an uptick in children with unexplained nosebleeds and diarrhea. Birds too lethargic to fly starred in a video that made the rounds of social media. Could these be symptoms of radiation poisoning, rather than the ストレス (stress) diagnosed by doctors?

Police inside the twenty-kilometer evacuation zone around the plant were said to be dying. Workers inside the plant were said to be dying: not the five or six that TEPCO admitted had passed away from conditions unrelated to their work but hundreds of them. If *yakuza* gangs had recruited them and the workers had never been properly registered, surely this was possible?[19] Gigantic potatoes and deformed tomatoes circulated on the Internet in virtual exchanges that labeled them as prizewinners or mutants, according to the political inclinations of the poster. Farmers near the exclusion zone continued to plant vegetables, because that was how they made a living, but some were afraid to eat the food they had grown. In Tochigi-ken families that had harvested wild plants from the forests for generations had to abandon their way of life as it became evident that mushrooms took up more than their share of radioactive cesium (Bird 2013). Local organic produce from these areas, which on March 10 commanded higher prices because they symbolized the safety of food grown under known local conditions, could not be sold at any price once 3.11 conjured the dangers of unknown radioactive exposures.

For all the attention devoted to *fūhyōhigai* or damage by rumor, the point was this: discourse became polarized between reassurances about safety and warnings about threat, with no way to adjudicate the difference. In that sense, whether people had recourse to rumor or the official pronouncements on NHK was not the issue, since neither offered access to any way of making this invisible thing called radiation tangible. Those who believed that they had woken up on 3.11 into a state of exception, like those who longed to verify rumors *and* government figures, did not want to wait to use the human body as a proving ground to register radiation's effects, for by then it would be too late to protect anyone from harm.

So some of them formed a human chain around the Ministry of Education to demand that it do more to safeguard schoolchildren. Some of them, like the writer Murakami Haruki (2011), gave speeches that contrasted the "illusion" fostered by utility company advertisements with the "reality" revealed by the accident: "Nuclear power plants, which were supposed to be efficient, instead offer us a vision of hell." Some of them, like Professor Kodama Tatsuhiko from the radioisotope center at Tokyo University, who worked with radiation every day as he tried to extend the lives of sick patients, gave impassioned testimony in which he estimated Fukushima Daiichi to have emitted the uranium equivalent of twenty Hiroshima bombs and called for the establishment of a center to study the efficacy of decontamination methods.[20] Some of them marched with drums and banners in the street to demand alternatives to nuclear energy. Some of them framed their demands with the English category "truth," as counterpoint to what they saw as an institutional investment in normalizing the situation. Some of them were shopkeepers who simply wanted to know whether it was safe for customers to buy whatever they were selling. These were scattered voices with different sorts of politics, united by worries that would not go away, much like the radiation itself.

This was the point at which some perfectly ordinary people took an extraordinary step: they reached for their wallets, or their soldering irons, and tried to put them to a new use. They decided to take matters into their own hands by taking their own radiation measurements, to become generators of knowledge about radioactivity instead of consumers who had to wonder whether to dignify the latest reports with the term *knowledge*. No need then to worry about the veracity of rumors or the accuracy of published figures, except to point out where they might be lacking.

In his early book *Risk Society*, Ulrich Beck (1992:54) distinguishes between two kinds of reactions to bad news in societies built upon trust in expertise and obscure supply chains: "Unlike news of losses in income and the like, news of toxic substances in foods, consumer goods, and so on contain a *double shock*. The threat itself is joined by the *loss of sovereignty* over assessing the dangers, to which one is directly subjected." (For "toxic" here read "radioactive.") Because radiation is a shadowy thing—tasteless, odorless, untouchable, inaudible, imaged but unseen—what it would mean to restore sovereignty over assessing danger after 3.11 was by no means obvious. But one thing seemed clear: Before anyone could come up with their own radiation measurements, before they could seize the means of knowledge production in any classic sense, they first had to seize the means of perception. And that meant getting their hands on some technology.

Technostruggle

Ever since nuclear testing began in the 1940s, one of the icons of the atomic age has been the Geiger counter. So perhaps it should come as no surprise that after 3.11 in Japan, when people attempted to determine how radioactively embodied they were likely to become and to minimize their exposure, the Geiger counter was the piece of scientific equipment they first enlisted. The apparatus was familiar, if only because the public had already seen countless images of Geiger counters used by officials to scan everything from evacuees to spinach. The apparatus was available to anyone who could afford it. The machine was also appealing, due to the way it parsed the presence of radioactive ions into a "reading" that could register with bodily senses. Both analog and digital models supplied visual feedback, in the form of a printed dial with a scale swept by a jittery "arm" or ever-shifting numbers on a screen. Turn on the sound and beeps or clicks served up an auditory stream of counts per minute (CPM).[21]

These machines also brought touch to the project of making radioactivity perceptible. "Personal" Geiger counters could fit in one hand; industrial models required the operator to hold a box while wielding a scanning wand. All styles cultivated haptic engagement, as bodies turned, bent, and twisted to scan various bits of the world. Geiger counters could also engage the body as a whole when excitement or fear generated by a ragged rhythm of accelerating CPMs made the heart race, staging a visceral drama that bioscience scripts as an endocrine system mobilizing for danger. Most importantly for a device taken up by nonspecialists, a Geiger counter was not technically difficult to operate and the readings it generated did not require extensive training to interpret.

What might not be immediately obvious from the proliferation of advertisements for Geiger counters on Japanese websites is just how expensive this equipment is, at least with respect to the budget of the average Japanese household. For people who lost jobs and homes or had to relocate following the tsunami, purchasing a Geiger counter was usually not an option, even if they thought it might be a good idea to buy one. But that did not keep people of lesser means from participating in this nascent movement to seize the means of perception. Tokyo Hackerspace and other community-based organizations sponsored workshops on how to make a DIY Geiger counter at far lesser cost than commercially marketed models. Independent software developers set about creating inexpensive applications that could turn the smartphones that most people in Japan already owned into radiation detectors. It was also possible to share equipment, of course.

What people were most likely to share, however, was not equipment but the readings they obtained from using the equipment. The Internet became the preferred medium for circulating the results of grassroots radiation monitoring, often in the form of videos that conveyed findings by documenting the monitoring process itself. Many of these videos chronicle journeys in which an unidentified person takes a Geiger counter onto a train and films the apparatus for a portion of the trip as it registers the presence of radiation, sometimes for twenty or thirty minutes at a stretch. One of many, many examples would be the video documentation of readings on a train ride from Nasu to Fukushima City posted to YouTube on April 16, 2011, about a month after the earthquake.[22] The title for this video is typical, insofar as it marks the highest level of radioactivity detected during the trip: "Summary of Shinkansen Radiation Nasu-Koriyama-Fukushima Max250CPM/2.5μSvh Low in Tunnels." This genre—and it has become a genre—of Geiger counter readings recorded on trains tends to feature dramatic contrasts, in which almost nothing registers when the train goes underground, whereas the instrument comes to life and displays elevated results (as many as 250 CPM in the case of the Nasu-Koriyama-Fukushima City clip) during later portions of the journey.

In other videos, the observer remains fairly stationary. "Playground Radiation in Kashiwa, Japan," recorded on June 20, 2011, linked Geiger counter readings to an emerging national debate about the safety of children by taking readings in a park.[23] After recording an extremely elevated reading of 6.46 microsieverts per hour in this city in Chiba, far from the nuclear plant, the filmmaker raises the camera to show kids playing nearby, their ignorance of a radioactive exposure now known to the viewer offered as a mute call to action. Corroboration of results for any video posted to the Internet in this way is difficult if not impossible, since neither the calibration of the instrument nor the location where the Geiger counter was placed can be verified, except by using landscape markers familiar to people who already know the locale. Yet the decision to film the process of taking a reading, rather than simply posting a series of numbers tagged with GPS coordinates, can arguably be read as a claim for veracity, since it conveys additional visual testimony in a bid to enhance the film's status as evidence.

This widespread deployment of Geiger counters, video cameras, software, dosimeters, and Internet postings with the goal of restoring sovereignty over knowledge about radioactive embodiment is an emergent form of *technostruggle*. In practice technostruggle exceeds the boundaries of any single technology such as the Geiger counter, however charismatic that technology might be. I use the term to describe what happens when people seize upon technology to wrest the production of knowledge from officials and experts, especially in situations where monopolization of the means of knowledge production can have that most intimate of consequences, life or death. For if, as Beck (1992:55) contends, "The investigations of risk researchers . . . take place with a parallel displacement in everyone's kitchen, tea room or wine cellar" and "each one of their central cognitive decisions causes the toxin level in the blood of the population to shoot up or plunge," then access to any sort of machinery that people can operate themselves in order to make less mediated assessments matters enormously.

In post-3.11 Japan, technostruggle also encompassed the rise of a populist version of the citizen scientist, someone with little or no formal training who equipped herself with the skills necessary to investigate what was happening to bodies in a world filled with new radioactive exposures. This expertise, which might be called self-taught except that in Japan people have often acquired it as part of a collective endeavor, sometimes went well beyond learning how to build a Geiger counter out of transistors and circuit boards. By networking through parent–teacher associations, nonprofit groups, and live blogs, people deciphered schematic drawings for boiling water reactors like the ones at Fukushima Daiichi, gained a theoretical understanding of the processes of nuclear decay, learned to tell a sievert from a becquerel, and so on.

"Ordinary people" are not the only ones who have worked as grassroots scientists in the wake of 3.11. Some professionally trained scientists and engineers also broke with the "official story" that minimized radioactive embodiment and began to apply their expertise from the standpoint of concerned citizens. At times the two groups have cooperated.[24] When citizen scientists armed with Geiger counters detect alarming levels of radioactivity at a site, for example, the next step is often to submit samples to a lab where technicians test the materials, and then to work with scientist citizens to lobby for action based on the results.[25]

Early on, Manuel Yang (2011) characterized this "people's 'measuring movement'" as the antithesis of the "capitalist quantification" embedded in Taylorist management. Rather than placing measurement in the service of profit and efficiency, people had resolved to measure "the radiation spewed out by nuclear capital, making visible the exploitation that is 'exposure.'" What I am calling technostruggle here would count, for Yang, as a form of class struggle, insofar as it involved the preservation of aspects of life—food, health, childbearing—critical to the reproduction of labor power.[26]

The scientific knowledge generated through technostruggle was not all newly acquired, as media coverage of "Geiger counter guerrillas" often suggested.[27] Japan's triple disaster reactivated the historical memory of the Pacific War bombings in complex ways, including ones that affected popular understandings of how radioactivity spreads. On the day after the earthquake, as news about trouble at Fukushima Daiichi diffused along with the isotopes, people living in the shifting paths taken by the wind reminded friends and relatives not to go outside if it rained. Radioactive particles would come down to earth, they warned, with any form of precipitation. Although most of them were too young to have lived through the war, they shared with earlier generations a postmemory of the "black rain" that brought radiation sickness when it fell on Hiroshima and Nagasaki.[28] Even on days without precipitation in the forecast, people sometimes referred to radiation as "invisible snow."

This wartime legacy of exposure to uncontrolled radioactive releases allowed Japan's 3.11 citizen scientists to draw upon an already existing version of biological citizenship of the sort that Adriana Petryna (2002) has described for survivors of the nuclear accident at Chernobyl. Japan, after all, is a place where hibakusha, as survivors of the atomic bombings of Nagasaki and Hiroshima, have long organized for peace and petitioned for the abolition of nuclear power.[29] Like the Chernobyl survivors, hibakusha have lived with illness, dispossession, discrimination, and medicalization. They have also grappled with the challenge of how to dramatize those experiences in appeals to the state and a wider public. After 3.11 the moral claims on the state mobilized by Japan's biological citizens would extend beyond human suffering to embrace the wounds of a suffering, irradiated landscape.

Such resonances between one nuclear disaster and another were animated by something at once more and less globalized than the "equivalence of catastrophes" proposed by Jean-Luc Nancy (2015) to critique the ways in which one sort of disaster plays out against another in this technologically complex and increasingly interdependent world. For nuclear catastrophe in Japan, of all places, had a site-specific history that could be—and was—mobilized to invoke the nation, in the guise of both wartime suffering and postwar restoration. As Lucy Birmingham and David McNeill (2012:173) note, "In a country with a unique nuclear legacy, Japanese popular culture is full of eerie warnings about such a disaster, from the radiation-breathing Godzilla to the Miyazaki Hayao eco-animation classic *Nausicaa of the Valley of the Wind*, set in a post-apocalyptic world where settlers live in constant fear of the encroaching poison from the toxic jungle." There are good reasons why ordinary people wielding Geiger counters knew, early on, to look for concentrations of radioactive particles along drainpipes, curbs, ditches, and anywhere else water would collect. How so many government agencies managed to forget these lessons is another story.

When citizen scientists and scientist citizens collaborated in techno-struggle, good things often happened. Consider a composite example: the "decontamination" of one among many playgrounds where parents used Geiger counters to detect harmful levels of radiation. What led to this form of collective action? First Kosako Toshiso, a Tokyo University professor and senior nuclear advisor to the government, resigned from his government post after officials refused to use his SPEEDI Projection system to alert the public to the likely paths taken by airborne radiation from the stricken plant.[30] Press coverage of his resignation, more diligent than usual due to the rare circumstance of someone of his stature breaking into tears on camera, raised awareness about the relevance of computer modeling to radiation detection, as well as the potential for highly radioactive particles to travel hundreds of kilometers outside the exclusion zone. Using trajectories plotted by such models, citizen scientists began to look for radioactive fallout where they might otherwise not have looked.

As informed citizen scientists, the parents who brought their Geiger counters to our composite playground would have realized that the top of playground equipment does not usually yield the highest radiation levels, so they also scanned the bottom of the slide where the rain runs off. When they detected disturbingly high readings in the place where children jump to the ground from the slide and stir up dust, they bagged soil samples from the spot. After completing their sampling and assessment, they had to request that the local government fund lab tests and pressure school officials to cancel the customary student-led cleaning of the school grounds, which would have included sweeping up radioactive debris. In the meantime, the parents created a no-go zone around the slide by marking the zone with the decidedly low-tech device of a can of spray paint. After receiving the requisite funding, they sent the soil samples off to a lab where technicians analyzed the samples with equipment not available at the household level. Finally, they petitioned politicians to decontaminate the site, which in this case meant power-washing the slide and removing several inches of topsoil. That did not solve the intractable problem of where to store the radioactive refuse, but the outcome of this collaboration would still be deeply meaningful for the children who played there, and for anyone else who understands the ways in which we are connected.

The Struggle in Technostruggle

Technostruggle can require courage. In the months immediately following 3.11, some citizen scientists traversed the country as self-styled sleuths with Geiger counters, video guerrillas pursued by the state, and whistleblowers with the courage to take on powerful corporate interests. They voiced fears of prosecution and took steps to conceal their identities (Sato Shigeru, Sakamaki, and Inajima 2011). In most of the Geiger counter videos posted to the Internet, the audience never sees the face behind the camera. Many of these videos also deliberately omit voiceover, relying on the machines to do the talking.

There is a certain romanticism, to be sure, that informs the figure of the Geiger counter–wielding superhero who shields his or her identity in order to help others. Yet neither were these fears totally unfounded, if one takes into account proposals to ban nonauthorized use of radiation detection equipment on the grounds that defective imported machines would generate erroneous readings and amplify those bothersome rumors.[31] (Why poorly calibrated machines should only err on the high side was never explained.) After receiving violent threats, sponsors canceled a lecture by one scientist citizen, Mayor Sugenoya of Matsumoto City, a medical doctor who had worked in Belarus after Chernobyl (Otake 2011). That a mayor who dared to speak on the topic of how to protect children from the dangers of internal radiation exposure would find himself in such a position is also a reminder of the fractures that run through government. Local officials, particularly in areas near the plant, often urged rather different courses of action after 3.11 than their national counterparts.

After the measurements and the lab tests began to come in, struggles only seemed to proliferate. Citizen scientists targeted areas for evacuation, decontamination, phyto-remediation, or exclusion, but who would authorize and fund these efforts? Small businesses declared their products tested and safe for use, but what would it take to get people to buy them again? Nonprofit organizations plotted the geographical distribution of readings, but what would happen when others questioned the validity of the documentation they produced? Technostruggle gave households the means to make more informed decisions about whether and where to relocate, but what if they didn't have the financial resources to move? What if members of a household disagreed? An organized or even random resistance of citizens armed with Geiger counters can spot radioactive isotopes after they enter the nation's playgrounds and rice bowls, but ideally speaking, isn't that a little too late? Shouldn't they have been pressing for more preemptive action?

Imagine the struggles embedded in a scenario multiplied across northeastern Japan, in which parents submitted radiation measurements taken on school grounds to local officials. In some cases, school administrators refused even a simple parental request to release their children from 掃除の時間 (sōji no jikan), a hitherto taken-for-granted practice in which students work together periodically to clean up their schools. Sōji can entail washing down surfaces and sweeping up leaf litter, the same activities that became central to decontamination efforts in areas close to the Daiichi plant. Having heard or read that removing fallen leaves from the forest lowers radiation levels, parents logically concluded that sōji could increase their children's exposure. New community groups, such as the Association for the Protection of the Children of Yokohama from Radiation （横浜の子供たちを放射能から守る会), emerged from similar conflicts over the implications of measurements taken by citizen scientists (see Bird 2012; Wilks 2011).[32]

Another instance of technostruggle began with a scan conducted by a resident on a bag of leaf compost purchased to nurture a home garden. When the compost registered high counts per minute on his personal Geiger counter, the concerned citizen alerted the Akita prefectural government.[33] In this case, officials followed up with their own tests, although due to the large number of alerts and the investments of various parties, that is not always the case. The compost registered eleven thousand becquerels of radioactive cesium per kilogram. To put that number in perspective, before the accident fifty becquerels per kilogram was often cited as the upper "safe" limit for everyday materials. Traceback efforts revealed that a company used leaves gathered in Tochigi prefecture about a month after the earthquake to produce the mulch.

But what then? Rather than laying things to rest, scientific confirmation of the presence of radioactive isotopes tended to amplify points of struggle. It was not necessarily clear what to do when traceback operations led to companies that refused to recall their products. What if a company argued, as TEPCO and many government agencies had, that a potentially harmful level of radiation should be considered safe?

By seizing the means of perception, ordinary people had acquired the capacity to monitor goods used in their daily lives for radioactivity, in an industrialized system of production that obscures the history and origin of those goods. But the knowledge about radioactive exposures that this form of technostruggle generates did nothing to rectify problems further up the supply chain. Plenty of people would have been irradiated from the time when workers gathered the leaves in Tochigi, to the time when shoppers carried home bags of compost held close against their bodies, to the time when a gardener thought to bring the family Geiger counter out to test a flowerbed. Technostruggle directed at the endpoint of consumption attains at best a rather restricted sovereignty over the production of knowledge about radioactivity, although that in no way lessens its accomplishments.

Another important example of technostruggle after 3.11 has involved the production of crowdsourced radiation maps that implicitly contest the limited threat displayed on the maps that the state initially disseminated. When the Japanese government decided to establish evacuation and exclusion zones around the Fukushima Daiichi plant after 3.11, it laid out those zones in neat concentric circles. The perfect Euclidean forms used to set their boundaries relied upon a linear notion of danger and dispersal: the closer, the more hazardous; the farther away, the better. Over time scientist citizens such as Professor Hayakawa Yukio of Gunma University began to use meteorological data to plot radiation contour maps. On these maps, areas of relative danger where "hot" particles had descended to earth extended tentacles hundreds of kilometers beyond the government-established twenty-kilometer zone, but not equally in all directions. It was around this time that the word ホットスポット (hot spot) entered the Japanese language, and with it the realization that people could not count on distance alone to shield them from radioactive embodiment.[34]

In response to this new understanding, community-based groups such as Safecast set about creating interactive radiation maps that anyone with access to the Internet could help build. Take a reading with your Geiger counter, upload it to the Safecast website together with the date and GPS coordinates, and voilà: you have asserted a measure of sovereignty over the production of knowledge about radioactivity levels at a given site. Because the coordinates are publicly accessible, others can corroborate your results. This type of technostruggle requires a more collective effort from the start than the leaf compost example just described. People had to orga-

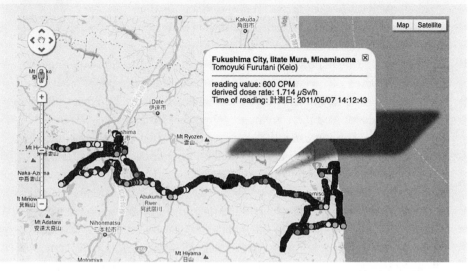

Figure 2.2. Screenshot of a section of Safecast's interactive digital radiation map taken early in the website's development [Credit: Safecast/Momoko Ito Foundation]

———

nize a group to run crowdsourcing software, maintain a website, recruit participants, and consider proposals to change public policy on the basis of the results. The site also created possibilities for intervention further up the supply chain by generating detailed site-specific knowledge that could be used to help keep radioactive ingredients out of manufactured goods.

Like any tactical form of engagement (and any form of technology), technostruggle does not carry an inherent politics. Much depends on what people do with the knowledge they generate after seizing the means of perception. Suppose, for example, someone goes outside, runs a Geiger counter over the ground, and comes up with a high reading. On May 2, 2011, a group of parents in Fukushima City who had done just that presented local politicians with a bag of radioactive dirt. They told reporters they decided to protest after their equipment generated readings at three-quarters of the schools in the city that exceeded the old standard for permissible radiation (J. Watts 2011).[35] In this case, they leavened their findings with a bit of drama to successfully pressure the local government into transferring the topsoil to a designated disposal site. But others alarmed by the frantic beeping of their Geiger counters embarked upon less responsible courses of action. Property owners who dumped radioactive topsoil in nearby forests only created new problems for communities whose common lands would otherwise have escaped the worst of the contamination.

Regardless of your politics, sometimes the apparatus you need is not the one you can seize. When journalists broke the story that manufacturers had rushed shoddy and defective radiation detection equipment to market after 3.11, even those who could afford the equipment realized that they lacked the means to check or recalibrate these technologies at the household level. And there are many things that surface scans performed with a Geiger counter cannot tell you, regardless. That is why some of the cows slaughtered for meals that included radioactive beef managed to pass Geiger counter tests with flying colors. Shopping centers and a few restaurants started installing gamma spectroscopy machines so customers could check their peeled and diced food for contamination with equipment that few could afford to purchase independently. Personal dosimeters, which register exposure over time, could also help fill in the gaps, but dosimeters cannot detect all radioactive isotopes, much less measure the bioaccumulation of radioactive particles in particularly vulnerable organs such as the liver, thyroid, and bladder. Whole body counts, arguably the most relevant to understanding the impact of radiation on the health of any given organism, require technologies such as scintillation detectors that are not widely available, affordable, portable, or familiar to nonspecialists. A laboratory assay of becquerels of plutonium was too expensive even for most city governments, much less families living as environmental refugees. These are all reasons that cooperation between citizen scientists and scientist citizens quickly became so important.

Political struggles waged over and via technology have a long history in Japan. One of the most famous examples dates back to the seventeenth century, when the Shogunate's *sakoku* (closed country) policy sought to control the importation of European scientific apparatus into the country (Screech 2002).[36] Arguably the most novel aspect of post-3.11 technostruggle was not the move to seize technology as such but the desire to generate knowledge about radioactive exposures in the first place. Japan, after all, is a society where people have not always attributed life-giving properties to knowledge about the state of one's health. In the annals of medical anthropology, Japan is famous for the common practice of withholding diagnoses of serious diseases from patients. Many people believe that knowledge of some threat to life can precipitate a health crisis, especially if disheartening statistics about probable outcomes accompany the diagnosis.[37] Of course, the idea that well-being can increase in the *absence* of knowledge assumes that the patient can safely leave that knowledge to medical experts charged with treatment. It is not incidental that efforts to generate data on radiation from the ground up coincided with a breakdown of trust in the ability or willingness of those in charge to come up with a proper diagnosis for the nation.

Considered in the light of all that is specific to Japan, it is also possible that sovereignty isn't quite the right concept with which to grasp the significance of the technostruggle that emerged following the meltdowns at Fukushima Daiichi. Sovereignty, after all, is a category derived from the history of European nation-states. In the case of post-3.11 Japan, where would sovereignty over the knowledge production achieved through technostruggle reside? With individuals? Households? Schools? The newly formed radiation dose neighborhood associations?[38] Shrines? Nonprofits like the Radiation Defense Project? And how well does sovereignty work to describe goals less territorially defined, such as care for the vulnerable bodies of children? The efforts of Geiger counter guerrillas, antinuclear advocates, activist monks, and worried parents seemed closer to producing the kind of "sovereign interdependencies" that Jessica Cattelino (2008:138) has described for Seminole communities, where assertions of sovereignty involved not autonomously acquired knowledge, not power *over*, but an obligation "to learn, to know, to remember, and to act upon a distinctive and valued way of being in the world."

To understand why the emphasis on popular sovereignty in social theory provides at best a partial insight into technostruggle, it helps to take a closer look at the continuous invocation of "protection" in Japan following 3.11. Rather than greeting each crowdsourced radiation map and playground cleanup as an instance of restored popular sovereignty over danger, or even knowledge, these struggles can be understood as novel appropriations of existing technologies by people trying very, very hard and very, very creatively to protect life.

Mamoru and the Radiation Divorce

"To protect"—守る (*mamoru*)—is an injunction that people in Japan have taken seriously since long before the triple disaster of earthquake, tsunami, meltdown. Shrines and temples sell a variety of *omamori*, or protective amulets, with customized applications to help visitors ward off everything from stomach upsets to traffic accidents. In Shintō protection does not issue only from amulets: it is something that trees, rivers, and mountains offer as well. While the majority of people in a random street sample would hardly characterize themselves as assiduous Shintō or Buddhist devotees, the notion of a world in which protection weaves itself into the landscape has a profound cultural resonance.

Immediately following the earthquake, when guests at my hotel requested confirmation of the news that something terrible had happened at a nuclear plant to the north, a desk clerk tried to reassure them this way: "Fukushima Daiichi is far away, almost two hundred kilometers. And anyway, the mountains will protect us." Whatever she had in mind, it is fair to say that the notion of protection she conveyed to the group of mostly Japanese guests assembled in the lobby was not limited to the effect of mountains on wind currents.

After 3.11 the language of protection—in both Japanese and English—seemed to pop up everywhere in public discourse on nuclear power. From the very beginning, news reports repeatedly referred to the "protective suits" worn by workers trying to control radiation at the plant. The phrase sounded reassuring, but obviously the suits could only afford limited protection at such elevated radiation levels. The practice of wrapping workers' bodies in "protective" gear also provided ideal conditions for heatstroke, which killed at least one worker at the plant.

Then, at a certain point, grassroots opposition to nuclear power began to mobilize around the slogan "protect children." The immediate trigger was an attempt by the state to raise the permissible annual radiation exposure for children to the limit previously designated for adults working in the nuclear industry. In areas of northern Japan where the government distributed dosimeters to children at school, parents began to ask why their children had not been evacuated if they needed dosimeters. They also questioned the decision to hand out the type of dosimeter that needs to be mailed to a laboratory for interpretation rather than the type of dosimeter that changes color or beeps to alert the wearer once exposure exceeds a certain level. That, at least, would have given children and the adults responsible for them immediate access to the measurements. Would they even receive the lab results, parents wondered, or had their children become lab rats in someone else's experiment?[39] Where, in other words, was the protection? Running a Geiger counter over the bento box to avoid sending your child to school with a radioactive lunch offered more protection than that.

Animals, too, began to appear under the sign of protection. In an effort to make visible the suffering of animals in restricted areas around the plant, farmers from Fukushima brought a black bull that had developed strange white spots on its hide to a demonstration outside the Ministry of Agriculture, Forestry, and Fisheries in Tokyo. The techno-intimacies described in the previous chapter on food chain surveillance would be of little help in a situation like this, since the animals' plight and location were already well known. The farmers appealed for research on the new maladies afflicting their herds and an end to burning contaminated vegetation that could otherwise be used as fodder by caretakers who had lost their incomes. Knowing that they could never sell these cattle for meat, they nevertheless jeopardized their own health by refusing to abandon livestock and pets in the way that they believed the state had discarded them (Kurtenback 2014).

While some people called for the protection of children or animals and took technology into their own hands to protect them as best they could, others worried about how to protect the trees, mountains, and streams that historically had made veneration and protection in a wider sense possible. Some Buddhist monks joined the Geiger counter brigades trying to track down hot spots and offered to store contaminated debris on temple grounds when no one else would take it (Villar and Nakao 2012). In an interview with a Reuters correspondent, Genyu Sokyu, a priest at a Buddhist temple west of Fukushima Daiichi, explained the spiritual complexities involved: "Mountains and oceans have purified us but now those mountains and oceans are contaminated. . . . We could see the very foundation for our religious beliefs break down, because it is no longer able to purify us" (Fujioka 2011). By situating protection in this spiritual/historical landscape, his comments illustrate how even calls to protect children, with their growing bodies and fast-dividing cells, tapped sensibilities specific to Japan.[40]

Takahashi Satsuki has pointed out that the words often translated into English as "decontamination" in discussions of "cleaning up" a radioactive site might also be translated as "purification," another category with deep resonance in Japan.[41] When the recommended course of action for the purification/decontamination of a watershed includes cutting down the trees with the power to protect you, soil erosion may be the least of your problems.[42]

And so it was with an emphasis on protection, not sovereignty, that the unwanted intimacy of radioactive embodiment came to affect relationships more conventionally conceived in terms of intimacy, such as kinship and spiritual ties. It is not a coincidence that playgrounds and school grounds were some of the first places parents headed with Geiger counters in hand.

The human chain formed around the Ministry of Education after 3.11 to demand better protection for children was organized by parents, mostly women. Parents also researched radioactivity on the Internet to be able to offer their children the kind of informal advice that can be followed without troubling anyone: when they serve lunch at school, don't eat the lotus roots, because lotus roots concentrate radioisotopes more than some other vegetables.

There are other ways to interpret these actions than as a simple bid for knowledge. In Japan, people would be more likely to characterize them in terms of what a person in a particular sort of relationship does to care for someone else. Technology can also be wielded to fulfill that sort of responsibility.

What happens, though, when people disagree on a matter as grave as radioactive embodiment in the context of their most intimate relationships? After 3.11 almost half the children in Fukushima living *outside* the government-established exclusion zone turned out to have thyroid exposure to radiation. Less than a year after the earthquake, thyroid cysts, usually rare in children, were already on the rise in Fukushima. The government insisted that these cysts posed no threat to health, since they were "benign," and probably reflected the results of more comprehensive testing. In 2012 the *Asahi Shimbun* pointed to the 36 percent incidence of thyroid cysts in Tokyo children in a longitudinal study whose inception predated the earthquake as evidence that such high rates were "normal" and could not be radiation-induced (Asai 2012). While the fact that none of the Tokyo children at the time of the study had gone on to develop malignancies was encouraging, the authors did not appear to have ruled out alternative sources of exposure to radioactive isotopes. Neither did they explain why the rates for the Tokyo children in the study were so much higher than those found in other parts of the world. For purposes of comparison, the rates for thyroid nodules in a study of two sites in the United States and England were 4.2 percent and 3.2 percent, respectively, a huge difference even allowing for variation in the sensitivity of testing equipment (D. Ross 2002).

Not surprisingly, some residents from areas near the Fukushima Daiichi meltdowns interpreted the data differently. They took these figures as evidence of hidden, delayed decimation of the sort that Rob Nixon (2011) has termed "slow violence," no less destructive because it occurs gradually. "They tell us, 'Please come back to your homes,'" explained one woman interviewed for the documentary *A2-B-C*. "It's the same as saying, 'Please murder your children here [あなたはここで子供を殺してください].'"[43]

The concept of slow violence highlights a creeping form of what theorists sometimes call "everyday violence" or "structural violence," which may include physical damage to bodies but extends well beyond bodily injury to encompass social conditions and institutionalized arrangements that help explain the inequitable distribution of harm. Sato Sachiko's (2011) testimony before MEXT officials in April and May 2011 attempted to situate the potential for injury associated with the nuclear *mondai* (問題, problem) in this sort of wider context (see also Hutner 2012). Sato, who introduced herself as a Fukushima farmer, a "simple housewife," and the mother of five children, emphasized that radiation as such was not the only concern: many "grandmothers and grandfathers," for example, had already died during the evacuation process after being forced to leave their ancestral homes.

Environmental activism around the world has often featured maternalist rhetoric, especially when women assume leadership positions in environmental movements.[44] Elders become "grandmothers and grandfathers" whose welfare lies in the hands of a middle generation of "mothers" (and occasionally fathers) who depict themselves as organizing not on their own behalf but on behalf of their children. It is a different sort of appeal than one that claims rights on the basis of humanity or citizenship. The pared-down kinship frame in maternalist rhetoric—no mother's brothers or father's sister's cousins here—travels easily across borders and frequently garners international press coverage. Japanese listeners might also discern in Sato's address a tacit appeal to the "good wife wise mother" ideology that has permeated the country since the late nineteenth century.

As time passed and the radiation spewing from the plant began to assume the dimensions of a chronic disaster, schools started to teach accommodation strategies for living with daily exposure to radiation. One went so far as to hand out advice on "how to get along with cesium."[45] If your child returned home from school with one of these leaflets, what would you do when your spouse found the advice reassuring, whereas you found it terrifying? If your partner dismissed your daily routine of scanning the rice and the seaweed with a Geiger counter before you served a meal as a silly obsession? If you woke up every day with the dream of moving your child to a place with lower levels of radioactivity, only to have your husband tell you to stop paying so much attention to harmful rumors?

Enter the "radiation divorce" (原発離婚, *genpatsu rikon*), a neologism coined to describe the separations that occurred after 3.11 when couples could not agree about what to do in light of the new knowledge about radiation exposure that technostruggle generated.[46] Although genpatsu rikon was sometimes characterized as the diffuse outcome of coping with the "stress" of living in or near a radiation zone, the archetypal radiation divorce involves a mother who decides to move with her children, over her husband's objections, to a place less contaminated by radiation. Critics drew upon the image of the *kahogomama* (過保護ママ)—the overprotective mother—to suggest that these women's fears for their children's safety were unfounded. Or they contended that women who filed for a radiation divorce were only using children as a cover for a step that they had wanted to take all along (see Onozawa 2013). Given the rise of a post-3.11 antinuclear movement framed by maternalism, however, it seems more likely that many cases of radiation divorce involved women earnestly troubled by marriage to a person who would not act to protect his children, even if danger lurked only in the guise of possibilities.[47]

Since relocation is expensive, radiation divorces required financial resources that not everyone possessed. How widespread would the phenomenon of radiation divorce become? Would a divorce boom follow the wedding boom that occurred in the shadow of the tsunami?[48] Had significant numbers of men also initiated radiation divorces when they perceived the dangers of radioactive embodiment to be more acute than their wives? Did radiation divorces affect gay couples or extend to childless heterosexual marriages? Were those who refused to move merely scoffing at the dangers of radiation? Or, like many who stayed behind, were they reluctant to abandon (見捨てる, *misuteru*) a larger network of relatives, animals, and places for which they felt responsibility? As the government called for resettlement of Kawauchi and other once-evacuated villages, how would tensions play out between the need to protect the more vulnerable bodies of youth and the need for young people to assist elders who returned?

With highly contaminated water from the triple nuclear meltdown still leaching into groundwater and overflowing into the sea, the answers to these questions remained unclear (Soble 2016). What did seem clear was that technostruggle had generated detailed knowledge about localized radiation exposures, knowledge that helped people care for one another, even if in some cases that meant breaking up a household.

In the end, there may be nowhere to run, although there will certainly be places judged better or worse. It is the hope of many who have seized the means of perception that some places judged worse can be made better. The dreamers who proposed covering northeastern Japan with sunflowers, which take up radioisotopes from the soil, weren't sure what to do with all those sunflowers once they finished growing.[49] Still, these dreamers were no more naïve than the decontamination troops armed with power washers, the inventors of robots that couldn't negotiate the stairs inside the nuclear plant, or the volunteers charged with stuffing radioactive debris into garbage bags by hand. Newly "cleaned" surfaces could become recontaminated, sometimes in a matter of days.[50] But not everywhere, not always. No one—no citizen scientist, no scientist citizen, no government agency, no corporation—knows how to do this thing called radioactive "purification" on the scale that Fukushima Daiichi demands, or indeed if it can be done. But the citizen scientists who have gifted technostruggle to the world insist that what can be done should be done, and people are bound to try.

CLIMATE CHANGE

———

Climate Change, Slippery on the Skin

"Look at me: I'm just dripping wet!" My great aunt Elsie chanted this re-frain through the sizzling Chicago summers of the 1960s, whenever the red line in the old mercury thermometer edged upward and conversation struggled to emerge from perspiring, drooping bodies. "No rain tomorrow. I'd feel it in my bones." A trickle of sweat escaped the white handkerchief draped around her neck in a vain effort to stem the rivulets that poured down her arms, off her wrists, through a crack in the floorboards, onto the ground below the porch where evaporation would speed even this bit of salty fluid on its way to the sea. Elsie would rock and rock to make her own breeze, with an economy of motion familiar in those days when home air-conditioning meant a box fitted to a single window and most working-class households in the United States had to make do with fans. She would rock and rock, as though a metal patio chair springing to life would be enough to stir the winds eventually.

Long before climate change skepticism appeared on the North Ameri-can scene, long before the fossil fuel industry paid lobbyists to spin cred-ible research on environmental damage into "junk science," people like my aunt Elsie were accustomed to consulting their bodies in order to decode shifts in both weather and climate. They also looked to the skies, of course, as well as the horizon and, eventually, to a new crop of college-educated professionals called meteorologists. As they weighed and integrated infor-mation from these various sources, many threw into the mix self-generated reports that offered up bodies as evidence of ever-shifting atmospheric conditions: "Look at me!"

Like my great aunt Elsie, some had proved highly skilled readers of corporeal signs. They were close observers of variations, large and small, in the way their bodies felt at work or in repose under different conditions, and they used those observations to make predictions. Secretions from the pores of the skin, pounding headaches, frizzy hair, creaking joints, and popping ankles found their way into debates about the meaning of changes in cloud cover, annual snowfall, foggy dampness, or the desiccation shared by tongues and rose bushes after too many relentlessly sunny days. These were not static "folk beliefs" or survivals from some preindustrial era. In these running commentaries on climate and weather, phlegm, thirst, and scaly patches on the elbows appeared as signs of larger processes that brought bodies into intimate engagement with the heavens and an industrializing landscape.

Perhaps it should not have come as such a surprise, then, that when the first popular accounts of climate change research appeared in the guise of global warming, one of the iconic responses in North America became "Global warming? But I'm not sweating!" It was tempting to dismiss this half-earnest, half-flippant reaction as some misguided rejection of scientific findings that were otherwise abundantly clear. On closer inspection, however, the appeal to bodies to evaluate predictions of ecological catastrophe made a certain cultural, historical, and *scientific* sense. Discussions of climate science that enlisted sweat (or the lack thereof) as evidence drew upon the time-honored, culturally situated practice of waking up, searching for that bit of breeze against the forehead, and not finding it, announcing, "It's going to be a hot one!" While those who puzzled over the seeming paradox of cool summers in a warming world might not have trained as scientists, they were the heirs to a long Euro-American history of using the body as a scientific instrument, both as a proving ground to test hypotheses and as a measuring apparatus in its own right. As scientists' warnings about the biosphere grew increasingly dire, bodies seemed to some to offer an additional source of evidence that could help verify or discredit those claims.

Could it be that at least some strands of climate change skepticism in North America owe their inspiration to science, rather than being hostile to scientific analysis? The only way to answer such a question is to set aside mythologies of the United States as a country filled with climate change "deniers," figured as irrational and anti-science, locked in combat with climate change "believers," portrayed as reliable reasoning subjects with the best interests of the planet at heart. Class tensions shadow this facile division into an "us" and a "them." Media accounts have all too often represented climate change skeptics as undereducated, misled, theologically driven yokels, while treating those who accept the reality of climate change as their betters in knowledge and clear thinking.

The classist "denier" narrative had become so well established by 2015 that a comedian like Jon Stewart could easily invert its terms by poking fun at "science-denying affluent California liberals" who refused to vaccinate their children (Luce 2015:7). But the political consequences were no joke. By uncritically reproducing this narrative, passionate advocates of reason had ironically aligned themselves with the corporate lobbyists that they pictured as opponents in the climate wars. Disdain for a presumptively irrational public had long underpinned corporate efforts to discredit the documentation of ecosystems in distress.[1] All this at a time when ecologically minded middle-class consumers regularly voiced what Andrew Ross (1991:33) once identified as a New Age suspicion of "technologies that are external to the body's holistic orbit."

There is little insight to be gained by battling phantoms: the "reality-based" thinkers who recognize the clear and present danger, versus the benighted ones with their heads in the sand. Poor ostrich, depicted on the cover of *Climate Change Denial* as the emblem of all that ails us! But maybe, just maybe, the ostrich has something to teach us. "Perhaps we would do better to keep our own heads close to the earth," suggests Peter Doherty (2013:19) in his work on the intertwined ecological fates of humans and birds, "so that we could look more clearly at what we are doing to it."

Even as it is evident to me that climate change is upon us and even as I work with my students to grapple with its implications, I want to bracket for a moment the grave warnings tendered by researchers and government panels in order to entertain a rather different set of questions.[2] What would it mean to take grassroots climate change skepticism seriously without necessarily subscribing to its politics?[3] To approach those who adopt a contrarian position as unconvinced, rather than casting them in evangelical terms as unbelievers? To jettison class snobbery long enough to ask whether certain variants of climate change skepticism might find tacit inspiration in science? Could a path be charted from climate change skepticism that enlists bodily sensation to the sort of citizen science initiatives that climate researchers might find valuable? For who is to say that there is not something to be learned from generations of aunts and uncles who have had recourse to the body as a technology for adjudicating truth claims about the world around them and getting their bearings in a world in flux?

We thought we knew heat then. What a season would bring. The extent of the damage a hailstorm or tornado could wreak. We thought we knew. How could we have been at once so right and so wrong?

The Body as Scientific Instrument

When schoolchildren in the United States learn their potted histories of the work of eminent scientists such as Marie and Pierre Curie, they encounter many examples of how bodies have long been integral to scientific inquiry. The Curies, of course, gained fame for their experiments with radium, sharing a Nobel Prize in Physics in 1903 with Henri Becquerel, whose name still surfaces in measurements of radioactive contamination from the nuclear meltdowns at Fukushima Daiichi. Marie's death in 1934 from the bone marrow damage associated with aplastic anemia circulates as a cautionary tale about the perils of radioactive exposure at a time when its consequences were not well understood. The flip side of that cautionary tale is a heroic saga of scientific discoveries that depended, in part, on the careful observations the Curies made as they charted the effects of handling radioactive substances on their fingers, arms, and hands.

The many radiation burns that the Curies endured were not all accidental byproducts of experiments. Taking the lead from Becquerel and others such as Friedrich Walkoff and Friedrich Giesel, the Curies deliberately created conditions that they knew would affect their bodies in order to, as Marie put it, "test the results" of the work of other scientists (Curie 1923: 117). These self-exposure experiments involved positioning sealed tubes or boxes filled with radiferous radium bromide and radiferous barium chloride close to the skin. Over time periods that ranged from thirty minutes to more than a month, they observed how "energetically" the radiation acted on their bodies. Scaly hands, red spots, inflamed joints, and peeling flesh all made their way into published articles. They also took precise measurements in centimeters of the lesions produced, with annotations that recorded changes in shape and color as the hours and days passed (Mould 2007:77–78).

When it comes to self-experimentation, the Curies have had plenty of company. In "Politics of Participation," Akhil Mehra (2009) recounts how early in the twentieth century a team of U.S. military scientists in Cuba led by Walter Reed deliberately exposed themselves to potentially deadly material in a quest to cure tropical diseases, experiments that led to identification of the mosquito as the vector of transmission for yellow fever. Lawrence Altman's *Who Goes First?* (1987) situates Reed's team in a long queue of researchers who have placed their bodies in the service of medical science. If a line of inquiry seemed promising, swallowing intestinal parasites (Claude Barlow), drinking a "cholera cocktail" (Max von Pettenkofer), daring a poisonous mamba snake to bite you (F. Eigenberger), or injecting yourself with white blood cells from patients with leukemia (Thomas Brittingham) was not out of the question. At the end of the nineteenth century, anthropology's Torres Strait Expedition provided yet another venue for self-experimentation, in this case by W. H. R. Rivers, who supplemented ethnological fieldwork with experiments in self-administered alcohol consumption, in order to test the theory that drug consumption represented an "evolutionary regression" (Kuklick 2008:172).

Nor were such experiments only performed back in the day, before scientists had established ethics panels and codified their procedures. Self-experimentation is still very much with us. Barry Marshall, co-winner of the 2005 Nobel Prize in Physiology or Medicine, downed a petri dish laced with *H. pylori* as part of a research program that established a link between bacterial infection, peptic ulcers, and gastric cancer. In order to gauge the impact of industrialized ecologies on human health, even filmmakers and investigative journalists have placed their bodies in harm's way. Earlier in the discussion of bio-intimacy we saw how the authors of *Slow Death by Rubber Duck* (2009) researched the effects of plastics, flame-retardant fabrics, and other products of synthetic chemistry by ingesting these substances or locking themselves in rooms where they would absorb high quantities of key ingredients. For his 2004 documentary *Super Size Me*, Morgan Spurlock restricted his diet to food ("food"?) from the menu at McDonald's franchises. Three weeks into the experiment, after his cholesterol levels spiked and his physicians began to worry about liver damage, Spurlock decided to quit, but the film he made stands as an indictment of the alliance between agribusiness and the purveyors of cheap, salty, nutritionally deficient meals.

Following the 2011 nuclear meltdown at Fukushima Daiichi, Yamakawa Yukio, a former television broadcaster, reported a range of health problems after intentionally eating irradiated crops he had grown himself:

> The harvested rice was contaminated, so I couldn't have my family eat
> it. However, I didn't want to waste rice so I had it myself. . . . I have

been eating it for one year and a half. *In a sense, it was an experiment on my own body.* When I fell down . . . I put a period to farming here. . . . It was for my personal consumption, but it is a matter of life or death for professional farmers. Radioactive contamination is really cruel.[4] (my emphasis)

Not all suggested links between self-experimentation and environmental impacts are so clearly articulated, but sometimes connections are there for the making. When a researcher like Stephen Hoffman sticks his arm in a box filled with mosquitoes to seduce them into biting, his goal might be a vaccine for malaria, but the ecological context for malaria's spread involves stagnant water that collects in paved-over landscapes, poorly designed irrigation systems, and the temperature shifts associated with climate change.[5]

J. B. S. Haldane, a well-known physiologist and geneticist who worked in the first part of the twentieth century, penned an essay called "On Being One's Own Rabbit" in which he recounted how he and a colleague (H. W. Davies) came to experiment on one another.[6] The goal of this particular piece of research was to improve the understanding of what it feels like when a human body becomes more acid and less alkaline, lowering the electrical charge of its colloidal substances. For research on pH, a rabbit should have been a likely candidate as one of the favored laboratory subjects of those pre–animal rights movement days. There was just one problem. As Haldane (1928:114) wryly remarked, "It is difficult to be sure how a rabbit feels at any time. Indeed, many rabbits make no serious attempt to co-operate with one." He did make a small exception for a bunny named Boanerges (Son of Thunder), who cooperated for "such a period as he thought reasonable," after which he pulverized any glassware left on the laboratory table and wandered off. "To do the sort of things to a dog that one does to the average medical student requires a license signed in triplicate by two archbishops," Haldane continued, only half in jest, so he decided to expedite things by leaving the rabbits, dogs, and medical students out of it.

After drinking hydrochloric acid, swallowing copious amounts of baking soda, and spending hours in a chamber with elevated carbon dioxide levels, he experienced raging headaches, heavy sweating, muscle spasms that could last for hours, and the shortness of breath that attends kidney failure. "Possibly my liver, had I been able to see it, would have resembled a Seidlitz powder [a laxative], but even had I had a window through which to watch the process I should have been too busy breathing to pay much attention," Haldane reported (1928:120). At the end of what sounds like an arduous path indeed, he published a paper that describes the results of ingesting ammonium chloride, which led to an effective treatment for babies who suffer from tetany, a condition in which muscles contract and contort the limbs once the blood becomes too alkaline.

In the matter of climate change, some have suggested that the radical acceleration of greenhouse gas emissions from burning fossil fuels amounts to a collective global self-experiment.[7] Any such "experiment" would amount to an unplanned exercise of madcap design rather than a trial inflicted with the deliberation of a J. B. S. Haldane. And to what end? Even Haldane held out, in his curiosity and his adventurousness, for self-experimentation undertaken with enough intelligence to test substances for which the probable effects were well understood, and then only in small quantities. In contrast, in the metaphor of a planetary-scale self-experiment, bodies serve as the litmus paper that will display the effects of climatic shifts down the road, as crops fail, refugees flee the submerged cities, phytoplankton cannot produce oxygen, and humans speculate their way toward an unsecured future.

But in addition to self-experimentation, there is another well-established way of wielding the body as technology in the history of science, one with arguably more relevance for explaining certain elements of North American climate change skepticism. From the period of medieval Islamic science through the heyday of natural philosophy in early modern Europe, researchers routinely enlisted the body as a sensing and measuring device. The eye did not simply see; it registered changes in what we might now call "data." The nose did not simply smell; it gauged acidity. The fingers might touch, but in so doing they could also render judgments about granular fineness. Before Pierre Daniel Huet, bishop of Avranches in France in the eighteenth century, designed an anemometer to measure wind speed, "holding a finger to the wind" represented more than a turn of phrase. As Alexis Madrigal (2011:270) puts it in *Powering the Dream: The History and Promise of Green Technology*, "Humans are excellent but imprecise wind sensors." When placed in the service of scientific investigation, the body's senses can become a sensory *apparatus* as integral to obtaining results as any crucible, astrolabe, or barometer.

Before the standardization of weights and measures, people stretched and lined up various parts of their anatomy as part of doing business, marking out a field, gauging the height of a draught animal, and so on. "Feet," which persist in the English system of measurement, were once accompanied by cubits (elbow to tip of middle finger) and spans (tip of thumb to tip of pinkie with fingers extended), fathoms (an arm's length) and hand-breadths. Before advances in optics led to the invention of telescopes, people who wanted to document the movements of heavenly bodies relied upon the eye to make their observations. Even then, mechanical equipment did not replace bodies altogether for the purposes of scientific inquiry. In the seventeenth century the sun's rays etched Isaac Newton's eyelids because he stared too long at the sun in a mirror in order to inspect after-images on his retina. Mid-nineteenth-century studies of the Doppler effect, which describes a change in the frequency of a sound wave as an observer moves relative to the source (or vice versa), used the ears of observers to register shifts in pitch.[8] Before the development of clinical blood tests and computerized tomography to detect gangrene, diagnosis began by having a friend or doctor take a whiff of the wound. Today, when much basic scientific research has become mechanized, the human body still serves as a prototype for understanding what innovative scientific instruments can do. To take but one contemporary example: researchers have made significant progress on breath testing devices that can identify the distinctive scent of various ailments, from toxic chemical exposure to lung cancer. When first introduced to the public, this sort of machine became known as the "electronic nose."

Self-experimentation primarily uses the body as matériel for scientific trials, transforming the researcher into a glorified test tube or petri dish. Investigations that employ the body as a sensing and measuring device, in contrast, lend themselves particularly well to variants of climate change skepticism that cite the presence or absence of corporeal sensations ("I'm not sweating!") as reason for doubt. That makes it all the more important to understand how the use of the body as a scientific instrument declined after the seventeenth century, and why some people should still find empirical observations registered through the body so compelling.

In "Empiricism without the Senses: How the Instrument Replaced the Eye," Ofer Gal and Raz Chen-Morris (2010) offer a telling account of this historical shift. The seventeenth century was the period when new technologies—most notably, the telescope and the microscope—allowed people for the first time to scrutinize phenomena both exceedingly distant and exceedingly small. To peer into one of these instruments was to embark upon a voyage of discovery to previously unseen worlds, an analogy built upon the voyages that European seafarers with their colonial mandates and letters of marque were undertaking at the same time. Yet these new technologies still had the potential to articulate with the human body in at least two radically different ways. They could figure as *extensions* of the senses (in the case of the telescope, as a kind of prosthesis that allows the eye to "grab" phenomena from farther and farther away). Alternatively, they could represent a *substitute* for the senses that, by virtue of its purported superiority, would sideline the human body for the purposes of scientific investigation. In the end, the substitution view prevailed: "For Kepler and Galileo, the new instruments did not offer extension and improvement to the senses; they replaced them altogether. To rely on their authority was to admit that the human eye is nothing but an instrument, and a flawed one at that. Rather than the intellect's window to the world, the human senses became a part of this world, a source of obscure and unreliable data, demanding uncertain deciphering. Accurate scientific observation meant that we are always wrong" (Gal and Chen-Morris 2010:121).

A new phrase, "the naked eye," entered the lexicon. In a subtle way, it marked the body's senses as a source of error and deficiency, rather than the mediators of all knowledge. Particularly bright novae, for instance, are now said to be capable of being seen *even* by the naked eye, with the eye imagined as the poor cousin of much more accurate and perceptive mechanical instruments: "Unlike optical predecessors such as the spectacles, the scientific instrument does not simply strengthen the weak eye. It thoroughly replaces the 'natural' function of the sense organ with reasoned procedure of observation, into which measurement and comparison are built and into which the eyes should be assimilated" (Gal and Chen-Morris 2010:122–23).

When first introduced, the significance of a new technology is not obvious; its cultural history has yet to be made, and it is not at all clear what social investments will be cast aside in the process. In the seventeenth century, some thought telescopes conveyed specters to the eyes, leading the mind astray with "bewitched and deformed" images. It is in this context that Gal and Chen-Morris read the well-known arguments between Galileo Galilei and Orazio Grassi over the comets that appeared in the European sky during 1618. These were treatises on Copernican astronomy, to be sure, but also polemics on the status of observations made using disembodied instruments.

Many Jesuit mathematicians at the time like Grassi "held onto the Pauline belief in the supremacy of 'face to face' acquaintance" via vision, a belief that still surfaces, as we saw in chapter 1, in nonscientific contexts from twenty-first-century banking to artisanal farming (Gal and Chen-Morris 2010:134). For Grassi, any mediation that interposed something between eye and star, between eye and planet, simply magnified the opportunities for error. But once people learned to treat new technologies like the telescope as *replacements* for the senses, it had the effect of naturalizing the body's sense organs, in a way that recast them as unreliable tools for scientific investigation. By the time Kepler devised his laws of planetary motion, vision had become not so much a scientific instrument in its own right as another mystery to be unraveled with the aid of mechanical devices.

Bodies, once naturalized in this way, no longer serve science in the guise of technology. This is the back story that helps explain why institutionalized science often dismisses out of hand any doubts about climate change that rely upon bodily sensation. At best, scientists have tended to treat such accounts as anecdotal reports submitted by well-meaning "amateurs down in the trenches who execute the ground game in the climate wars" without realizing that they are pawns in a bigger corporate game (Mann 2012: 71). Twenty-first-century bodies serve up unreliable assessments, scientists suggest, which are fleeting, impressionistic, imprecise, and limited to the life span of the observer. Since climate oscillations have unfolded over the course of centuries, it is tempting to conclude that there is not much those salty drops trickling down your neck can tell you.

Or is there? Easy enough, once the body loses its status as instrument, to scorn observations about the corporeal effects of atmospheric shifts as foolishness or to refute them as a category error that confuses climate with weather (about which more in a moment). A view of the climate change debates through eyes that peered into the skies before Galileo, Grassi, and Kepler suggests that it is possible to read this sort of climate change skepticism differently. Through those eyes, what gets brushed aside today as unreliable testimony could just as well be characterized as an aspect of field research, and play all the differently for it.

When someone wields her body as technology for the purpose of registering sensations, a report that "I'm dripping wet" (in August)—like "Why are we shivering?" (in June)—supplies a bit more than anecdotal evidence and rather less than a longitudinal study. Charles Wolfe and Ofer Gal (2010) call this research method *embodied empiricism*, perfectly respectable in the seventeenth century and something that still shadows scientific investigation today.[9] In their guise as instruments, bodies yield empirical observations that can assume evidential status. Sweating is not shivering, after all. Taken together and in quantity, those particulars accumulate and can be subjected to inductive analysis just like any other observation. Self-experimentation would be meaningless were that not the case.

There are even ways to build quantifiable measurements into embodied empiricist techniques. In the Bollywood hit film *Bhaag Milkha Bhaag,* a biopic based on the life of the runner Milkha Singh, Olympic hopefuls wring their perspiration-soaked shirts into a cup on their way around a track. The level of sweat in the cup rises as they complete lap after lap, providing a marker of effort expended and training accomplished (as well as a laugh at the expense of the character who raises the cup to his lips, expecting a drink of water).

Of course, an empirical observation does not an empirical investigation make, and therein lies the rub for those who have subjected climate change discourse to the test of the senses and found it wanting. But for the purposes of understanding the peculiarly North American intransigence on the topic of climate change that many scientists, like progressives, have found so mystifying, there is a key takeaway point here. Arguments that cite bodily sensations as a reason for doubt are not necessarily antagonistic to science. Neither, *secunda facie*, is climate change skepticism.

When skeptics try to understand what, if anything, is changing by noting the conditions that prompt them to reach for an extra sweater or run their wrists under water to cool off, they effectively adopt an empiricist stance. From a philosophical standpoint, the idea that sense experience is the source of all knowledge can be problematic. Yet the conviction that knowledge derives from experience (*empeiria*) also conferred value upon observation and experimentation as tools for understanding the world. Without that conviction, European science would never have become European science.

Embodied Empiricism, Corporate Campaigns, and Thinking Publics

"It will be interesting to see how the science approach sells," wrote William Brier in an Edison Electrical Institute (EEI) internal memo, speaking of one of the earliest corporate advertising campaigns deliberately devised to bring the concept of climate change into disrepute. Three fossil fuel and utility industry associations, including EEI, were behind the ill-fated formation of ICE, the campaign's sponsor.[10] Founded in 1991 for the express purpose of discrediting research on what was then known as global warming, ICE adopted an intentionally bland name—Information Council on the Environment—the better to conceal its corporate ties. One ICE-sponsored ad targeted residents of the Twin Cities with the question, "If the earth is getting warmer, why is Minneapolis getting colder?" Versions of the same ad aired in Kentucky, North Dakota, and northern Arizona, with local place names exchanged for "Minneapolis."

The idea behind the advertising blitz was never to attack Science with a capital "S" but rather to cultivate the impression that scientific conclusions about climate change could not stand up to scrutiny. This was a middling gambit well suited to a country with a history of repeated bouts of antievolutionist fervor, on the one hand, and on the other, an enduringly positivist "mania for facts" that David E. Shi (1995) traces back to the mid-nineteenth-century promulgation of realism by then newly professionalized scientists.

Most scientists, of course, would agree that data should be scrutinized, verified, and interpreted with care. That is the point, after all, of submitting research for peer review by other scientists before publication. That is also the reason scientists attempt to replicate each other's findings. What raised suspicions and later raised hackles was the revelation via leaked documents that ICE had staged an old-fashioned disinformation campaign to manipulate public perceptions. In the wake of the scandal, ICE dissolved, but corporate-funded attacks on the scientific evidence for climate change continued. And they continued to appeal to science.

This was not a new pitch. Long before anyone entered the fray in the name of climate change, trade associations for the chemical industry had hired public relations firms to save chlorine. Like many chemicals, chlorine has a double face: it can work as a disinfectant in household cleaning products or as a lethal poison gas in time of war. For years activists had argued that chlorine poses health hazards that outweigh the benefits of its antimicrobial properties. The fact that chlorine combines with organic matter to form dangerous trihalomethanes was reason enough, they contended, to stop routine chlorination of drinking water in the United States. Rather than directly addressing scientific findings on trihalomethanes, the chemical industry claimed that a ban on the use of chlorine would halt scientific research that might eventually cure diseases such as cystic fibrosis (see Rampton and Stauber 2001:147). Fight science with science.

The stakes were high for the chlorine industry, as they would later be for their corporate cousins in the executive suites of "big coal." Revenue from alkalies and chlorine manufacturing in 2015 amounted to $7.1 billion, with an estimated gross profit of 46.76 percent.[11] Had industry executives believed that a broad swath of the public in the United States was resolutely antagonistic to science, it would never have made sense to build a high-profile public relations campaign around alleged threats to scientific progress in biomedicine. By the time climate change became a matter of public debate, such PR strategies had established a template for any business that wanted to direct attention away from the ecological harms associated with their products.

From 2003 to 2010, in addition to direct corporate funding, the climate change countermovement (CCCM) in the United States received an average of $64 million annually from conservative foundations (Brulle 2013). The merchants of doubt, as Naomi Oreskes and Erik Conway (2010) dubbed them, might have opened their coffers to war against climate science, but they did so through the ingenious maneuver of positioning themselves as champions of science. First they paid a small number of scientists to conduct studies with conclusions that would favor industry. Then they promoted *junk science* as a catchall term that industry representatives could invoke whenever the results of a study didn't suit them. Another new term, *sound science*, went mano a mano with *junk science*, since every evil twin needs its likeable oppositional other.[12] This stealth marketing strategy for continued reliance on fossil fuels enlisted the authority of science, even as it undermined confidence in particular scientific findings. By the late 1990s the bad science/good science dichotomy had made such headway that even many courts of law found these terms admissible, leading Gary Edmond and David Mercer (1998) to dedicate an entire article in the *Stanford Technology Law Review* to "Trashing 'Junk Science.'"

By any measure, the climate wolf in scientific sheep's clothing created by high-powered corporate campaigns had a tremendous impact. Right-wing radio shows, think tanks, blogs, and podcasts gleefully amplified the message. Rajendra Pachauri was chair of the United Nations Intergovernmental Panel on Climate Change (IPCC) at the time of Climategate, when someone hacked into scientists' e-mail accounts at the University of East Anglia in order to cast aspersions on their work. In an interview with the *Financial Times*, an exasperated Pachauri said he believed the attacks were sponsored by companies looking to protect their profits, "the same people who deny the link between smoking and cancer . . . who say that asbestos is as good as talcum powder—and I hope they put it on their faces every day" (Kazmin 2010:6). My great aunt Elsie would have called such antics "shenanigans." But then again, she might have been convinced.

It is one thing to craft an advertising pitch; it is quite another to make the sale. Even the most carefully seeded clouds do not always bring forth rain. Why did so many people in the United States find the corporate take on climate change so persuasive, or at least persuasive enough to share their doubts with neighbors and friends, in a classically embodied form: "It's freezing out here! So much for all that talk about global warming." An opinion poll taken in 2006 found that a mere 56 percent of Americans thought global temperature averages had risen, at a time when climate scientists had nearly reached consensus on this point (Oreskes and Conway 2010:169).

Rather than incorporating testimonials from scientists to lend legitimacy to their claims, the ICE ads featured cartoon characters: a man holding a snow shovel (for Minnesota), a horse in earmuffs (for Kentucky). Campaigns like these rely upon simple visual associations (earmuffs = cold), but they can also traffic in science of a sort. By encouraging people to ask themselves whether they had, indeed, felt warmer during the era of "global warming," such commercials played to an embodied empiricism that called upon skin, nerves, and breath to register the temperature.

Now it is certainly true, as Chris Mooney (2005:57) puts it, that "not every skeptic is necessarily a Galileo." And there are, to be sure, varieties of climate change skepticism that should not be dignified with the term *skepticism*. If you decide that the conditions for human life on earth cannot possibly be deteriorating because your best friend or your pastor or a talk show host told you so (again and again), then you have not mastered the arts of inquiry that skepticism requires. If you uncritically accept the verdict of someone who writes "PhD" after his name, you are trafficking in cultural authority rather than scientific inference, as much in thrall to celebrity or credentials as the next person. Damian Thompson (2008:2) has called this miscarriage of observation and reasoning *counterknowledge*, a term he applies in a sometimes reactionary, sometimes insightful way to the recent "surge in the popularity of propositions that fail basic empirical tests." By Thompson's reckoning, counterknowledge would encompass creationism and intelligent design, but not religion as such, because claims about the existence of a god or gods remain untestable.[13]

Critics often lump climate skepticism together with antievolutionist creationism as a fundamentally irrational species of pseudoscience. Both have found fertile soil in North America, with 46 percent of U.S. residents in a 2012 Gallup poll subscribing to the statement "God created human beings pretty much in their present form at one time within the last 10,000 years or so" (Newport 2012). But climate skepticism comes in many guises, and it is that very particular guise called embodied empiricism that interests me here, because it has the potential to transform dismissal into dialogue. In his work on Christian Pentecostal communities in California, for example, Josh Brahinsky (2012) describes devotional practices that cultivate a "modern sensorium" that positions the body as a vehicle for spiritual understanding. With this sort of bodily cultivation already underway in many communities, the appeal of using the body to attempt to verify truth claims accorded the status of science becomes more legible.

If empiricism by definition generates claims that can be tested by evidence of the senses, embodied empiricism produces bio-intimacy in a slightly different register than the ones described in earlier chapters. Embodied empiricism choreographs a bio-intimacy of detection and assessment, which registers conditions through membrane, skin, and retina, then uses reason to sort out the results. In that sense it matters little whether your "environment" embodies you, or you it, or both.

Everyday attunement of the flesh to humidity, wind, and hydration only begs a series of larger questions: If embodied empiricism can count as a scientific form of inquiry, why, when applied to climate change, has it yielded such errant results? Once corporate campaigns redirected awareness to the body, why didn't those beads of sweat yield a different form of doubt, directed at the campaigns themselves? Shouldn't skeptics who had recourse to empiricist methods, after paying careful attention to the evidence of their own bodies situated in the world, have come to the conclusion that the case for climate change is, at a scientific minimum, plausible and called for further investigation?

Social Skin in the Game

These are urgent questions, not rhetorical ones: questions whose answers might well require people to live differently. It is worth hazarding a few responses, if only because it has been so difficult in the United States to mobilize the political will to address climate change without them. The first possible explanation involves what anthropologists call the social skin; the second, a category error; and the third, a populist reaction to the eclipse of empiricism by Big Science. Some of these explanations turn on matters of methodology, which sounds dry until you realize that a subtle methodological reorientation might help make embodied empiricism useful for confronting climate change after all.

When anthropologists talk about a "social skin," they mean more than the fact that, as Terry Turner (1980:111) famously put it, "Man is born naked but is everywhere in clothes." Sensation may be sensation, but perceiving, describing, and interpreting it is site-specific. Does that tingling sensation represent a cultural category called "anxiety," a cardiac event, a healthy manifestation of qi, or ghosts in the neighborhood? Would it matter if the sensation occurred at the fingertips instead of the back of the neck? The sense that people make of the sensations that their bodies register varies profoundly from one sociocultural context to another.

This is not just a matter of dueling "cultural logics" of the sort anthropologists are accustomed to seek. For a phenomenologist such as Maurice Merleau-Ponty, there can never be such a thing as "pure sensing": "The red patch I see on the rug is only red if the shadow that lies across it is taken into account; its quality only appears in relation to the play of light, and thus only as an element in a spatial configuration" (Merleau-Ponty 2012:27). In *Phenomenology of Perception*, he argues that bodies participate in a dialectic that situates them as a "third term" somewhere between subject and object. Sensation depends upon relationality.

Once the doors of perception open, they open to political persuasion. What you see may be what you get, as the old song goes, but what you get is not always what you see. Embodied empiricism has proved vulnerable to corporate spin that appeals to science, despite but also because of the pivotal contributions of empiricism to the codification of science itself. That any evidentiary quality should be attributed to sweat on skin is a profoundly sociohistorical move.

In an effort to explain climate skepticism, scientists have suggested yet another reason for attachment to contrarian thinking. The problem, they contend, lies in a category error that mistakes weather for climate (see, e.g., Mann 2012). Weather can be highly variable, with winds blowing hot or cold or not at all on any given day, whereas climate materializes over time, quite a bit of time: the *longue durée*. Climate assessments must therefore take historical trends into account, above and beyond the current appraisal that any bodily sensation can offer. In the case of climate change, the pace of a shift also matters. While it might be true that the camel's ancestors did indeed once roam the Arctic, that was three and a half million years ago, which gave their descendants plenty of time to migrate and adapt to a changing environment (Rybczynski et al. 2013). What worries scientists are the sharply accelerating trends they have measured recently, with ice sheets vanishing in a matter of decades, leaving creatures precious little time for adaptation.

As alarming as these trends are, the category error explanation is not as compelling as the one that takes the sociality of skin into account. To argue that weather and climate should not be confused is to forget that the two often overlap in the ways that human activity engages them. Corporations that sell farmers crop insurance regularly monitor weather forecasts, even as the actuarial tables developed to underwrite crop insurance are based on climate histories. Engineers in Tokyo who argue for better flood defenses have appealed to both "unusual [climatic] conditions" and changing "weather patterns" to secure support (Cooper and Matsuda 2013). German periodicals sometimes include sections on *Bio-wetter* and *Wetterfühligkeit* that tell readers what effects they might experience in their bodies— headaches, disrupted sleep—as barometric pressure drops or a cold front moves in.[14] Climate trends affect *Bio-wetter* as surely as the latest snowstorm. In practice *and* in bodily sensation, climate and weather often go hand in hand.

Even Michael Mann, who has identified category confusion as something that leads climate change skeptics astray, points out that weather and climate meet through a cyclical process called the seasons. "Just because certain aspects of the weather and climate are chaotic in character," he writes, "does not mean that climate changes are unpredictable, as anyone familiar with the rather easily forecasted climate phenomena known as *winter* and *summer* is no doubt aware" (Mann 2012:94). Winter and summer are readily accessible to empirically embodied investigations that are, in turn, accessible to living memory.

Seeking out the eldest among us, like my great aunt Elsie, to inquire, "Do you ever remember it being this hot?" is one way to go about linking climate to weather, keeping in mind that an untrained memory can prove as frail as teeth or limbs. Another way is to read the body for signs, as farmers have done since long before the meteorologist was invented. When the blue-streaked *perti wha* bird shows up in Maharashtra, tribal elders say it is time to plant because rain is on the way. According to them, this mobile, highly localized harbinger of precipitation has provided more accurate predictions than the regional forecasts issued by the national weather bureau (Pallavi 2009). But when no one sees the *perti wha*, and not for want of looking, what then?

The point is this: people who use eyes, wrists, and perspiration to search out evidence of changing climatic conditions may not always be "confusing" weather with climate so much as puzzling out the relationship between the two. After all, as the climate scientist Shang-Ping Xie so cogently puts it, "no one lives in the global average" (Sumner 2015:6). When sleepers cast aside their blankets in Himalayan mountain valleys where apple orchards no longer receive sufficient chilling hours to bear fruit, they come to realize that daily fluctuations cannot explain it.

Recently planners at the Indian Meteorological Department have had to revise the "climatic parameters" for the onset and withdrawal of the annual monsoon due to "deviation from normal dates" that were themselves based upon averages calculated in the 1940s (Sachan 2011). At the same time, they have come to recognize that averages have their limitations when it comes to predicting what an altered climate holds in store. As James Lovelock (2006:60) has cautioned, "We should expect climate changes of a kind never even thought of, one-off events affecting no more than a region." Scientists themselves have begun to devise ways to look for the "climate change signature" of otherwise singular events (Raloff 2012). To most people, a one-off incident that takes the shape of a monster cyclone or hailstorm looks a lot like weather, even as they testify that no one remembers experiencing anything like it before.

Whether the use of bodies to evaluate claims about climate change is likely to lead people astray has less to do with *if* someone consults the weather than *how* she consults it, and what she does with her observations. It matters that her orientation to the weather forecast is often a visceral one. Beyond faith and fashion and culture, she wants to make an educated guess about sun, wind, and rain in order to determine how to array her body before walking outside. How much protection? How much reveal? What sets climatology apart from sticking one's head out the window before deciding what clothes to wear are (among other things) good records, multiple observations, and a longer (much longer!) time frame.

These days climatology is as deeply indebted to ice core analysis and computer modeling as it is to the humble backyard weather station.[15] New techniques for investigation can be prohibitively expensive, beyond the reach of replication by a curious public. Like other areas of organized inquiry, climatology has participated in a wider shift away from the "small science" that gave rise to embodied empiricism and self-experimentation, toward the kind of Big Science that requires well-funded laboratories, drilling rigs, server farms, grant applications, and expeditions. All of which raises a third possibility: that the reluctance of some climate change skeptics to accept the latest computer models of a shake-and-bake future for the planet may have less to do with a distrust of science as such and more to do with being asked to take expert testimony on trust.

Most people cannot fly out to Greenland, hire a drilling rig, and store the ice cores in a freezer out in the garage until their citizen scientist friends can come over on the weekend to see if their findings corroborate the climate data that university researchers have reported. They can, however, have recourse to their bodies. And while a single body on any given day can only supply anecdotal evidence, reports that enlist multiple bodies on multiple occasions begin to look like data. In places where oral testimony still counts for something, people consult the elders, not the elder, for a reason.

It might be objected that self-reports can only ever amount to a rough-and-ready version of "subjective experience," useless for detecting the fractional shifts in average temperature at the heart of a worldwide phenomenon like climate change.[16] It is true that people's bodies are not well calibrated for this sort of investigation, and in any case, we don't need them. We have thermometers for that. (Although in an age of cybernetically enhanced bodies, one can equally well imagine people donning wearable digital devices with heat-measuring capabilities that could adjust for body heat and transmit readings as people moved through their days, in effect crowdsourcing ever more fine-grained temperature data.) But when it comes to climate change, temperature is only a linchpin in a cascade of interacting effects, many of them amenable to fruitful investigation by sight, smell, hearing, taste, and touch.

If climate consists of patterns measured over decades, there is no reason that bodies, located and sufficiently sampled, cannot contribute whatever the senses, configured as instruments, apprehend. Want to improve the mapping of severe storms? Lend your eyes, ears, and hands to a citizen science project like the Community Collaborative Rain, Hail, and Snow Network. Need to know more about how climate change is affecting the leafing and flowering of plants? Join Nature's Notebook, sponsored by the National Phenology Network, and begin uploading your observations.[17]

One of the less celebrated features of the citizen science movement lies in its reclamation of the value of qualitative data for tackling contemporary scientific questions. Citizen scientists do make plenty of metric assessments as they gauge stream quality, build do-it-yourself lab equipment, and so on. But many also honor the scientific practices of an earlier era by keeping field journals that include self-report. In *The Incidental Steward: Reflections on Citizen Science*, Akiko Busch (2013) creates an American lineage for this type of "public amateurism" that runs through Thomas Jefferson's naturalist notations, Henry David Thoreau's journals at Walden Pond, and Franklin Delano Roosevelt's field notebook of migratory birds. Climate historians have put all three sources to a use their creators never envisioned: documentation of a dangerously warming world.

Details about what bodies register can help establish patterns and catch instances of unexpected divergence, as well as provide evidence that numerical measurements cannot capture. Centimeters in a rain gauge tell you nothing about whether rain lashed the fields and destroyed the crops or nourished them with the gentle steady patter that farmers in Maharashtra call a *jhad*. Eyes, ears, and skin are perfectly serviceable tools for discerning the difference.

As the organizers of the volunteer bird counts that take place on multiple continents will tell you, these old-fashioned embodied instruments are sometimes the *most* effective way to document quantitative and qualitative changes in phenomena, especially in an era of budget cuts. The Common Bird Monitoring of India project has produced valuable insights into changes in migratory behavior by recruiting ears and eyes to produce tallies, allowing volunteer bodies to momentarily escape their latter-day reputation as collections of unreliable or "naked" instruments. Brian Wynne's (1996) classic essay, "May the Sheep Safely Graze?," recounts how farmers in Cumbria in the UK drew on what they learned while working with their flocks to determine that the radioactive contamination of their fields originated not from Chernobyl, but from the nearby Sellafield nuclear fuel reprocessing plant. Wynne calls what the farmers possessed "lay expertise," an empirically derived expert knowledge developed through careful everyday observation, often without the aid of specialized equipment.[18] Lay expertise unfolds in the interstices between unreflective approaches to ordinary life and the professionalized realms of Big Science. Credentialed scientific authorities often resist recognizing lay expertise, as the Cumbrian sheep farmers discovered when they attempted to make their case.

If there is an error in the climate change skeptic's appeals to the body, then, it has nothing to do with embodied empiricism as such. Systematically organize those individually embodied observations, date them, record them, place the narrative passages in context, expand the number of observers, and see what happens.

Grassroots Climate Science: The Good, the Bad, and the Corporeal

During one of those lost years when Elsie and I used to sit out on the front porch to conjure the wind, the phones at WLS-TV in Chicago started ringing off the hook. John Coleman, the local meteorologist, was in the midst of delivering his live nightly weather forecast, which featured an unqualified prediction: zero percent chance of precipitation. "Step out on the fire escape," callers urged him. He came back after the commercial break, his dress shirt spattered with rain, to stage a mea culpa.

You could take this story as a warning about the dangers of trafficking in absolute values, the importance of leaving yourself a little wiggle room, or the ways that the world will surprise you. But you could also read it as a good old-fashioned populist dig at the experts, particularly if you took the viewers' delight into account when Chicago's favorite meteorologist came back on the air to retract his forecast. By now the sentiment should be familiar, since there is more than a little populist delight in the embodied empiricist variant of climate skepticism that urges people to stick out their hands to feel for raindrops before coming to their own conclusions.

American variations on populism have spanned the political spectrum from left to right historically, but most draw upon what Michael Kazin (1995:2, 13) calls a producer ethic, which emphasizes the creation of knowledge and wealth through one's own efforts and "practical intelligence." As Ernesto Laclau (2007:176) points out, "Populism . . . is not a fixed constellation but a series of discursive resources which can be put to very different uses." This is why Laclau can speak of populist *reason* instead of reducing all populism to an irrational, politically naïve, easily manipulated reaction to disenfranchisement. There is a difference between skepticism (a species of critical thinking, à la Hume) and ostrichism (heads buried in denial). Those who hope to understand, rather than simply deride, the contingent of thinking climate change skeptics with whom they differ—admittedly a subset of the larger whole—could learn a thing or two from Kazin's and Laclau's analyses. For whatever its shortcomings, populist reason is not always and everywhere faulty.

The embodied empiricists accused of climate change denial could equally well be credited with *refusing to succumb* to denial, in the sense that they have refused to deny the evidence of their senses when encouraged to take climate model projections on trust. These intertwined rhetorics of evidence and trust are begging for cultural analysis. In *Trust Us, We're Experts!* Sheldon Rampton and John Stauber (2001) open their discussion of skepticism about expert verdicts in North America with a story about what happened the year the U.S. Environmental Protection Agency (EPA) decided to promote sewage sludge as a farm fertilizer. Internal EPA documents complained about "an irrational component to public attitudes about sludge" grounded in "the widely held perception of sewage sludge as malodorous, disease causing or otherwise repulsive." Translated into the vernacular, the EPA had come to the conclusion that "people are irrational because they think sewage stinks" (Rampton and Stauber 2001:1). (A conclusion that reeked of irony for anyone with even a passing knowledge of the history of state-sponsored campaigns to educate rural and immigrant publics about the importance of soap.) In another case, chemists hired by industrial meat producers in the United States fielded complaints about the nauseating odors emanating from rendering plants by installing "scento-meters." When the chemists duly declared the smell negligible on the basis of machine data, these captive researchers implied that "the evidence of neighbors' noses couldn't be trusted" (Rampton and Stauber 2001:1). In both cases, credentialed experts judged lay knowledge to be "anecdotal," no matter how many bodily sensors replicated the results, while they categorized machine data as "scientific" by definition.

The same public that occasionally succumbs to an onslaught of ads filled with horses in earmuffs is well aware that both government and industry hire experts to manage perception. They don't call it public relations for nothing. At the same time, "the public" is neither a group nor a unified subject, which guarantees that perceptions will vary. A rendering plant, like a sludge-strewn field or a paper mill, can smell like money to anyone whose job depends on it. Regardless of what side in the climate wars individuals came down on, these were not the credulous masses.

The generations targeted by the merchants of doubt had lived through Watergate, exposés about Cold War medical experiments conducted on un-suspecting citizens, efforts by the state to downplay the dangers of above-ground atomic testing, and the failure to verify satellite photographs of alleged weapons of mass destruction in Iraq.[19] In their experience, expert testimony had not always passed the stink test.

Of course, as S. G. Collins points out in his clever visual exposition of why the U.S. government could never have faked the moon landing given the state of photographic technology at the time, "that step from know-ing that you've been lied to, to believing that everything else is a lie, is a big step."[20] There may be a reason many Europeans think of conspiracy theories as a distinctively North American preoccupation. Still, as George Marcus (1999) and colleagues argue in the aptly titled volume of case studies *Paranoia within Reason*, deceit administered by experts and offi-cials can increase the appeal of conspiracy theories to the thinking woman and the reasoning man. In the United States, people who were old enough to remember spoke cynically about the swine flu vaccination campaign of 1976, which painted a picture of dire consequences that never materialized. They were less likely to consider the kind of temporal paradoxes that pre-occupy epidemiologists, in which successful efforts to quash the spread of a disease can lead to the impression that those efforts were not necessary in the first place.

In North America, nonspecialist understandings of what researchers do or don't know are also informed by consumer-oriented health reports that present the results of scientific studies piecemeal. On Monday celebrity doctors appear onscreen to tell viewers that coffee (the national beverage) can help prevent type 2 diabetes. On Tuesday viewers are assured that coffee can protect them from liver cancer. By Friday they wake up to warnings that coffee may lead to spikes in blood pressure that could send them to an early grave. Since viewers have no way to adjudicate such claims, many report they have stopped paying attention.

Global warming, in contrast, seemed like a theory that ordinary people could put to the test rather than leave to the determination of Big Science. This was particularly true in the early days of the climate wars, when advocates of greenhouse gas reductions assured a wary public that climate change would soon create impacts that would affect everyone, impacts they would *feel*. Feel, as in: apprehend with the senses.[21]

This is where researchers who believe that all climate change skeptics misunderstand how science works may themselves be missing the point. In *Global Climate Change: A Primer*, for instance, the authors feel compelled to explain to a potentially skeptical audience that "criticism and discussions between scientists are the way science is conducted and not an indication of weakness or uncertainty" (Pilkey and Pilkey 2011:13). Here they are talking past grassroots empiricists who have greeted scientific discussion of the details of computer models and climate histories as an *invitation* to weigh in with their own embodied evidence.

At this point in the chapter, readers who have positioned themselves as defenders of climate science might be experiencing some discomfort. If you are one of those readers, try tabling your views long enough to approach the variant of populist reasoning embedded in the climate wars with a spirit of generosity and understanding. Rather than imagining every skeptic as resolutely opposed to evidence produced through observation and testing, think of some of them as taking a stand in favor of something: their own embodied apprehension. Look carefully enough, and the embodied empiricist version of grassroots climate change skepticism starts to resemble citizen science.[22]

As shown in the discussion of technostruggle in Japan in chapter 2, citizen science has the potential to hold governments and corporations to account by making sure that experts with access to greater resources serve future generations rather than shadowy moneyed interests. In a global marketplace saturated with bids to manipulate perception, grassroots climate skeptics in the United States have accordingly used their bodies to adjudicate disputes, develop their own claims to expertise, and deliver their own assessments of climate projections. This move was only possible because the human body is, in a certain sense, a technology available to everyone, not just credentialed researchers with grants and institutional affiliations. How tragic, then, that embodied empiricism in the individualized way that climate change skeptics have employed it in the United States has ended up playing right into the hands of vested interests.

When Japanese experts portrayed people who took their own radiation measurements after the nuclear meltdown at Fukushima Daiichi as irrational actors who gave too much credence to harmful rumors, it was easy for progressives in North America to embrace the efforts of these citizen scientists as a form of heroic resistance. But when American experts portrayed climate change skeptics as irrational actors with their heads in the sands of denial, many progressives were a bit too quick to concur. There is nothing progressive about dismissing a politics before you understand how people have come to it. As it has become clearer that facing up to climate change will require more than better communication about scientific findings, there are calls to investigate other things that may have gotten in the way, from hopes and fears to political partisanship, overreliance on market mechanisms, ambivalence about the place of human beings in the world, stymied decision-making processes, a decline in pragmatic reason, and a reluctance to part with creature comforts (see Hulme 2009; Jamieson 2014; Klein 2014; Washington and Cook 2011).[23] Perhaps the embodied claims to knowledge that empiricism generates should be added to that list.

Like citizen scientists in Japan after the nuclear accident at Fukushima Daiichi, the early climate change skeptics in the United States who looked to bodies for signs of a world in trouble had reason not to trust blindly. Like citizen scientists in Japan, these particular North American climate change skeptics hoped to compile evidence and reason their way through official pronouncements rather than take them on authority. They simply availed themselves of the kind of ballpark measurements that a technology of the senses could register, rather than producing digital readouts with the aid of Geiger counters or other sorts of machines.

To generate meaningful scientific results, it would only take legions of observers rocking their way through the summers like my great aunt Elsie to record their sensations more systematically and share their reports: crowdsourcing, by any other name. Instead of backyard weather stations documenting conditions that yield patterns when amalgamated over time, think bodies, differentially calibrated, perhaps, but geographically distributed and closely observed. Citizen scientists working on climate change would have the advantage here, since bodies wielded as scientific instruments have no trouble detecting temperature shifts or extreme weather events, whereas nuclear technologies tend to alienate people from their own senses because they cannot tell when radiation is present without an assist.[24] Like other forms of citizen science, embodied empiricism could serve as a tool that complements rather than competes with existing lines of research.

In a 2009 essay on sea-level rise in Bangladesh, Timothy Finan (2009: 175) proclaimed, "In all corners but the most intractable, the debate over climate change is over." Well, yes. And no. If opinion on the matter in North America had really begun to turn, it probably did have something to do with changes in the seasons and dramatic weather events, corporeally apprehended, year after unprecedented year (see "The Greening of America" 2007). Perhaps that old "confusion" between climate and weather, much lamented by scientists, was not so disastrous after all. While researchers locked horns over the question of whether Arctic warming had encouraged the jet stream to wander, people in the middle latitudes added "polar vortex" to their vocabulary and wondered whether they should get used to seeing daffodils in February. Attribution science set out to demonstrate that specific incidents such as an out-of-season hailstorm or an unusually destructive flood could be linked to climate change by documenting historical shifts in the odds of such a thing happening (see, e.g., Peterson, Stott, and Herring 2012). As for corporate interests, they had begun to display their own rifts. Global reinsurance companies such as Munich Re could no longer afford to ignore the rising number of weather-related catastrophes in places like North America (Suess 2012). They had become less interested in spinning the science than in exploring the costly possibility that climate change might have something to do with all those "extra" thunderstorms and cyclones.

If the North American climate change debates have made anything clear, it is that a preponderance of scientific evidence is not automatically convincing, since "preponderance" encodes a judgment that people may not have the means to corroborate, and "evidence" may entail methodologies that not everyone values. In 2013 the U.S. chapter of the nonprofit Union of Concerned Scientists still perceived the need to title an essay "It's Cold and My Car Is Buried in Snow: Is Global Warming Really Happening?" The reader's body had achieved recognition as a sensor but still fell short of qualifying as a technology that any certified scientist would want to enlist.

Unlike a mango (ripe or unripe?), a massage (deep tissue or shiatsu?), or a desk (hardwood or veneer?), climate change presents would-be observers with what Timothy Morton (2013a:4) calls a hyperobject, that is, a geographically and historically distributed object that is tricky to think, by virtue of its distributed effects and, one might add, its late-breaking constitution as a scientific object. Yet for all that, climate change is and will be lived. Candis Callison (2014:42) considers it an "emergent form of life" that calls forth as it calls upon different vernaculars, when differently situated constituencies attempt to bridge "direct present experience and the conceptual future."

Embodied knowledge of a hyperobject can only ever be partial. Suppose though, for that very reason, that the problems with the conclusions reached by empirically oriented climate change skeptics have had less to do with empiricism as such and more to do with the fragmented way in which individuals have gone about making their assessments. What would it take to organize the scattered empirical *observations* of North American climate change skeptics into an empirical *investigation* that could subject truth claims about climate change to the test of the senses without necessarily rejecting the body's value as a scientific instrument or finding those senses wanting?

In her discussion of grassroots environmental politics in southern India, Monamie Bhadra (2013) tells the story of a fisherman who brushes away the numbers that the developers of a nuclear power plant brandish to reassure him of its safety. Who needs charts of temperatures? He explains that he can better gauge the warmth of ocean water—and thus its habitability for fish—by sticking his hand in the water. Now imagine a flotilla of fisherfolk concerned about climate change who use their hands to make such measurements, reporting on different patches of water, in different seasons, at different times of day, with an eye to documenting the relative changes from one measurement to the next. Cooler or warmer? A shift of greater or lesser magnitude? And how was the fishing that day?

Embodied empiricists, in all their skepticism, have a similar opportunity to contribute to projects that document surface temperatures, sea level rise, drought conditions, and the like. Brittle leaves that crumble in the hand, the sour smell of sap from a dying tree: these, too, can become data. Crowd-

Figure 3.1. An image used in the Sweatuation campaign to promote public awareness about climate change [Credit: The Franklin Institute]

sourced maps of the sort that Safecast produced for radiation hot spots in Japan could make corporeally sourced reports available for inspection, comparison, and corroboration. By placing embodied observations in a wider context, such projects would also encourage people to work together to interpret what their bodies tell them, so that a week of cool breezes and dry armpits in summer cannot so easily be mistaken for a sign of ecological well-being.

Citizen science might seem the obvious way to enlist embodied empiricism in the struggle to reduce greenhouse gas emissions, but it is only one of many possible routes. Here is another: Early in the twenty-first century, a public service campaign with the tagline "Here's the Sweatuation in Philly" hit the streets in Philadelphia, sponsored by the Climate & Urban Systems Partnership in association with the Franklin Institute.[25] Campaign graphics featured locals going about their daily routines with perspiration dripping down their faces and sweat stains spreading across their clothes. A website explained how to "improve your sweatuation" by installing rain barrels, planting trees, looking out for neighbors, and celebrating the measures that the city had already adopted to combat climate change. Anyone who snapped a "sweatie selfie" could enter it in a contest to win a bike and start riding to work in "eco-friendly style." In answer to the question "Why is Philadelphia getting hotter and wetter?" the website referred to scientific findings, but it also warned Philadelphians to expect "more swugs, swecks, swarmpits, and swellies," as well as more serious afflictions such as heat exhaustion. The implicit message to the merchants of doubt, with their appeals to bodily sensation, had become "Two can play at that game."

Of course, bodies can't appraise everything, and they are better suited to examining some things than others. Only studies that invest in remote-controlled equipment can determine things like vertical heat distribution in the world's oceans, which may have absorbed up to 90 percent of the heat added to the global climate system in recent times (see Balmaseda, Trenberth, and Källén 2013). But there are already many examples of cooperation between professional scientists and citizen scientists that enlist human sensory faculties such as sight and pattern recognition. In a bid to "crowd-source the cosmos," Galaxy Zoo has recruited people without technical training to help with the daunting task of classifying astronomical galaxies according to shape.[26] If nothing else, embodied empiricist investigations of climate change could help distinguish skeptics who want to bring the evidence of their own senses to bear on expert testimony from "skeptics" who are committed to an obstructionist politics of doubt, come hell or high water. Very, very high water.

WATER

4

_____

The Greatest Show on Parched Earth

"Who's there?" she calls out, but no one answers. "Who's there?" she asks again, as the tap-tap-tapping grows ever more insistent. She is moving toward the door when a trio of feathered heads at the window catches her eye. It's a troupe of jungle babblers pecking at the glass, expending unthinkable amounts of energy in the languid heat of a northern Indian summer. They have come to demand their daily water ration. The terra cotta bowl my partner sets out for them on the veranda ledge lies neglected this morning and the babblers will not leave until they have had their due.

Water from the faucet, when it comes — and it comes here but twice a day, on a good day — does not satisfy. Its variegated shades of amber, tan, midnight sludge, ash, and crystal are too fickle for these birds to find palatable. Motor oil, chromium, mercury, pesticides: who knows what produces the ever-changing colors? The babblers may not know the industrial recipe, but they know enough to reject tap water, in favor of the best that urban water-filtering technology can provide: a glistening offering from the reverse osmosis machine in the kitchen. Once served, they stay to play, sipping, wrangling, bathing, and splashing their way through the thick premonsoon air.

In short, the babblers put on a show, for passersby inclined to turn spectator. And therein lies a lesson for anyone inclined to reduce the sociality of water to thirst, politics, and profit. It is not that thirst, politics, and profit do not matter, especially in the semiarid regions that ring the Indian capital.

Figure 4.1. Filtered water for the birds next to a bottle of tap water
on a *kala pani* ("black water") day [Credit: Author photo]

Gautum Budh Nagar District in Uttar Pradesh, where Noida and Greater
Noida are located, received just 359 millimeters (14 inches) of rainfall in
2013.[1] Without water, humans and birds alike perish, and without politics
or profit it becomes increasingly difficult to tell the story of how any creature these days can manage to stay hydrated. But thirst, politics, and profit
do not bring down the curtain on explanations for the range of things that
people do with water, much less what entices them into unsustainable uses.

To understand the visceral pull exerted by lively displays of water in a
region of water depletion—to understand that visceral pull in a register
other than thirst—we have only to travel twenty-nine kilometers from the
veranda as the babbler flies to the New Delhi suburb called Greater Noida.
For years an entertainment and business complex called the Grand Venice
has been rising on its allotted plot, by stops as much as starts.[2] This is the
kind of project environmentalists love to hate: water-hungry, dependent
on a diminishing "resource," bending an already polluted aquifer to the
whims of patrons and investors, capitalizing on the impression its façade
conveys of access and excess, a million square feet of retail space that must
be watered daily.

Technoscientific mastery undergirds its every allusion to the "real"
Venice, with a realness that washes up both on Mediterranean shores and

on a strip of casinos in the North American desert. None of this homage rises at all without the wizardry required to arch a roof over the tiered balustrades that frame the atrium, without the engineering know-how to sink tubewells deep underground in order to fill a gondola basin in the interior. None of this homage rises, either, without the artisanal skill that sends intricately patterned tile and *jali* (lattice) work cascading past the entrance.

Environmental critiques directed at megaprojects like the Grand Venice frequently strike a pejorative key, branding them regrettable examples of hubris, spectacle, ecological harm, profit-seeking, financial chicanery, mimesis, and/or nationalist aspiration. Add a dash of scarcity discourse plus utilitarian reasoning, and readers with even passing acquaintance with water politics would be forgiven for thinking they know where all this must be heading. Bad, bad, bad project, right? Another folly in the desert that even a good monsoon cannot remedy!

A folly, perhaps, but not necessarily in the sense that ready critiques bring to mind. Architecturally speaking, the Grand Venice has something in common with the follies concocted by eighteenth-century landscape architects such as Lancelot "Capability" Brown, who conjured Merlin's Cave in Kew Gardens for Queen Caroline as an extravagance and a playful allusion to an elsewhere that invited aesthetic contemplation (J. Brown 2011: 221).

If play does not conventionally appear among the usual suspects in accounts of water politics, there is an argument to be made as to why it should. And not just any sort of play, but the kind of play that involves turnabout. The National Capital Region (NCR) is a place where people commonly follow the media's lead in characterizing the region's most powerful river, the Yamuna, as "a sewer." At night its middle-class inhabitants sit down to watch actors lavish a gaze otherwise reserved for the beloved on glasses of clear water in ads for household filtration systems on television. Mothers who would never dream of letting their children take a dip in the polluted rivers send their children to water parks (if they can afford it) where the kids can cultivate a lighthearted connection with water, but not during the monsoon months for fear they will catch waterborne diseases. In such a place, as they play—play!—against ecological damage and images like these, the "scintillating and mesmerizing" attractions brokered by the Grand Venice are simply over the top.[3] What follows, then, is a bit of street theater in which the streets are canals, paved with liquid assets or fool's gold, as the case may be.

The Cast

The Grand Venice, a water-themed building complex on the outskirts of Delhi in Greater Noida, which has long promised to endow the subcontinent with an aquarium, shopping mall, canal basin, gondola rides, office suites, 270-room hotel, plus India's first mermaid show. A chorus of jungle babblers, leaning on their local reputation as silly mischievous little chatterboxes, annoying and entertaining by turns. The Yamuna River, the longest tributary of the Ganga (Ganges), assuming various incarnations as she/it flows past New Delhi. A roster of supporting actors that includes the artisans and contractors who have given form to the Grand Venice; Worlds of Wonder, a water amusement park; mafias and investors of various sorts; a contaminated, diminishing aquifer; and villagers who depend upon the Yamuna floodplain for their livelihood.

With a cameo appearance by Mikhail Bakhtin, conjuror of dialogism and heteroglossia, tamer of polyphonies, for one night only, bringing to life on this very stage his world-famous notion of the carnivalesque.

And withal, the play.

The Greatest Show on Parched Earth

O for a Muse of water, that would ascend / The brightest heaven of invention.[4] What is it about a desert that wants a fountain? Or, for that matter, some mirage of a city of canals etched into scrub and sand? First onto the global stage comes the Venetian, a luxury hotel and casino in Las Vegas, built atop the rubble of the old Sands Hotel in the 1990s. At the time, celebrity and razzmatazz eclipsed any premonitions of the dire threats to Las Vegas's water supply that would emerge two short decades later. The newly opened Venetian had sounding trumpets, clouds of doves released into the sky, brasseries that showcased chefs of renown, Sophia Loren expertly piloted under a replica of the Ponte di Rialto by a singing gondolier. Then came the Venetian Macau, bankrolled by the Las Vegas Sands group and opened in China's casino capital in 2007. Now it is Greater Noida's turn.

For three years I have been traveling out to Plot No. sh-3, Site IV, Greater Noida, to watch an edifice clamber skyward atop a foundation of investments and deferrals. What was not so long ago a *jangli* place, filled with deer, monkeys, cows, thatched huts, hand pumps, and *kikar* (acacia) trees, finds itself increasingly hedged in by the gray concrete skeletons of buildings. Developers peddle unfinished flats and offices in these complexes,

Figure 4.2.
Exterior of the
Grand Venice during
construction [Credit:
Author photo]

located on relatively cheaper land at the moving periphery of India's pricey NCR. Buyers hope their own units will near completion before the developers go bust or lose interest as they use the deposits to bankroll other projects.

Bhasin Group,[5] the corporation that broke ground on the Grand Venice and once fielded questions about the suitability of the location, stands vindicated: A place that represented the middle of nowhere (to Delhiites) at the project's inception in 2007 has become an edge city, replete with its own university, traffic jams, fast-food outlets, and expressway. Folded into such metropolitan signifiers are pockets of villagers, old-time shops, migrant laborers, and light industry.

Because this radical transformation has occurred in living memory, developers have been able to capitalize on the area's rural roots by adding "eco" features to residential blocks in an effort to brand them (however misleadingly) as multistoried countryside retreats in which residents will live lightly on the land. The Grand Venice's neighbors in luxury include high-end Jaypee Greens, where the concept of "green" encompasses both lush landscaping and a golf course. Supertech Ecovillage IV, a bit further out, offers prospective buyers a "*vaastu*-friendly fengshui layout" and pledges to run its backup generators on cleaner CNG fuel rather than diesel whenever the lights go out, as they regularly do on the east side of the Yamuna in Uttar Pradesh, which sources its electricity from a different grid than Delhi proper.[6]

This foggy December night in 2014, however, is all about the lights coming on, not off. My partner and I are headed to the Grand Preview Soft Launch of the Grand Venice. The serendipities of research like this include not only the stumbled-upon but also the almost-never-happened. Shortly after arriving in Delhi, a half-page ad in the *Hindustan Times* alerts us to the event, so long anticipated that, just like the investors, I have almost stopped anticipating it. Jet-lagged, I breeze right past the ad en route to a second cup of coffee, only to be called back by my partner's keener eye. After a flurry of phone calls, explanations of my research program murmured into sympathetic office workers' ears, attestations to publication prospects as glowing as any investment prospectus, a delivery by courier that fails to arrive, and a madcap taxi ride during rush hour to a deserted storefront office, our combined efforts yield one slightly crumpled invitation-only couple entry admission pass.

That admission pass is the key to an evening's entertainment, to be sure, with "Magical Music by MIKA," a Panjabi bhangra/rap artist (not to be confused with the Lebanese British pop singer) whose repertoire extends to Sufi music. But the pass is also an entree to something more. Backstage is about to become *the* stage. After three years of attempting to gain access to what lies within, a glimpse of the Grand Venice's inner workings is nigh.

As our car spins off the roundabout at Pari Chowk, I crane my neck until a clock tower modeled on the one in the Piazza San Marco comes into view. Only this one comes complete with logo: Grand Venice (as in, "Grand Venice: A Dream Destination"). And what could be a more fitting landmark to guide tourists to an enterprise configured as a fantasia than Pari Chowk, with its Golden Fairy (*pari*) sculpture auspiciously presiding over a traffic circle draped in a whirl of auto rickshaws, commuter cars, and two-wheelers?

Naïvely expecting a preview of an all-but-finished space, our entrance to the mall offers instead a study in contrasts. Approaching the complex

Figure 4.3.
Grand Venice clock
tower [Credit:
Author photo]

from behind, with the upper levels of the hotel still in the concrete-and-cinderblock phase, I had not recognized it at first, especially with all the new buildings coming up in the vicinity. From the front, however, there is no mistaking it. Windows in the intricately patterned tile of the façade evoke the Venetian Gothic of the ones in the Doge's Palace. Julius Caesar rises high and gilded on his plinth. A fresco recasts itself into the burnt-orange pigments of commercially sourced paint and finds its vanishing point in the wall. As dusk falls, lights animate the baroque outlines of Greater Noida's very own *Fontana di Trevi*, a cataract of allusions to creatures governed by its watery ruler, Neptune/The Sea. The original of that particular fountain graces Rome, not Venice, but no matter: the point is to create a bit of "Italy in India" (or, as the construction contractors put

it, "something European"). There is also a finely wrought display of orna-
mental latticework over the main door in the style of a jali screen, flanked
by domed *chhatri* ("umbrella") pavilions at the corners of the piazza, but
tonight these go unremarked.

After inspecting our admission card, an usher directs us to remain on
the upper level. Long rows of chairs for the likes of us skirt the bannis-
ters on either side, overlooking the atrium at the heart of the mall. Seat-
ing on the main floor is reserved for large investors, members of the Bhasin Group and their relatives, politicians, foreign businessmen who have
pledged funds for the yet-to-be-realized aquarium in the adjoining yet-to-
be-opened hotel, and others who fall into the VIP category. Without the
requisite stamp on one's pass, even the escalators are off-limits. Two bounc-
ers arrayed in elegant yet slightly menacing shades of black regulate access to a super-VIP section in front of the stage furnished with upholstered
white sofas. When the super-VIPs overflow their designated abode, clouds
of additional sofas float down the aisles to accommodate them.

A spiral staircase bridges the multiple levels of the atrium visually, albeit
at an angle intended to call forth the Leaning Tower of Pisa. Spotlights
bathe the gathering crowd in lime, gold, and fuchsia, as if to counter the
winter chill wicking up through beautifully laid floors of Indian marble.
Seemingly no expense has been spared to stage this event. Video cameras
supply more vantage points on the festivities than a typical Premier League
cricket match. There is even a camera with a microphone boom set up on
rails for dolly (tracking) shots, projected live onto giant pixelated screens.
The effect is to enhance the beauty of the space cinematographically while
adding a dash of Bollywood to the mix.

"They need to keep investors on board," observes a man next to me in
the process of pushing forward to get a view of the stage. Of which, it turns
out, he is one. "How much work has gone into this! So many times they
have run out of money." He believes the barrage of advertisements for the
Soft Launch was directed primarily at investors, not the public. Like others
literally relegated to the sidelines on the mall's second tier, he speaks guard-
edly, but he implies that unless the developers secure another round of
funding, they may have lost their shirts. While he seems hopeful about the
prospects for bringing the project to completion, he does not sound convinced.

All these money troubles occurred in the context of a slew of building
projects in the region that had landed deeply, perhaps irretrievably, in debt.

A 2015 *Financial Times* article on the woes of Indian infrastructure projects titled "If You Build It, Can They Come?" alluded to the chicken-and-egg problem of schemes that failed to attract successive rounds of funding without buyers and clients yet had a hard time enticing anyone to commit when the projects might never be completed (Sender 2015). The struggles of Jaypee Group, developers of a Formula One racetrack as well as the luxury residential complex that was supposed to build up the area around the Grand Venice, were profiled in the piece.

My partner strikes up a conversation with an affable man on her right who purchased shop space in the adjacent hotel-to-be some time ago. "Until now, cash flow is outflow!" he laughs. According to him, costs ballooned as developers proceeded from one phase of the project to another, until the initial projections had more than tripled. The key elements of the mall are finally in place, but not the finishing. In its current state, the mall can open for the occasional site tour, special event, or gondola ride, but not for regular retail trade.[7] India's latest "mega tourist destination" has a way to go. Neither he nor his wife are particularly troubled by the delays that have plagued the project, however, since they receive 1 percent monthly interest on their investment. Even in an inflation-prone emerging economy like India's, 12 percent annually amounts to a healthy return.

The devil, as always, is in the details. The plasterwork on the railing where we have been cooling our heels looks alluring under the glow of gel lights but roughly executed up close. Turn your back to the stage at this freeze-frame in the project's development and you will find the enticing pastels of the atrium give way to banks of dusty plate-glass windows where the shops should be. Wires exit the walls at odd angles. Ghostly stairways lead to storage lofts that do not yet exist. The only commodities behind the glass have commenced their second or third lives: broken plastic barrels, lengths of dusty pipe, a pair of abandoned *chappals* (slippers), chunks of discarded marble, the occasional beat-up mattress for the security guards.

After a few false starts, dignitaries and developers assemble to introduce the mall to the crowd. The Chief Minister of Uttar Pradesh imparts support for the project via a crackling videoconference connection. Malaysian investors hold out their arms to receive prestations of flowers. Satinder Bhasin thanks all and sundry. Everyone heaps praise upon this first iteration of "Venice in India," until the prospect of shopping at a mega-mall begins to acquire the nationalist glow of Nehruvian industrialization projects from the bygone days following independence. The discourse of "India's first" ex-

Figure 4.4. Julius Caesar on his plinth

Figure 4.5. A security guard finds shade under a *chhatri* pavilion, a common design element in Rajasthani architecture (below)

Figure 4.6. Grand Venice foyer (next page)

[Credit: Author photos]

Figure 4.7. Grand Venice atrium with Leaning Tower of Pisa staircase
[Credit: Author photo]

tends to many new attractions in this aspirational economy, where newspapers relentlessly hawk India's "1st Live [sic] Sized Animated Santa," "1st Inflatable Human Snow Globe," and the like.[8]

Next onto the stage comes Pranay Sinha, a consultant who got to know the Grand Venice's "mammoth story" after the project was already underway. "It's very difficult," he explains, "to create something India doesn't have." He paints a sumptuous vision of a fully functional Grand Venice that will serve as a domestic tourist destination for the fifteen million Indians who travel through Delhi annually "on their way to the mountains, the deserts, the forests, wherever, and don't have anything special to see." Anything, that is, "besides the old sites." In the space of an earnest sentence the Grand Venice claims a place beside Delhi's Qutb Minar (twelfth century, World Heritage Site), Humayun's Tomb (sixteenth century, World Heritage Site), Purana Qila (the Old Fort renovated by Humayun), Lodhi Gardens (with its monumental tombs from the fifteenth and sixteenth centuries), the Red Fort (seventeenth century), and the lively maze of bazaars in Chandni Chowk (once the market for seventeenth-century Shahjahanabad). Still, in its own way, the edifice that envelops us *is* grand, with its soaring ceiling and allusive ambitions.

The pride these developers take in the imminent realization of their *sapna* (dream) proves infectious. Right here in Greater Noida, Sinha proclaims to a round of applause, tourists will discover the pleasures of a mall "with a Venetian backdrop, a Venetian innovation, but an Indian soul." PowerPoint slides splash onto the screens. We rip through a series that pairs photographs of Italian monuments with their Greater Noida namesakes. The Campanile di San Marco (aka the Bell Tower), Julius Caesar, Trevi Fountain, Pisa's perpetually leaning tower: it's all there. Sinha asks his audience to imagine a series of internationally branded stores unfolding in the next few months on either side of them. "Behind me you've also got Zara [the Spanish-based clothing retailer]. Can you believe it? Zara in Greater Noida, India!?! . . . And before it opens all over the country, it will open here. Because this is where we can showcase the store to the rest of India."

To the delight of younger members of the audience bored by the speeches, MIKA finally steps up to the mike and launches into a *qawwali*-inspired number calculated to appeal to the entire family. As the evening progresses, we wander over to the gondola basin, where from our mezzanine perch we can watch a female gondolier kitted out in striped shirt and beribboned straw hat help her aging VIPs into the boat. With MIKA's amplified band filling the arcade, it is impossible to tell if the gondolier croons as advertised while she poles the craft around a corner toward the other end of the ersatz canal, where another row of uninhabited storefronts lies tucked away. Next to us couples lean precariously backward over the bannister in search of the perfect selfie. Underwater floodlights, positioned to dazzle by illuminating the *acqua* itself rather than the boaters or the bystanders, complicate their task.

At first glance, the concept behind this "concept mall" appears to be Venice. And, of course, it *is* that, in a domesticated, sales-oriented, boosterish sort of way. Look again, however, and the concept becomes water. Dangle your hand to skim the surface of the water as your gondola rounds the bend. Look down and you can actually see the bottom of the canal, unsullied by sediment, plastic wrappers, or bottles (a feat unrivaled by Italy's Venice). Crane your neck to scan the roofline of the atrium for a glimpse of the relief sculptures of idealized rural Indian women carrying pots filled

Figure 4.9. The Gondola Basin [Credit: Author photo]

Figure 4.10.
Overlooking a canal
[Credit: Author
photo]

with water on their heads. As the electrified music envelops them, Mother India enters the digital age. On your way out, stop to watch the spray of fountains cycle through pinks and greens. There, too, you can liquefy your visit to the mall (and, in a hotter season, cool off) by caressing the spray. If everything goes as planned, these wonders will be augmented by sharks at play and bubbles trailing from the mouths of divers costumed to look like sea nymphs. Penguins, walrus, an octopus, and dolphins have also been sighted on the wish list for Indian Ocean World, the proposed aquarium.

The Grand Venice surely intends to sell clothing, fancy coffee, a night at the movies, designer luggage. But it also markets engagement, an encounter with gallons and gallons of water so clear you can see through them. In a place where clear water materializes sparingly in the see-through tanks of reverse osmosis machines for the few that can afford them, that, too, is a marvel.

Filtering Out the Fun

At the time of the Grand Venice Soft Launch, headlines with titles such as "Noida Water Unfit for Drinking, Cooking" regularly appeared in the local section of national newspapers, accompanied by photographs of aggrieved residents holding up bottles of muddy brown liquid. The Noida Authority had euphemistically acknowledged that "hard water" posed a problem for the district, making no mention of the dangers posed by the industrial effluents and heavy metals that appeared to have leached into the ground-water pulled up by tubewells. In response, the city engineered a switch to softer Ganga (Ganges) water (HT Correspondent 2014b; Rajput 2014a). While the Ganga was not as polluted as the Yamuna or Yamuna tributaries like the Hindon that idled past Noida and Greater Noida, its own condition was sufficiently compromised that international campaigns had dedicated crores of rupees to "saving" it.

Experience had shown that securing a supply of higher-quality water, in and of itself, was no palliative. After Noida's neighbor, Ghaziabad, re-ceived a share of Ganga water, its municipal authority ended up mixing the Ganga water with water sourced locally to meet demand, generating fur-ther shortages and cross-contamination (HT Correspondent 2013b). And from the point of view of the rivers themselves, redistribution only made things worse. In order for these waterways to regenerate themselves, hy-drologists recommended greater, not lesser, ecological flow: the opposite of the drawdowns created by diverting water to new locations. Shuttling more or less contaminated water from one place to another might have a salutary effect on the chrome showerheads of the wealthy, but it could hardly solve the bigger problems.

When citizen scientists from the Federation of Noida Residents Wel-fare Associations (FONRWA) tested water supplied to households by the Noida Authority in 2015, they discovered high levels of Total Dissolved Solids (TDS) containing mercury and nickel at levels sufficient to cause disease.[9] FONRWA duly pronounced the water "not potable" and recom-mended that people avoid cooking with it unless they filtered it first (Sri-vastava 2015). Given the high cost of alternatives, the unregulated quality of locally bottled water, and the inadequacy of household single-filtration systems under such challenging conditions, many people had no practical choice but to use the municipal supply untreated. People living on the pavement were lucky to find water at all.

Researchers from New Delhi–based TERI (The Energy and Resources Institute) confirmed the suspicions of humans and babblers alike that water from the Yamuna watershed fell far short of palatable. A two-year UNICEF-funded study of a stretch of the Yamuna that passes through the NCR identified elevated heavy metal concentrations in water used for drinking and irrigation, as well as in the soil and crops grown in the river basin.[10] While water from the relatively new jurisdiction of Greater Noida had yet to be extensively examined, another study conducted in Noida proper in 2011 found that the "quality of the potable water has deteriorated to a large extent at many sites. High concentrations of TDS, Na, Cl, So_4, Fe, Mn, Pb and Ni indicate anthropogenic impact on groundwater quality and demand regional water quality investigation" (A. Singh Tewary, and Sinha 2011:523). In 2014 the National Green Tribunal petitioned the government to prevent "fresh-looking" vegetables farmed along the riverbanks from making their way into cooking pots (D. Singh 2014a:2). Residents, for their part, had had their fill of investigations. They longed to see a liquid emerge from the tap that looked, felt, tasted, and digested like something more compatible with life.

More and better sewage treatment constituted another practical remedy, perpetually proposed and just as perpetually deferred in any effective implementation. "STPS [sewage treatment plants] lie inactive because financially constrained urban local bodies are unable to pay for the electricity needed to run them, and sewage networks carry only a fraction of the design load because last-mile connections to individual households have not been made" (Ruhl 2014). Although a journalist penned these words about the Ganga, he could equally well have applied them to any of the streams in the Yamuna basin. Delhi's Centre for Science and Environment has suggested that a more appropriate solution for India lies in decentralized sewage treatment that does not itself require vast amounts of water for processing. Leachfields, manufactured wetlands, waste stabilization ponds, reed beds, soil aquifer treatment, activated sludge package plants, anaerobic sludge blanket reactors, biocatalysts, rotary biodiscs, and urine-diverting toilets all offer antidotes to the imported "flush and forget mindset" (Centre for Science and Environment 2005:iv). The alternative that is no alternative requires unobtainable amounts of clean surface water to be pumped to households and recovered through costly sewage treatment plants that are difficult for emerging economies to afford, much less to link into a single integrated system.

Monsoon season brings more water woes to the NCR, as people struggle to make their way through inundated streets, sinkholes swallow roadways, viral fevers spread, and flooded transformers in the parks electrocute random pedestrians. After months without a drop of water falling from the sky, the refrain switches to "water, water, everywhere, yet (still) not a drop to drink." What to do with so much of the blessed liquid, arriving in a rush on those few special weeks?

At this time of year, the typically pragmatic cast to local discussions of water politics manifests in calls for more rainwater harvesting to store the bounty for future need (Tankha 2013b), or, as the case may be, in calls to repair recently built but already nonoperational downspouts and cisterns (Sanon 2014). Even the fiercest critics are careful to lay the blame for seasonal waterlogging not on the monsoon as such but on cemented and trash-clogged drains, on the deposition of silt from "cleaned" *nullahs* at roadsides where it waits to be washed back into the drains, on neighborhoods designed without outlets for stagnant water, and on lack of maintenance generally (see, e.g., HT Correspondent 2013a, 2013b, 2013c, 2013d, 2013f, 2014c; Tankha 2013a). India needs, and treasures, its monsoons. The same cannot always be said for the administrative decisions of local authorities.

New building complexes like the Grand Venice appear to work at cross-purposes with any tangible remediation of the water supply by placing outsized demands on a contaminated, shrinking aquifer. It was not for nothing that bus stops on Delhi's Ring Road at the time of the Soft Launch featured wraparound public service ads with graphics of a leafy green tree set against the backdrop of a desiccated plain. The pitch (delivered in English): "Save Water. Think today . . . tomorrow will be too late." If these were scare tactics, they took their cue from some genuinely scary projections about what lay ahead for the National Capital Region. Readers of Noida's *Mail Today* had already had two years to ponder this warning: "The unregulated extraction of groundwater by builders may leave Noida almost dry in the next few years, environment experts say. The city has already been placed under the 'semi-critical' category by the Central Ground Water Board (CGWB)" (Vashishtha 2012; see also Rajput 2014c).

When viewed in light of the hardships imposed on so many lives by limited access to water of dubious quality, the demands on local ecologies made by the Grand Venice could easily seem profligate. Most obvious was the

Figure 4.11. "Save Water" wraparound ad at a bus stop on New Delhi's Ring Road
[Credit: Author photo]

water required to realize the Venice theme: shimmering canals, flush toilets, fountains, ocean-in-a-tank. But water was also the liquid asset hidden inside the building's very structure, not to mention the consumer goods soon to vie for the shopper's eye. A single pair of blue jeans requires hundreds or even thousands of gallons of water to produce. Add to that riverbeds dredged within an inch of their lives by the sand mafia that illegally supplies grit to the "land sharks" who pour concrete, and the backstage demands posed by a development like a mall are as awash in water as any gondola basin.

Scarcity discourse and utilitarian reasoning pervade water politics in emerging economies like India. "My mother always explains we are responsible citizens," admonishes the line sketch of a schoolboy in a 2013 campaign sponsored by the Government of India's Ministry of Water Resources. "Wastage of water in one home makes the other houses go dry. How will my friends get ready to go to school if I waste water?"[11] When controversy arose the following year over the vast amounts of money sunk into India's *Mangalyaan* Mars Orbiter Mission, clean water and toilets became the talismans brandished by critics who argued for "best use" of funds.[12] Not food for the hungry or jobs for unemployed youth or aid to distressed farmers, but water and toilets.

At the local level in communities such as Noida, conversations about ecology and livelihood tended to circle around the question of "what is to be done?" This is a crucial question, but one whose very pragmatism drains water politics of a host of resonances that make all the difference for understanding how people engage with a place like the Grand Venice.

Ethnographies of India and elsewhere have offered a much-needed corrective to the assumption that water is only, or mainly, for use, by drawing attention to the importance of power, culture, and representation for understanding any outcome where water is concerned. J. Stephen Lansing's (2007) classic work on the water temples of Bali shows what can happen when administrators fail to grasp what rituals and religion could possibly have to do with water supply. Ben Orlove's (2002) *Lines in the Water* follows the struggle to retain control over fishing grounds waged by villagers at Lake Titicaca with the Peruvian state, with implications for the meaning of "development" and "sustainability." Ajantha Subramanian's (2009) *Shorelines* depicts the emergence of new geographies of citizenship in the places where land meets the sea when South Indian fisherfolk avail themselves of the courts. Shaylih Muehlmann's (2013) *Where the River Ends* and Veronica Strang's (2013) *Gardening the World* explore the importance of identity and ideology for water politics in Mexico and Australia, respectively. Götz Hoeppe (2007) sets his sights on the production of water-based knowledge. But even in the most exquisitely nuanced accounts, joy, levity, frivolity, and mirth have somehow gone missing.

The onset of the monsoon in northern India offers a hundred thousand playful vignettes of what scarcity discourse and utilitarian reasoning cannot capture. In wealthy and poor neighborhoods alike, people rush outside, forget for a moment their soon-to-be-inconvenienced lives, and raise their faces to the sky as they dance. No umbrellas are wanted here: just raindrops sizzling on skin, eyes blinking their way into a newly watered world. People greet the monsoon with joy, not as some hostile elemental force arrayed against them. Good monsoons presage traffic jams and floods, to be sure, but also good harvests and a welcome relief from steadily climbing temperatures. Water quenches many things, only one of which is thirst.

From "*Neti-Neti*" to "Yes-And" Thinking

There is a way of making one's case in India called *neti-neti* that dates back at least to the *Upanishads*.[13] Rather than go directly to the point and argue for it in no uncertain terms, a person embarks on the path of persuasion by setting up alternative interpretations or possible objections and knocking them down, the better to prepare the ground for whatever it is she favors. "It's not this, you see. And it's not that. Neither is it the other thing." That's neti-neti, not-this-not-that, thinking. By the time listeners arrive at the end of a long string of negations—if, indeed, they haven't tuned out—they often find their thinking clarified as to what, precisely, *is* going on, since it cannot be this and it cannot be that.

If this methodological preamble sounds a bit dry, I can assure you that water politics is just the thing to bring it to life. From an environmentalist's perspective, constructing a neti-neti argument about the unsavory effects of a water-themed shopping mall seems simple. It goes something like this: Whatever sapne, whatever dreams, might have provided inspiration for the Grand Venice, inspiration cannot shepherd its accounts into the black. In the long term, profitability must guide its development. If that requires making money at the expense of local ecologies, won't ecologies suffer? In a region plagued by water scarcity and contamination, the Grand Venice is not ecologically sustainable. Neither is it well integrated into the landscape. Touched by hubris, a project like this ignores at its peril sinking water tables and inadequate or nonexistent sewage disposal systems. Neither can its nationalist aspirations compensate for whatever ecological damage it will cause. And what is so nationalist anyway about a project that imitates buildings in Singapore, China, Japan, or indeed Venice itself? Because this sort of concept mall transforms water into a spectacle, can it really encourage people to relate to water in more intimate ways that would teach them to treasure it? More likely, this mall recruits capital to create an urban outpost in the wider project of monetizing what Bram E. Büscher (2014) has called "liquid nature."[14]

So the structure of the neti-neti environmentalist critique of a project like the Grand Venice looks something like this:

- *Not* guided simply by dreams but by profitability
- *Not* environmentally sustainable but rather ecologically damaging
- *Not* well integrated into the local landscape but teetering on a foundation of hubris
- *Nothing* but a derivative
- *Not* an enterprise that meaningfully animates intimacies with water, but an enterprise that turns water into a spectacle, the better to distance people from it

Staggering under the weight of mounting objections, what's not to dis-like? Taken individually, these are familiar critiques that could be applied to any number of construction projects in both emerging and developing economies. But notice how the collective structure of neti-neti argumenta-tion paints developers, investors, workers, and "end users" alike into a cor-ner marked by false consciousness. The implication is that they must either be too desperate for money, too indifferent, or too ignorant (as the case may be) to take proper account of the dire ecological impacts of such projects. Otherwise why would anyone build it? Why would anyone come? What possible appeal could they find in a gondola ride that troubles the waters of this semiarid land, a journey unmoored from its "original" context in a city with a sea-fed lagoon?

To indulge in a bit of neti-neti argumentation myself, it is not that these critiques are without merit: there really are serious problems with water quality and water supply in the capital region, after all. It is simply that the overwhelmingly negative force of neti-neti argumentation can obscure things about a project like the Grand Venice that are important if you want to understand its impact and its draw. The carnivalesque intimacies with water that the Grand Venice promises emerge not from the utilitarian calculus that informs lists of neti-neti objections but from a much more visceral sense of how water figures in the daily lives of people in India's northern cities. To grasp the power of the carnivalesque to enlist, even as it sidesteps, worries about degraded ecology requires a shift from neti-neti to *yes-and* thinking.

"Yes-and thinking," as I use the term, abandons refutation for a more capacious approach to the analysis of tensions and contradictions. Yes-and thinking helps explain why, in the face of neti-neti critiques that they find compelling, people can nevertheless find themselves captivated by things that the critiques encourage them to renounce. As the section on the carni-valesque will make clear, yes-and thinking also helps explain how a project like the Grand Venice, built with little regard for its impact on local ecolo-gies, depends for its very appeal on the ways in which those ecologies labor under burdens imposed by unchecked development.

Put another way, yes-and thinking might accept all the neti-neti cri-tiques listed above yet go on to embrace everything playful, topsy-turvy, and irreverent about the Grand Venice by way of grasping its ability to entrance. Yes-and thinking does not in any way downplay the importance of debates about scarcity, best use of "resources," and equitable distribution of "resources."[15] Yes-and thinking is also perfectly compatible with Nikhil

Anand's (2011) "hydraulic citizenship," which emphasizes how water creates belonging as it flows, when people mobilize politically to access it. It is just that none of these frameworks, engaged as they are with logics of allocation, contested claims, and management, can do what a concept like the carnivalesque does. So *yes* to all of that, *and* something more may still be needed.

In contrast to neti-neti argumentation, the structure of a yes-and argument looks more like this:

- Was the Grand Venice conceived in the hope of turning a profit, even at the expense of local ecologies? Yes, and . . .
- Is the enterprise likely to prove environmentally unsustainable over the long run? Yes, and . . .
- Is the construction of such ecologically voracious developments in a semiarid zone an act of hubris? Yes, and . . .
- Is there something derivative involved? A qualified yes, and . . .
- Doesn't the Grand Venice configure water as a spectacle that maneuvers people into a contemplative stance, distancing them from whatever is on display while distracting their attention from the hands reaching for their wallets? Yes, perhaps, and . . .

Profit-driven? No one would pretend otherwise. Developers, environmentalists, investors, and most certainly the Punjab National Bank (which provided the initial round of funding) agreed on this point, however divergent their politics. Local journalists wrote freely about the speculative operations of "land mafia" and "sand mafia" in areas like Greater Noida, cabals of companies alleged to have cornered the real estate market, draining wetlands and raiding riverbeds for materials to mix all that soaring concrete.[16] For the investors who attended the Soft Launch, realizing a profit was obviously a key reason for underwriting the enterprise, although not necessarily the only one. They left conspiracy theories to the journalists, instead portraying the quest for profits as reconcilable with nationalist dreaming. Those dreams, in turn, rested on joint ventures with multinationals like the U.S.-based Starwood Hotels and the Singapore-based Andover Leisure. Profit-driven? Yes, and . . .

Environmentally unsustainable? This was not a question the developers of the Grand Venice had ever addressed directly, at least as of this writing, but clearly a complex of this size raises concerns when it taps groundwater indiscriminately, especially in an area with a falling water table. If plans for sewage treatment and gray-water recycling existed, promoters did not publicize them. Developments in Greater Noida could piggyback on the reputation established by its older sibling, Noida, with its leafy squares and "Clean Noida, Green Noida" refrain. By no stretch of the imagination, however, could the Grand Venice be considered a conservation-as-development project. Throughout Greater Noida, sponsors of the building spree invoked economic development as "pure play" without regard to ecological consequences, but with a sweetener: glory for the nation. Environmentally unsustainable? Yes, and . . .

An exercise in hubris? The kind of pride that sets up the presumptuous for a fall? Long before high-rise buildings bequeathed modernity a skyline and set developers to dreaming, the road to commerce in the drier regions of northern India featured oases of one sort or another. Weary travelers could count on a drink from the water cisterns that collected rainfall in caravanserai and even quite humble households. Larger settlements maintained tanks (reservoirs) to provide water for ablutions and bathing. During the Mughal period, grand establishments sent water cascading through interior rooms over angled slabs of intricately carved marble—a precursor to electrified air-conditioning, if you will—then channeled it outside to nurture gardens laid out to create a miniature of paradise (Moynihan 1979). Even today, in certain wealthier neighborhoods of Delhi, residents station a *ghada* and dipper near the street, offering water to passersby as a kind of *daan*. But when an oasis from the heat takes the form of a cavernous shopping mall, dependent on coal-fired utility plants, diesel generators, and above all water that may not be there in some years' time, it is hard to argue with confidence that this does not represent overreach. Hubris? Yes, and . . .

Incorporated into yes-and thinking is a certain complexity, particularly in a postcolonial context. Take the allegation that an edifice like this mall is simply derivative, modeled as it avowedly is on Italian "originals" as well as similarly monumental shopping schemes set up in other countries. In his work on colonial mimicry, Homi Bhabha (1994:85–92) made the definitive case that what looks like mimesis in a colonial or postcolonial context may be many things, but it is never simple. For Bhabha, colonial mimicry encodes an ambivalently appropriative relationship to power, at once aspirational and subversive. "I want what you have!" can be quite close, indeed, to "Why should you have what I haven't got?" Anyone who dismisses mimicry as mindless imitation will miss the nuanced politics that simultaneously joins and demarcates these two stances. As Partha Chatterjee (1993) famously pointed out, nationalism flourished in India as a derivative discourse, yet that did not prevent it from undergoing powerful transformations as activists appropriated it and bent it to the struggle to end British rule.

At the Grand Venice Soft Launch, "Why shouldn't *we* have?" was the cry from the stage that roused the audience to applause. Why shouldn't we in India also have the best of what the world has to offer? Why shouldn't the developers be allowed to pay homage to something that inspires them, without having others confuse homage with "mere" imitation? So derivative, yes, but derived as much from a legacy of anticolonial struggle, with its nationalist-inspired calls for justice, as from the canals of Italy, the casinos of Las Vegas and Macau, the "underwater sea maids" that graced San Diego's Sea World in the 1960s, or shopping complexes like the one outside Tokyo modeled on Versailles. Bianca Bosker (2013), in her work on "architectural mimicry" in China, calls such designs "original copies."

At the same time, the derivative aspects of the Grand Venice are extremely selective. There will be no attempt, presumably, to replicate Venice's seasonal *acqua alta*, when tourists detour onto elevated walkways because the city is sinking ever deeper on its wooden pilings while climate change causes sea levels to rise. There are also iconic Indian elements deliberately inserted into the Grand Venice's design to disrupt any seamless references to Italy. Far up on a wall near the atrium ceiling, easily missed, was that plaster relief sculpture of women with water containers on their heads: thoroughly on-topic for a water-themed concept mall, yet derived from a clichéd image with local resonance. Added by artisans, perhaps? Above the mall's entrance and therefore not to be missed was a gorgeous piece of jaliwork, arguably the finest piece of craftsmanship in the mall. Its intricately carved marble leaves and twining branches looked familiar, but it took me some time to place them: ah yes, a reproduction of the famous screen from the sixteenth-century Sidi Sayyid Mosque in Ahmedabad, Gujarat.[17] The screen's central figure, the Tree of Life, has extended its roots into many border-crossing forms of art and commerce in recent years. That it should show up in latticework at a for-profit venture catering to tourists in Greater Noida is surely no more remarkable than the exhibition of a Tree of Life created from decommissioned weapons by artists in Maputo and exhibited at the British Museum, or the colorful graphic of a Tree of Life that adorns bottles of Ambo mineral water for sale in Addis Ababa. Derivative, yes, several times over, and . . .

A shopping mall staged as a spectacle? No doubt. At the time of the Soft Launch, malls had come to dominate entire sectors in the NCR, yet there

Figure 4.12. Tree of Life jali screen over the entrance to the Grand Venice (above)

Figure 4.13. Tree of Life graphic on a bottle of Ambo mineral water, Addis Ababa, Ethiopia (left)

[Credit: Author photos]

———

was nothing remotely like the Grand Venice anywhere in India. Gondoliers and fountains in a region edging over into desert are meant to be marvels, especially in a wash of pink and green lights synchronized to *bhangra* and *qawwali*, interspersed with bars from *The Skaters' Waltz*. The big screens set up in the atrium at the Soft Launch for viewers who already had a direct line of sight to the stage recalled the installation of jumbotrons at concerts and sporting events. But if viewers cared to peer more deeply into what the spectacle owed to those screens, they might find themselves back in the 1920s, when television broadcast technology began to generate the kind of rapidly circulating images that Guy Debord (1995) considered integral to the production of a "society of the spectacle." As commodities began to circulate in the mediated forms known as advertisements, they acquired a dual character, at once material and ethereal.

While the once rare imported merchandise slated to materialize in Grand Venice shop windows had become a relatively common sight since India opened up its economy in the 1990s, exhibits of world-traveling goods still had the capacity to enchant. Rural tourists might not have seen much of them, older generations remembered when foreign goods were hard to get, while middle-class youth who took them for granted still found pleasure in hunting for the latest brands. As for those who could afford only to window-shop—and that would describe a goodly number of the patrons of these burgeoning malls—spectacle was what they largely consumed.

What distinguished the Grand Venice from its sister malls down the road was the way it organized its consumer delights around an architecturally inspired sound and light and *water* show. Water was both the motif and the tangible substance that floated its rather disparate attractions. Susan Davis, who conducted an ethnographic study of Sea World, introduced the concept of "theme-parked nature" to describe attempts to offer "an immediate, seeable, touchable consumer experience" focused on killer whales, say, or replicated jungle settings (Davis 1997:19).[18] If "theme-parked nature" is an industrial product of corporate capitalism that promises to bring the remotest regions of the world into proximity with consumers, then the Grand Venice worked a variation on this established theme. By showcasing water in the form of a cityscape within a cityscape, the installation had created its own urbanized niche for "Nature." Why water itself should have the power to signify Nature—and attract customers—has much to do with the condition of the waterways in urban Delhi.

Rather than having water serve as some taken-for-granted medium there simply to support sharks, sea urchins, and divers with glittery tails, at the Grand Venice on any given day water could steal the show. Its sparkling expanse in a city where water seldom glistens constituted a spectacle in its own right. That made the Grand Venice different from a tiger reserve or even a safari park, with their cultivated impressions of the remnants of a pristine wilderness, set apart from the concrete jungle. Acre-feet of clear water right in the midst of Delhi's hustle and bustle: that was the marvel, and part of the draw.

This particular way of displaying an urbanized Nature was not without what Paul Greenough (2012) would call its *bio-ironies*. The wave of urban expansion that made the Grand Venice potentially viable involved extensive draining of lakebeds and encroachment upon floodplains. Historic water bodies disappeared as builders mysteriously and illegally acquired plots in eco-sensitive areas. Even the forms of Nature cultivated on land set aside for animals during an earlier period of industrialization had come under threat.[19] Wildlife preserves like the Okhla Bird Sanctuary and the Bil Akbarpur wetland were dying so that Nature, rolled up into tree-lined parks and skimmed by boats corralled into basins, might live (see Rajput 2013c, 2014b, 2014d; Ramnani 2014). Spectacle, yes and . . .

A resounding yes, then, to each of the above appraisals: profit-driven, unsustainable, hubristic, derivative, spectacular. *And* if you stop there, you will see in the balustrades of the Grand Venice only shadows of what you think you already know: well-worn critiques of ecologically damaging development. But yes-and thinking does not stop there. In the case of the Grand Venice, yes-and thinking goes on to ask why this sort of water-based spectacle, in particular, should have become the stuff of sapne, providing abstracted ingredients for retailed dreams. What were all the fuss *and* the fun about?

Carnivalesque, Or, Turnabout Is Fair Play

Even the most pragmatically designed water management systems often find themselves caught up in a bit of play, with or without the blessings of their designers. The Thames Barrier, a massive bit of industrial kit installed in the 1980s to protect London from tidal surges, now faces the deadly serious problem of climate change–induced rises in sea levels that threaten to overwhelm it. But that has not stopped authorities from installing a children's playground next to its somewhat dilapidated museum. When the barrier's gates rotate into action, the best view is from the top of a slide.

On a more humble scale, irrigation canals and sprinklers do double duty

Figure 4.14. London's Thames Barrier with playground [Credit: Author photo]

across the world, watering mischievous kids and thirsty plants alike, as well as the occasional heat-stressed adult. In the inner cities of the United States, where shade and gardens still come at a premium, people have illegally opened fire hydrants in the summer since hydrants were invented. It is true that they open those hydrants in a practical effort to avoid roasting in the sun, but they frolic as they do so. Children run through the spray, teasing and splashing their companions; adults laugh as they cup hands to faces and shake their wet locks. These are small pleasures, tactile pleasures that coexist with the hydrant's potential to do quotidian service as a piece of life-saving equipment. During the deadly Chicago heat wave of 1995, the image of a fire hydrant gushing into the street became an emblem in media coverage of the disaster (Klinenberg 2003). Opening the hydrant lowered water pressure in the system, a dangerous condition in the case of fire, but opening it also brought visceral relief to those who would have died from heat stroke—or boredom—otherwise. Yes, and . . .

Johan Huizinga's (1971) classic, *Homo Ludens: A Study of the Play Element in Culture*, has attracted a new generation of readers as game developers reflect upon the cultural variability and significance of play. Perhaps environmental scientists and eco-critics should be reading it, too. Huizinga intended his "Playful Man" to serve as counterpoint to the usual list of earnest suspects who populated social science texts: Economic Man, Darwinian Man, and their kinship-oriented and ritually obsessed cousins. Those who have subsequently stood on the shoulders of this giant have done so mostly to peer down into a minor subfield called the Anthropology of Play. But Huizinga himself hoped that his book would serve as more than a clarion call for scholars not to forget about play when they studied the roster of human behavior. His very title—*Homo Ludens*—positioned play at the heart of what it means to be human. Were he writing today, he might have had room for the occasional jungle babbler as well.

What would it mean to apply Huizinga's insights to eco-intimacies of the sort that the Grand Venice fosters? First and foremost, it becomes less satisfying to attribute every human stance toward water to the Unquenchables, those antiheroes who know no limits when it comes to depleting the earth's aquifers, especially when there is money to be made. In reductive characterizations like this, utility, necessity, and "greed" eclipse playfulness, until once again Homo ludens comes up missing. Neither does she surface in discussions of "sacred waters": calls to stop polluting the Yamuna out of respect for the river goddess (Jain 2011), celebrations of the feast day of San Isidro by the water-sharing associations that maintain *acequias* (irrigation ditches) in northern New Mexico (Rodríguez 2006).

Animistic accounts likewise often fail to reckon with Homo ludens. In Sanjay Bahadur's (2008) novel *The Sound of Water*, based on the 2001 Bagdighi colliery flood, water is the Beast who stalks miners deep underground. The Beast relishes provoking one of the worst mine disasters in Indian history, while the miners respond with fear and perhaps, just perhaps, the desire to outwit an opponent: little room for levity there. Or consider a case from North America: When a group of Native Americans decided to walk the length of the Mississippi in order to heal the river and "give her a taste of herself," they brought along a bucket filled with water from the crystalline headwaters at Lake Itasca. By journey's end, when they emptied the pail into the turbid waters of the Chemical Corridor where the Mississippi reaches the Gulf of Mexico, they hoped to draw attention to the river's plight but also to help the river remember: "This is how you started off; this is how we wish you were again" (Lemay 2013:30). Reporters focused on the threats to water quality and the sincere determination of the walkers.

The point is, you would never suspect the existence of a playful side to such intimate encounters with water from reading about them. Rodríguez's analysis of the acequia system mentions the annual party that follows the prayers and blessings for San Isidro, but what happens at the party remains in the margins of her book, treated as something ancillary to the serious business of how rituals can support resource management. For anyone who knows Native American and First Nations communities, it is hard to imagine a dedicated group completing a 2,552-mile journey along the Mississippi on foot, however honorable its purpose, without someone cracking a joke. Even the miners trapped in Bahadur's gloomy novel indulge in a bit of banter to keep despair at bay.

So what sort of creature is this Homo ludens, and what form might she take in the burgeoning environs of a place like New Delhi? Someone who steps outside to gambol in the first refreshing monsoon rain, it seems. Yet play is not a synonym for enjoyment. Video games can become obsessive; shopping is not always fun, even if it materializes in a whimsical venue like the Grand Venice. Thomas Malaby (2009:206) accordingly defines play as a *disposition* rather than any sort of activity per se, "an attitude characterized by a readiness to improvise in the face of an ever-changing world that admits of no transcendently ordered account." Now we're talking. Play in this sense is something that people on the subcontinent well understand. Many take pride in *jugaad*, the improvisational art of cobbling things together in the face of the unpredictable circumstance that is India. Rules may be bent, workarounds encouraged, and materials creatively repurposed. Business writers have even performed jugaad on jugaad by bending its informal principles to serve the corporation's need for innovation (see Radjou, Prabhu, and Ahuja 2012). There is satisfaction in jugaad, as there is in a well-played chess game.

If play speaks to disposition, then it is a very particular sort of disposition that makes the Grand Venice so interesting, one that goes beyond play as such. The disposition I have in mind is the one Mikhail Bakhtin (1984) called the carnivalesque. Bakhtin invoked the festival of carnival to begin to theorize how certain literary devices could set the world on its head. At the annual carnival celebrations across Europe, women lorded it over men, servants bossed bosses, and the very humblest souls let loose in grand fashion. Things could be said that were otherwise better not. No one was exempt from ribald humor. People roamed the streets masked, and drunk. Nothing—or everything—was as it appeared. Carnival privileges what Miguel Sicart (2014:14) calls the disruptive aspect of play, when play "appropriates the objects it uses to come into existence" by unraveling or even taking over the context in which it occurs.

Allied with such extraordinary play with power is a second key element in Bakhtin's carnivalesque mode: the grotesque. In *Rabelais and His World*, he focuses on the banquet images in François Rabelais's satirical works, which are filled with distended bellies and monstrous anatomical exaggerations. Diners tuck into armies of sausages that march across their plates *as* armies. They discover they cannot fill their insatiable appetites with games of dice. They do manage, however, to bring the dead back to life with a riot of food, drink, and laughter. And, of course, what goes in must come out: "The bowels study the world in order to conquer and subjugate it" (Bakhtin 1984:301).

In the sensuous disarray and repulsiveness of these scenes Bakhtin finds the seeds of a historical materialism, as well as a history of laughter:

> [Laughter] unveils the material bodily principle in its true meaning. Laughter opened men's eyes on that which is new, on the future. This is why it not only permitted the expression of an antifeudal, popular truth; it helped to uncover this truth and to give it an internal form. And this form was achieved and defended during thousands of years in its very depths and in its popular-festive images. Laughter showed the world anew its gayest and most sober aspects. Its external privileges are intimately linked with interior forces; they are a recognition of the rights of those forces. This is why laughter could never become an instrument to oppress and blind the people. It always remained a free weapon in their hands. (Bakhtin 1984:94)

At a glance, the images of untrammeled consumption at the carnivalesque Rabelaisian banquet might appear politically reactionary, just like the scenes of gondolas gliding past high-end shop windows at the Grand Venice. Surely this staging of luxury and excess simply amounts to another incitement to privatized consumption? But Bakhtin argues for a more subtle interpretation: "The popular-festive banquet has nothing in common with static private life and individual well-being. The popular images of food and drink are active and triumphant, for they conclude the process of labor and struggle of the social man against the world. They express the people as a whole because they are based on the inexhaustible ever-growing abundance of the material principle. . . . Finally, they are infused with gay time, moving toward a better future that changes and renews everything in its path" (Bakhtin 1984:302).

"Gay time" in Greater Noida might ally itself with a forward-looking belief in progress or with the kind of nationalist egalitarianism that cries out, "Why shouldn't India have?" But "gay time" spent circling an ersatz Venice also suggests more ecologically oriented questions. Might the carnivalesque encounters with water staged at the Grand Venice have the potential to "renew everything in its path," even as they draw down precious water reserves? To reanimate relationships with neglected or exploited surroundings that critics assume to be evacuated of care and meaning, even as the developers put added pressures on workers and ecologies? The answers are yes, and yes, but to know why, one first has to understand what makes the Grand Venice carnivalesque.

During the colonial period, carnival put down roots in many parts of the world, most famously in Brazil, the Caribbean, and New Orleans. Although Delhi is not a place with a carnival tradition, Bakhtin's work on grotesquerie and the playful turnabout of accepted hierarchies speaks powerfully to some of the ways in which people in northern India are trying to make ecological sense of their relationship with water. It also suggests why, counterintuitively, the wasteful waterworks and ever-flowing fountains of an over-the-top installation like the Grand Venice might just help them do it.

First to the grotesque. It has become commonplace in recent years to describe the highly polluted Yamuna as a "sewer." This enduring trope circulates in all sorts of venues, from casual conversations and testimonials to court decisions. To take but a few diverse examples:

- A gleaming toilet bowl positioned on the riverbank dominates the cover of *Sewage Canal: How to Clean the Yamuna* (Seth and Suresh Babu 2007).
- A headline in *The Times of India* reads "Yamuna Reduced to Sewer Canal Again" (2014).
- Sarandha Jain opens her book, *In Search of Yamuna: Reflections on a River Lost*, with an attempt to explain why things that can seem incongruous to outsiders might not seem so to people who have grown up in India. To make her point, she describes "rivers in India being putrid with filth and shackled by dams, while also serving as deities in temples and goddesses in the Hindu pantheon. To me, this wasn't absurd at all. 'Of course the Yamuna is a sewer, it has always been' ... 'Of course the Yamuna is a Goddess, she is mother to all'" (Jain 2011:1).
- In a controversial 2002 decision on encroachment in the Yamuna flood plain, the High Court of Delhi singles out "sewerage water" in its description of the river's degraded condition, assigning all remaining pollutants to the residual category of "other filth" (Ghertner 2011:146).

- The Noida Authority proposes to plant "4,000 trees having aromatic effect" along the Shahdara Drain "to counter the foul smell" (Rajput 2013a:8). Residents complain that in addition to smelling bad, the effluents in the drain give off vapors that eat away at refrigerators and air conditioner components in their homes.
- Petitioners file an official RTI (Right to Information) request to find out why the Yamuna is called a river rather than a drain (i.e., a channel dedicated to carrying away waste). The DPCC (Delhi Pollution Control Committee) responds that it does not know why. Delhi's Environment Department claims such questions cannot be asked. Not to be outdone, the CPCB (Central Pollution Control Board) insists that the Yamuna is a river "because the maps published by Survey of India say so" (D. Singh 2013).

Now it is true that the river tasked with relieving the parched throats and cleansing the sweaty bodies of millions in the capital region receives the stinking effluents of those same millions. Coliform contamination from feces is a major problem for the water supply. Fish have difficulty surviving in the Yamuna's waters because aerobic decomposition of the excrement of warm-blooded mammals reduces dissolved oxygen. Although sewage treatment plants dot the watershed, not all are operational and historically they have captured only a fraction of what bodies in the fast-growing metropolis expel. A sewage treatment plant set up in 2013 in Greater Noida, home to the Grand Venice, had a capacity to process 137 million liters per day but initially received only 20 million liters because sewage lines had yet to be connected. Periodic appeals by NGOs to *jal* (water) boards to decentralize sewage treatment in order to make it more effective have made little headway (HT Correspondent 2014d:3; Seth 2013).[20] Flow is also at issue. As a reporter on the environmental beat for the *Hindustan Times* put it, "No matter how many treatment plants are built, the river cannot survive only on sewer water" (Singh 2014b:6).

At the same time, the Yamuna's condition is hardly improved by the vast quantities of chemicals, heavy metals, and other industrially synthesized materials that it carries. This is not sewage. Wherever those billowing suds and oil slicks come from, you can be sure they did not emerge from anyone's butt. That makes it all the more meaningful that human viscera, via the trope of the sewer, have come to stand in for the cause of all that ails the watershed today: Not nasty discharges from factories, not unauthorized dumping, not dams that restrict water flow, not lax enforcement of environmental regulations. Not even all of the above. Just bodies.

Other severely polluted waterways around the world have acquired the epithet "sewer": the Snake River in Idaho in the United States, for instance, where the primary culprit is industrialized agriculture. Effluent from cows packed into feedlots drains directly into the river. Calling the Snake "Idaho's Sewer System" has drawn attention to the dubious water politics that lie at the back end—literally—of some of the farming practices described in chapter 1 (see also Manning 2014). The sewage trope has also made its way into less genteel forms of political protest. In the 1980s a campaign against pollution in California's Santa Monica Bay staged a publicity stunt called the Dirty Toilet Awards, in which organizers flushed effigies of local politicians down a commode for the benefit of the cameras and then sent the real-life politicians certificates "suitable for framing or wiping" (Sharpsteen 2010:160).

In the Indian context, however, the imagery of river-as-sewer has its own political/cultural/class history. (Hint: It is not a history of protests that allude to toilet paper, which often signifies there as a foreign commodity, a woefully inadequate sanitation device, and/or an expensive luxury.) In the high court ruling referenced above, the specter of legions of eating, evacuating bodies stationed at the riverside became a rallying cry for slum clearance, with 35,000 huts razed and 150,000 residents displaced in 2004 in Pushta alone (Ghertner 2011:146). Slum demolition acquired the fervor of a purification drive, at a time when the Hindu nationalist Bharatiya Janata Party, or BJP, was a dominant force in government. D. Asher Ghertner (2011:146) describes how the court's metonymic association of slums with contamination and environmental damage invoked a "green aesthetic" about how the city should look that trumped scientific evidence about sources of pollution. "Cleaning up" the Yamuna provided a rationale for evicting the river's poorest neighbors to open up spaces for pricy waterside development.

Close up, the Yamuna is a working river, not an aesthetic object. I do not mean "working" in the fashionable sense that depicts waterways as service providers who undertake the "jobs" of irrigating crops, transporting goods, and accomplishing what waste scavengers used to do in the night.[21] If viewed through a different lens, some of the villages in the floodplain, with their water buffaloes, bicycles, immaculately tended fields, and "sustainably constructed" huts, lend an unexpectedly pastoral heart to the pulsating city. Boatmen labor harder than ever for their rupees as traffic takes to the bridges. Devotees place offerings at riverside shrines to their gods. Below the water's surface microorganisms toil away, part of what James Lovelock once called the invisible proletariat, an "underworld of nature" (Lovelock 2006:111). In nearby canals, people engage in the hazardous labor of flinging rags across the water's surface to soak up oil for recycling. Youngsters troll the river depths for coins using magnets. There is even a place to wash wedding elephants between ceremonies (see Pepper 2007; Trautmann 2015).[22]

Close up, the Yamuna is a playful river as well. Scampering children, yoga practitioners, and the occasional magician grace the shores. Kingfishers practice their aerobatics for the birdwatchers in the sanctuary. Desperate souls hide in the reeds to gain an advantage in cat-and-mouse games with the authorities. All this activity, all these forms of liveliness and livelihood, disappear into the mists of a grotesquerie that holds (some) licentious bodies responsible for fouling the waters people must drink, while letting industry conduct business as usual, however much it contributes to the deterioration of the river.

Ghertner (2011) implies that the high court's eviction order took arbitrary cognizance of poor riverside settlements by editing out all the other factors that make a polluted river what it is. A nod toward the carnivalesque, however, suggests that more than arbitrariness is at play. The grotesque trope of the river-as-sewer indulges in just the sort of hyperbole that Rabelais cultivated, insofar as it exaggerates the power of human bodies alone to reconstitute the elements of an industrially reformulated waterway like the Yamuna. Concealed behind the masked character of the river-as-sewer is a vision of the Yamuna basin—every pipe, every tributary, every canal, every peed-up patch of ground that drains back into the river—as one giant prosthesis for living shitting bodies from Noida to Paharganj. Even the cement rabbits placed around Noida parks to keep them "clean" digest their trash and discharge it through holes with anatomically correct locations below their tails, a design that disconcerts those charged with cleaning them but would have delighted Rabelais.

In the absence of effectively organized sewage treatment, all those tributaries and drains, all those networks of pipes and impromptu lavatories, become visceral extensions of the grotesque body that amplify its reach and magnify, even celebrate, its power to wreak ecological havoc. It is a twisted form of scatological humor that attributes so much to the naturalized bodies of the poor and so little to the institutions charged with managing bodily effluents, much less to all the other classes in the grip of that

Figure 4.15.
The "Green Noida Clean Noida" rabbit: rubbish container in a Noida park [Credit: Author photo]

great equalizer, "the call of Nature." Rabelais's Gargantua and Pantagruel had nothing on it.

So much for the grotesqueries on display during the interval. Now as to the turnabout: the second element of the carnivalesque that, in this case, depends upon having a discourse of the grotesque firmly in place. To fathom the visceral pull of lively displays of water at the Grand Venice, you have to perceive those displays, in their astonishing clarity, as a play on the grotesque. That is to say, as counterpoint to the murky displays of water encountered in kitchen basins and river basins on a daily basis. While you might not want to cup the hand that trails in the water beside your gondola and raise it to your lips for a drink, the chemistry of the water in the gondola basin is beside the point.[23] It's for drinking with the eyes.

Spectacles are notorious for mystifying social relations, not least divisions of class. There was a world of difference between the way that water figured in the lives of the Grand Venice's developers, who appeared to be financing forward by using investor funds to jumpstart their next ventures; the contractors, who had to down tools more than once in order to get

Figure 4.16. Contractors down tools at the Grand Venice in a dispute over pay
[Credit: Author photo]

———

paid; the artisans, who added their own interpretive touches to liquefy the design; and the laborers charged with cleaning the tiled fixtures. Security personnel might well deny those on the lower end of these hierarchies admission to the mall unless they had work to do inside. As Erik Swyngedouw (2004:27) puts it, there is a "city in a glass of water," complete with unequal access, social control, divisions of labor, the domestication of water by private capital, and more.

Yet the carnivalesque character of the watery connections animated by the Grand Venice also allows this aspiration of a mall to amount to something more than just another extravaganza for the monetarily endowed and playfully inclined. As spectacle, but more than spectacle, the Grand Venice plays with as it plays against the everyday appearance of water, which is contaminated in ways that the senses can often readily detect. In the process, its carnivalesque pleasures momentarily sever local associations of polluted waters with excrement. *This* water entices businessmen to dream. *These* cascades beckon to middle-class mothers who would not dare send their kids to a water park in the monsoon season for fear the children will come back with typhoid. Water acquires a new character for the mall's guards and sweepers, too. Although they cannot afford to be too picky about the quality of the water they drink or touch in this unjust world, they register the sheer clear flowing excess. It is a site-specific marvel. It is also a place that prompts awareness of things that are no longer there. For all these people, differently situated as they are, the Grand Venice recalls to memory what the jungle babblers feel entitled to demand: water that takes the form of the luminous, nourishing substance that once made H_2O a signature of life.

While the waters at the Grand Venice may not live up to this phantasmatic promise in terms of their organic composition, they call out to the Yamuna's guardians to do better. Even as the mall inflicts ecological damage on its surroundings, its glistening displays urge the river to abandon her trickster character. Grotesquely polluted waterways like the Yamuna deliver sustenance on Monday, dysentery or heavy metal poisoning by week's end. Bringers of life, bringers of death.

The play's the thing, is it not? So which is it to be? Come back for the final act.

KNOWING WHAT WE KNOW,
WHY ARE WE STUCK?

———

_____

Political Ecologies of the Precarious

In *The Age of Stupid*, Fanny Armstrong's (2009) speculative documentary of a future in which climate change has decimated life on Earth, the narrator, speaking from an underground vault, seems mystified by what he perceives as a failure to act.[1] Flanked by a global seed bank, carefully preserved stacks of computer archives, and an elephant taking its final swim in a bath of formaldehyde, he calls up digitized footage from 2008, when the magnitude of the threat posed by climate change had become clear and people still had a chance to do something about it. "What state of mind were we in," the Last Man wonders, "to face extinction and simply shrug it off?"

Like much contemporary environmental commentary, the film title imparts a cognitive spin to this refusal to act: it was a matter of stupidity, apparently, a lack of intellectual comprehension. Yet there is also something obdurately affective at play in the paradox articulated by the Last Man, and without a better sense of affective attachments than political ecology has thus far been able to provide, there can be no meaningful answer to the Last Man's question.[2]

What does it mean to know but not to grasp, to have realization end in a shrug? To have the arms, once they do reach out, reach for the very things that are killing you? It is an intimate stance that links two forms of unstable attenuated connection. First is the shrug, a collective gesture of resignation. Next, regardless, comes the sweet embrace of toxicity. Governments seize tribal lands for mining ventures. Cosmetics applied to protect skin from a damaged ozone layer turn out to be known carcinogens. New factories gift desire a carbon footprint.

This attenuation marks a failure to make a connection that has already been made. It emerges from a historical moment in which the dire consequences are already foreshadowed, with innocence assigned to a rapidly receding golden era of industrialism when factories still signaled job security and pollution had yet to be codified as a cause for activism. "You may not be interested in extinction," writes Deborah Bird Rose (2011:51) from the interiority of that moment, "but extinction is interested in you." A peer-reviewed study in *Science Advances* affirms that Earth has entered the "sixth mass extinction" in its 4.5 billion-year history, with "human-induced species loss" accelerating at an alarming rate (Ceballos et al. 2015). Political leaders take notice. To the sound of virtual trumpets, they announce steps to mitigate when leaps are called for: the bodies, flexible; the policies, flexible; the species, infinitely flexible, even unto death.

What has fostered such an intimate engagement with ecological demise, at a time when the notion of climate change has raised the specter not of displacement from one earthly place to another but displacement from the planet itself?[3] What has prevented that intimate engagement from having more salutary ecological effects? Rather than address such questions by relying on analytic categories such as "the corporation," "the body," or "the state," as though people could ever viscerally fathom such abstractions, this final chapter seeks to move political ecology toward a more embodied and affectively oriented understanding by embedding analysis in a series of passages framed as ethnographic "stopgaps." Most obviously, these passages—sited in Chicago, New Delhi, and Venice—allude to the promising yet utterly inadequate stopgap measures currently advanced to address ecological degradation. As the chapter unfolds, it should become clear that they also constitute a nod to the sporadic and perpetually disrupted character that eco-economic precarity lends to environmental politics.

If any single piece of machinery can illustrate how technologies (in the extended sense) have schooled people into adopting a sensual, toxicity-infused attachment to what they have taken to calling "the environment," it would be that iconic product of the Fordist era, the automobile.[4] Considered in a pedagogical light, a car is not some free-floating symbol of the open road (in North America) or an export economy temporarily on its knees (in Japan) or class mobility and modernization (in South Asia). Rather, it represents one of many technologies that are intimately and corporeally implicated in the cultivation of new ways of inhabiting the very ecologies they modify. In different ways on different continents, Henry Ford's first love, the automobile, has helped consolidate the affective stance that reassures us we can poison the world without limit by extending contemporary relations of production into the future, even as we recognize that a limit must be out there somewhere. In this dreamworld, the ecological limit to capitalist expansion arrives like the calculus, with a boundary that logically and relentlessly approaches but cannot be breached through visceral experience.

Precarity Enters Ecological Discourse

With the precipitous decline of manufacturing and the shift to service sector jobs in wealthy nations after the 1970s, a literature on post-Fordism emerged that focused on the precariousness of new labor regimes.[5] That literature, in turn, contributed to a master narrative of globalization in which the relatively stable institutional arrangements associated with unionized factory work and welfare capitalism yielded to demands for flexibility in all aspects of production, including employment.[6] Job tenure had become more uncertain, sustenance harder to secure, employment more intermittent, health rather difficult to maintain. Middle-class confidence in the efficacy of planning began to suffer. Unemployment hit record levels in many parts of the European Union. Families ended up living in the parks after Japan liberalized its labor laws. Increased productivity, celebrated as good for "the economy," translated into many people's lives as higher workloads with no corresponding increase in pay. Cultural critics such as Lauren Berlant (2007), along with ethnographers such as Anne Allison (2013), Carrie Lane (2011), Guy Standing (2014), and Kathleen Stewart (2007, 2012), have offered moving, even gut-wrenching, accounts of how labor market insecurity in developed economies has reorganized older forms of sociality, power, and attachment.

In emerging economies where manufacturing was rising rather than waning, working people could not look back nostalgically upon an industrial past that symbolized security, yet they, too, had experienced economic precarity linked to urbanization, displacement, liberalized trade regimes, and the industrialization of agriculture. While their counterparts in Japan, Europe, and North America hankered for the sanctuary of a bygone era of job security and ample employment, they took refuge in yearning for the affluent future promised by "development." On either side of the old North/South divide, millions longed for a less precarious existence.

While labor conditions destabilized in venues across the globe, a seemingly unrelated discourse emerged that focused on precarity of another sort. This one highlighted the increasingly precarious hold on existence of life itself: life in the sense of biological life forms, not body by body (which has always been so), but on a planetary scale. A sense of fragility entered the lexicon of environmental politics through studies of what was first called global warming, then reformulated as climate change. In one 2010 poll, 50 percent of Americans—in a country that had become notorious for climate change contrarianism—described themselves as worrying "a great deal" about global warming (Jones 2010). New social categories such as the "environmental refugee" emerged to mark the tenuous connection to place ushered in by recent ecological shifts. When computer models imaged the consequences of steadily increasing greenhouse gas emissions, the continued survival of many species, not to mention ecosystems, no longer seemed assured. A heightened language of crisis and catastrophe pervaded even sober assessments of the threat that climate change might pose (e.g., Hansen 2009; Kolbert 2006).

It is this environmental counterpoint to anxieties about making a living during the period of neoliberal or late capitalism that I characterize here as a discourse on *political ecologies of the precarious*. From their inception, political ecologies of the precarious have displayed certain features customarily attributed to post-Fordist economies, including but not limited to nostalgia, flexibility strategies, niche marketing, and just-in-time inventories of solutions.[7] Nostalgia in this context trades on images of an unspoiled planet, imaginatively located just before the onset of industrial production or, alternatively, the invention of synthetic chemicals. (Imaginatively, because the periodization that undergirds such nostalgia cannot easily accommodate, say, the deforestation that occurred in medieval Europe well before the Industrial Revolution, much less the late twentieth-century rebound of forest cover in eastern North America.) Responding to a pervasive sense of loss, nostalgia seeks a way back, which turns out to be a way forward, since it is the linear march toward a future that climate change has subjected to doubt.

Finding a way "back," most governments have agreed, demands a coordinated response. Under the auspices of the United Nations, they duly set about negotiating a series of international protocols on the reduction of greenhouse gases. Some provisions in these accords incorporated the classically post-Fordist language of flexibility, to whit, "flexible mechanisms" for implementing low-cost, market-driven emissions trading.[8]

Businesses in wealthier countries rolled out niche marketing schemes targeted at a newly minted tranche of green consumers who had decided to do what they could to address ecological degradation at the household level, whether or not governments faltered. "Eco" laundry detergents, reusable shopping bags, lamps made of recycled chopsticks, and edible landscapes supplemented high-ticket items such as solar hot water heaters. Futurists and engineers, for their part, retailed just-in-time inventories of as-yet-unrealized technologies as remedies for the havoc wrought by climbing carbon dioxide and methane levels. Maybe a new liquid energy source will be discovered. Maybe mirrors launched into space can deflect sunlight. Maybe seeding the oceans with iron can mitigate the acidity that is killing the fish, without too many unforeseen consequences. Maybe.

Before moving on to consider the part that a mass-produced artifact like Henry Ford's automobile has played in keeping people affectively mired in political ecologies of the precarious, a caveat: The perception that environmental changes are rendering life more precarious is not to be confused with an apocalyptic narrative, although the two may feed off one another. Meteor strikes, nuclear winters, and climate change–induced disasters all draw audiences to cinemas, especially in North America, but these stories focus on the end game, the time when human history stops, not the insecurities of a now. With their teleological bent, apocalyptic accounts are affectively quite distinctive.[9] Apocalypse derives pleasure from its own inevitability, from the magnitude and impact of the disaster, while precariousness solicits a reassurance that, in the context of Christian heritage, may take on a variety of salvific forms. (Think electric cars, Energy Star–certified air conditioners, or any number of "resource-intensive" products that promise to "green your life.") Apocalypse looms, then descends, or is headed off by courageous action. In contrast, political ecologies of the precarious seduce people into participating in their own demise, often in the guise of working against it.

Intoxicated with Ecological Ruin: An Ethnographic Stopgap, Chicago

How did it come to this? How did any number of people end up embodying a contradiction that encourages them to shrug off the life-threatening consequences of events they foresee as impending, even as they make incremental changes to become more "environmentally conscious" and train themselves in new habits of worry? (Note that I am focusing on an affective tension here rather than working with the type of critique more commonly directed at climate change, which interrogates a state of conviction called "denial" or theological matters of "belief.")[10] Since closely reasoned argument alone cannot dislodge affective paradoxes, perhaps a bit of ethnography can be of assistance.

Our first stop is a car dealership outside Chicago, circa 1969. Watch the salesman in the burgundy sweater as he takes customers for a spin. Before a customer turns the engine over, the salesman always uses the same opening line, although he makes it sound like a new sensation that has just washed over him. "Ah," he says, inhaling deeply. "There's nothing like the smell of a new car, don't you agree?" Most prospects follow his lead, taking a long breath, letting it out slowly, the corners of their mouths turning up to echo the salesman's. They look satisfied, relaxed, even giddy.

Nothing like it, indeed. Decades later, laboratory tests would confirm that the much-vaunted new car smell consisted of an unpredictable mix of volatile organic compounds (vocs), potentially carcinogenic and certainly not conducive to health. Adhesives, polymers, and solvents used in the manufacturing process generated emissions that accumulated in passenger compartments to produce the readily identifiable scent. Automakers monitored voc levels in vehicle interiors, not out of concern for the passengers' welfare but because they knew they had to keep the compounds below a certain level in order to prevent the windows from fogging up (Fedoruk and Kerger 2003; Ritter 2002).

Across the United States, the odor of vocs signified (and still signifies) luxury, as well as the capacity to afford the latest products rolling off assembly lines. Since the fumes diminish over time, they index newness. Go to any new car dealership today and you will likely hear variations on the salesman's pitch: "Ah, that new car smell!" Despite widespread publicity about the dangers, you will still find people in thrall to what they now know may come to ail them. It is a visceral as well as an emotional attachment. When asked—as though they needed to be asked—they will affirm that the interior of a new car smells good to them. Better than good. Great.

There is a corporeal intimacy to chemical synthesis and "resource extraction," fashioned over the course of years of relating to mass-produced objects such as automobiles. Sweaty fingers grip the steering wheel, feet kick tires, and lungs suck in whatever gases are on offer. In the process, the car exerted a pedagogical effect, teaching people to relish what might harm them. And in the process, they not only came to sense and feel and signify differently; they were materially altered, down to the cellular level. Through small gestures—a breath!—en route to homes and schools and dealer showrooms, they learned to luxuriate in aspects of the "mutant ecologies" spawned by synthetic chemistry and nuclear testing, which reshaped ecosystems in unprecedented ways from the mid-twentieth century onward.[11]

Yet there is nothing inherently noxious about fumes or radioactive isotopes, however damaging, in their *meaningful* apprehension. The factory smoke that "casts a pall" over a city in reviews that tourists post on the Internet can just as easily represent jobs to a worker or the "sweet smell of success" to a shareholder (who at any rate has the means to inhale from a distance). "As a boy I was always fascinated by smoke," writes Carlos Schwantes. "The thicker and blacker the plume rising from a row of smokestacks, the better. . . . Back in the prosperous 1950s I never considered a relationship between smoke and environmental degradation. I do not believe, in fact, that most Americans did back then. As I recall it, factory smoke in those days clearly symbolized power and prosperity" (2009:125).

The view that Schwantes describes may have been dominant, but it was hardly consensual. Throughout the nineteenth and twentieth centuries, fumes also figured prominently in agitation for industrial reform in Europe and North America. Charles Dickens set his novel *Hard Times* in Coketown, a dystopian vista of "machinery and tall chimneys, out of which interminable serpents of smoke trailed themselves for ever and ever, and never got uncoiled" (1854:32). Friedrich Engels's proto-ethnography, *The Condition of the Working Class in England in 1844*, noted that factories had deposited "a long string of the most disgusting, blackish-green, slime pools" on the riverbank in Manchester, "from the depths of which bubbles of miasmatic gas constantly arise and give forth a stench unendurable even on the bridge forty or fifty feet above the surface of the stream. . . . If any one wishes to see in how little space a human being can move, how little air—and *such* air!—he can breathe, how little of civilisation he may share and yet live, it is only necessary to travel hither" (1892:48, 53). Although the health effects of fumes, particularly on factory workers, were much debated throughout this period, it still took time for industrial smoke to become "pollution." In nineteenth-century Britain, there were those who praised coal smoke for its ability to dispel the unhealthful miasma produced by the decomposition of organic detritus that littered the streets (Thorsheim 2006).

Dickens had used the trope of fumes in an earlier novel, *Nicholas Nickleby*, to explain how the effluvia of profit-driven societies might just as well appeal as repel: "For gold conjures up a mist about a man more destructive of all his old senses and lulling to his feelings than the fumes of charcoal" (1839:4). In this formulation, money casts a sensory spell that works simultaneously as an illusion, a form of damage, and a seduction. Yet the pervasive enticement of that new car smell for retail customers, who stand only to lose money on the deal as the vehicle depreciates, suggests that something more than profit began to work its sensory magic during the Fordist era.

Although Henry Ford was a staunch opponent of labor organizing, he famously contended that wages should be set at a level that would allow people to purchase the goods they manufactured. An assembly line worker at the Rouge River plant, in other words, should have the purchasing power to drive home a Model A. This is a familiar chapter in the oft-narrated story of the rise of Fordism in North America: the implementation of a family wage, the growth of a stable middle class, and the shift away from hailing workers as producers to hailing them as consumers.[12] Rarely perceived, much less acknowledged, are the ways in which, by taking its signature product to the masses, the Ford Motor Company went beyond the reinvention of factory production to reinvent the masses affectively.

In the long run, autoworkers (like other workers) would shape-shift into buyers with moods assessed under rubrics such as "consumer sentiment." In the more immediate sense, these workers-cum-consumers provided a vastly expanded pool of new recruits for the fold of North American tinkerers, including Ford himself, who had long applied "Yankee ingenuity" to the creative modification of existing technologies (see Hounshell 1985). What made this episode different from earlier experiments with plows, looms, and harvesting equipment was its scale, yes, but also the intimacy with industrially produced chemicals that was an outcome of integrating them into "domestic life."

Early car models were so unreliable that spare parts and fluids had to be taken on the road, forcing drivers to double as mechanics. Lavishing care and affection on a vehicle was a matter of necessity but also a response to the incitement to accessorize that these vehicles tendered by virtue of their incompleteness when they rolled off the assembly line (Muehlebach and Shoshan 2012). By the 1950s, American workers regularly ministered to family vehicles on weekends, in garages that had become a requisite extension of mass-produced housing. The same people who exulted in the scent of a new automobile might wear dioxin-laced oil streaks on their overalls as a badge of pride, or, if less mechanically inclined, stock their garages with toxic substances such as transmission fluid. As the big automobile manufacturers moved leaky oil pans, coolant, tire patching goo, and VOCs into the realm of everyday experience outside the factory, they helped turn contact with industrial chemicals into a mass experience.

Discerning new car buyers today know all too well that they inhale with the windows closed at their peril. An enterprising attorney in Colorado even staged a new car smell defense on behalf of a man charged with leaving the scene after he crashed into a bicyclist. The VOCs in his client's month-old Mercedes-Benz had exerted an intoxicating effect, the attorney argued, ultimately causing his client to lose consciousness (Rudolf 2010). It remains to be seen, however, whether fears incited by exposés and critiques buttressed by studies can reorganize social relations in a way that would meaningfully disrupt this on-again, off-again love affair with toxic industrial products that appear to be rendering life, qua life, ever more precarious.[13] One suspects that they need not, since fear can ally itself with other affective stances, such as thrill, rather than prompt a change of course. William Mazzarella (2008:298–99), who treats affect as structurally integral to modernity, contends that as a consequence, "any social project that is not imposed through force alone must be affective in order to be effective." Carefully reasoned critiques make many valuable contributions, but they do not do that.

And there is still the unresolved matter of nostalgia. "The scent," observed Walter Benjamin, "is the inaccessible refuge of *mémoire involontaire*. . . . If the recognition of a scent can provide greater consolation than any other memory, this may be because it deeply anesthetizes the sense of time" (2003:335). In at least some contexts, political interventions have to counter nostalgia in order to carry the senses.

After the exposés on VOCs began to appear, a company called Lane's Professional Car Products began to niche market an item called "New Car Scent." Car sales might have plummeted in the United States in 2008 as the Great Financial Crisis clicked into gear, but for a mere $11.50 anyone could afford the ambience of a freshly minted vehicle. Simply spray a bit of this bright pink liquid of unknown provenance, alleged to be nontoxic, on the surfaces with which passengers interact and—voilà!—the driver of an old car can capture the aroma (never "fumes") of a vehicle that just came from the dealer. However successful a product like New Car Scent might be in terms of marketing, it hits another affective register entirely with its promise of *a substitute that offers salvation*, even as it preserves the form.

Even in North America, where the steady decline of factory production had reduced the manufacturing sector to just 11 percent of the economy by the early twenty-first century, the car emerged as a leading protagonist in quest narratives of the path to an ecologically viable planet. In a certain sense, this was not a new development. With concept cars and expos devoted to showcasing the latest technology, the big automakers had long billed their products as windows onto a future.[14] Toyota even named one of its models "Mirai" (未来), Japanese for "the future" (literally, the "not yet come"). The difference this time was that, as debate about climate change quickened, media coverage routinely linked cars with sustainability and sustainability with cars. Start-up companies began to experiment in earnest with alternative sources of propulsion. Major automobile corporations dusted off research on electric vehicles and moved them back into mass production. University researchers collaborated to develop a recyclable electrochemical fuel. If the breathless accounts of automotive innovation were to be believed, reengineering would be all that stands between an environmentally problematic today and a perpetually renewable tomorrow.[15]

Take, for example, the review of Expo 2010 in Shanghai that was published in the *Economist*, intriguingly titled "The Bubble Car Is Back" (2010: 86–87). The article characterized the EN-VS (Electric Networked Vehicles) on display as successors to a fifty-year-old design that was once commercially produced in Europe but popularized in North America primarily through drawings and futuristic cartoons such as *The Jetsons*. Fifty years later, Americans, at least, finally arrived at their future, in a way that set up the possibility of nostalgia for a future past that was never lived but merely animated. In addition to a source of thrust portrayed as less environmentally harmful than the internal combustion engine, the EN-VS featured a two-wheel balancing system, small size, and excellent maneuverability. Sensors and a global positioning system equipped the vehicle to drive itself, automating the task of valet parking and allowing drivers to retrieve their cars with a phone call. Crowds who got a chance to see the EN-VS in action at the expo were reportedly "enthralled."

Such celebratory accounts occasionally mention the environmental costs of electricity generation, especially by coal-fired power plants, but they tend to ignore the life cycle (cradle-to-grave) impact of producing all those sensors and polycarbonate plastics. A similar disconnect occurs in discussions of hydrogen-powered cars, which are often said to produce only "natural," "harmless" water emissions, taking no notice of effects of scale. Water vapor is itself a potent greenhouse gas. Imagine tens of millions of vehicles emitting it on a daily basis.

Somehow, even in a time of perceived ecological crisis, the automobile refuses to be upstaged. From an ecological perspective, many new automotive technologies do offer something better than their predecessors. To question the automobile's centrality in narratives of sustainability is not to adopt an anti-technology stance but to ask, rather, how it is that a vehicle associated with the introduction of industrialized mass production and the paving-over of wildlife habitats has become fetishized in such a way that it promises to deliver the world from the very evils it appears to have wrought. The Christian subtext here is not incidental. There is a palpable irony in looking for salvation to an automotive industry that has effectively subordinated the welfare of living creatures to the course of its own expansion. It is an irony mediated by an affective bond to the automobile that remains visceral in its sensory attachments yet exceeds the configuration of desire through the sense of smell described above.

To ask why the car should have emerged as a leading protagonist in quest narratives of the route to a perpetually inhabitable planet is to ask about the relationship of sensation to prosthetic embodiment of the sort that the automobile teaches, that is, the kind of embodiment in which industrial products, however toxic, return to people as extensions of their own physicality. Here it helps to turn to Henry Ford's own account of what the test drive, a routine part of his manufacturing operations, revealed about the limits of standardization:

> We build our cars absolutely interchangeable. All parts are as nearly alike as chemical analysis, the finest machinery, and the finest workmanship can make them. No fitting of any kind is required, and it would certainly seem that two Fords standing side by side, looking exactly alike and made so exactly alike that any part could be taken out of one and put into the other, would be alike. But they are not. They will have different road habits. We have men who have driven hundreds, and in some cases thousands of Fords and they say that no two ever act precisely the same—that, if they should drive a new car for an hour or even less and then the car were mixed with a bunch of other new ones, also each driven for a single hour and under the same conditions, that although they could not recognize the car they

had been driving merely by looking at it, they could do so by driving it. (1923:11)

If people can readily distinguish one mass-produced vehicle from another by apprehending them through another register—in this case, touch rather than vision—there is a kind of customization without design that drivers produce when they take a car out for a spin. The sameness that undergirds mass production may be partially an optical effect. Not all aspects of mass production, in Henry Ford's time or ours, occur en masse.

Once the car is understood as a pedagogical instrument and not just as a carrier of passengers, cargo, or aspirations, the importance of sensation in differentiating one vehicle from another, so as to personalize it, acquires another aspect.[16] Here it can be useful to distinguish between sensation, feeling, and affect, along the lines laid out in some schools of Buddhist philosophy.[17] Sensation encompasses touch, smell, hearing, vision, taste, and (in this philosophical lineage) mind. Feeling takes sensation as its matériel, working it up into a stance of attachment, ignorance, or aversion toward its objects. Affect describes the sort of dream palace created with injunctions, assertions, and narrative, as people create stories or even throwaway comments about what these feelings and sensations are supposed to mean. What starts with the sensation of air brushing along the contours of a body filters through feeling and becomes an affective confection that intones, "I love the feel of the wind in my hair when I put down that convertible top. I've never felt so free." Or: "I hate this traffic. Close the windows. Those diesel fumes are really getting to me. But I shouldn't complain. That's the price the country has to pay for progress."

Customization began as an embodied process, long before Ford retailed accessories for its Model T and lowriders in North America started to make symbolic statements by integrating hydraulics into their cars. Henry Ford's account of the variable, even unique, sensations produced by each test drive hints at the way in which the automobile would become a sort of prosthesis, an amplification of the human body that augments its sensorium in the process of generating the novel sensations associated with traveling at speed. Through *sensory customization*, driver and driven are inextricably transformed, each becoming a vehicle for an expansion of the other's capacities. In English, cars even have bodies; instead of checking them into hospitals or spas after accidents, owners take them to body shops for repairs.

The highly personalized sensations generated when a driver engages steering wheel or clutch have fostered an intimate attachment to the vehicles themselves, but as affective attachments, they have also sutured people to larger narratives such as nationalism and the emergence of an economy that can transcend poverty. To gaze at the flyovers (elevated roadways) springing up in major cities in India is to witness a country's advance, or so the story goes, repeated by drivers, residents, even bicyclists. To dethrone the automobile from its privileged position in a landscape is to give up the story. For many, that seems as unthinkable as a world without cars.[18]

So the clamor arises for salvation by substitution, and the search is on for a greener automobile, or, for that matter, a greener way of producing the concrete that goes into all those flyovers. Bill Ford, heir to old Henry's automotive empire, sets out to bring the Rouge River plant into the twenty-first century by installing the world's largest living roof atop the old 1917 complex, with no fundamental changes in the system required. "This is not philanthropy," the younger Ford insists. "It is sound business" ("Ford Motor Company's River Rouge Truck Plant" 2010). There is a whiff of just-in-time inventory here: sustainable designs arrive just in time to stave off environmental disaster and, incidentally, preserve capital.

Of course, the green roof at Rouge River is a commendable initiative and not to be dismissed. But the larger questions remain: How have such viscerally affective attachments to the automobile managed to reproduce themselves across the globe in market after market opened to capitalist production? Is the automobile-enhanced and automobile-extended body compatible with a planet that can nourish bodies of a less mechanized sort? To the extent that car access generates "pathways to inequality" — by, for example, requiring poorer households to spend more on mobility than food — some of those bodies would still be malnourished (see Lutz 2014). And even if the answer could be a qualified yes, in some yet-to-be-engineered guise, why should the automobile now, given its environmentally deleterious effects, have become the poster child for securing a future?

Nano Technology: An Ethnographic Stopgap, New Delhi

It's a tricky thing, always, to talk about air and water pollution in a postcolonial context, after the lengths to which colonial powers went to associate the majority world with "dirt" (see Ashenburg 2008; McClintock 1995). A hundred years and thousands of bars of Pears soap later, the portrayal of one really existing fly in Nairobi can activate an arsenal of demeaning and racist imagery in a way that that same fly never would when spotted elsewhere.[19] Still, political ecologies of the precarious inhabit postcolonial societies, just as they do the former metropoles, however distinctively configured in each case.

Over the Yamuna River, a bridge called the DND Flyway links the metropolis of New Delhi with the adjoining state of Uttar Pradesh, where it empties out into the mixed residential/industrial community called Noida. Tolls imposed on the privately operated bridge thin out the fierce Delhi traffic, which makes driving on the DND as close as one can come to an experience of the "open road" in a city where residents register up to one thousand additional vehicles daily. Reports on the environmental safeguards put in place during construction of this serpentine roadway litter the DND website (www.dndflyway.com).[20] Like all roads, the DND extends an invitation to be used, which sends a somewhat different environmental signal.

At night the flyway glimmers through the winter smog-fog like a neon page out of Dante's Inferno. Billboards line the sides of the roadway. If the Inferno had had corporate sponsors, it might have included these: the manufacturers of air conditioners to combat rising average temperatures, "green" housing developments that chew up the desert, insurance companies ready to sell you a policy on your pollution-diminished life.[21] The hoardings are almost always lit, even when the power fails, as it frequently does, especially on the Noida side. At those times, there is a surreal quality to the pitches for electronic gadgets that even the middle-class consumers who can afford them will not be able to recharge without an inverter when they finally reach the darkened landscape of their rainwater-harvesting homes.

If it is foggy on the bridge, you do not need to see the Yamuna to know that the river flows beneath you. There is a whole world down there on the floodplain—cows, village, rickshaws, farmers, fields—but it is the kind of community that India's new concrete thoroughfares pass over, not through, when they do not displace them altogether. By the time the river's glacier-fed waters flow through Delhi, they have accepted direct discharges from paper mills, factories, utilities, tanneries, and sugar refineries as well as enough fertilizer runoff and excrement to reduce dissolved oxygen levels to the lowest of all rivers in the country. Yet you might still be moved to take a deep breath. In this case, a middle-class you breathes not to savor the chemical mixture like some new car aroma but to gauge your position on the flyway, and more specifically, whether you are about to reach the point where your mobile phone signal will be lost.

That is when you spot the Nano. It might be just another compact car,

Figure 5.1. Newspaper advertisement for the Tata Nano [Credit: Author photo]

ignored in the race to get to the tollbooth, except for the press coverage the vehicle has received by virtue of its record low cost. Rumor has it there are quite a few Nanos on the road down in Mumbai, but in Delhi in 2010 they are a novelty. This Nano's electric yellow bodywork illuminates the night as it toddles along on miniature wheels. Economizing moves are evident in the single wiper blade, but the overall impression is of something gleaming and spanking new: a mode of transport that can secure a better tomorrow, for the customer as for the nation.

Tata Motors initially portrayed its Nano as "The People's Car," another in a worthy line of automobiles designed to bring previously unaffordable technologies to the masses. Like the original Volkswagen—the people's mobile—the Nano targeted an emerging middle class. Its debut was supposed to symbolize progress, especially for those for whom a better life remained aspirational while riches accrued to Indian elites. From the beginning, however, the project elicited skepticism. Would such an inexpensive car stand up to the punishment of India's climate and unevenly maintained roads? Wouldn't it have made better ecological sense to leapfrog an old technology like the combustion engine in order to produce an electric or CNG-powered vehicle?

Villagers in Singur, West Bengal, where Tata first proposed to manufacture the Nano, waged a successful two-year battle to retain their lands, in a reminder that not all the environmental impacts of an automobile issue from the tailpipe.[22] Tata relocated production to Gujarat, but controversy still dogged the project even after cars began to roll off the assembly line. When several Nanos spontaneously caught fire, the company offered the owners compensation and upgraded "safety equipment" but refused to apologize. Sales plummeted. Leaving aside safety issues, Ratan Tata, then chairman of Tata Sons Limited, cited the Nano's reputation as a "poor man's car" as a "stigma" the company would have to work to undo (HT Correspondent 2012).[23]

Tata accordingly intensified its advertising campaign for the Nano, sticking with the slogan "*Khushiyon ki chaabi,*" the key to happiness, or to the things that make for happiness. Not, then, just a key to a car. One of the images from the initial campaign enlisted the sense of touch in an effort to attract buyers. In the ad a young girl in school uniform, braided hair neatly tied off with a ribbon, leans across the vehicle. Her cheek rests gently on the hood as her eyes close and a smile spreads across her face. The hug she gives the Nano is not an appeal to the tactility integral to a test drive but an attempt to elicit the viewer's identification with a figure too young to drive the vehicle. Benefits for the masses recede as an ambiance of *khushi*, happiness, individually and intimately tailored, takes hold. In the still shot used at one point on the Nano website, there was not a road in sight, just a car parked in a field of lush green grass, with animated specks of birds flying across the screen into the pristine hills beyond.

Back in Delhi, there have been periodic calls to clean up the river, if only to honor the Hindu goddess Yamuna for whom it is named, a goddess the river incarnates for believers. In 2010 a group of farmers from Allahabad demanded that India's Supreme Court investigate why, despite more than four billion rupees spent to treat the Yamuna's waters, levels of pollution have only continued to rise. To increase awareness of the untenable situation, the farmers took to the road. Not in motorized vehicles, however. These marchers journeyed to the capital the old-fashioned way, on foot, staging a *yatra* (pilgrimage/procession) with an ecological dimension ("Allahabad Farmers" 2011).

During the winter months, when atmospheric inversions trap pollutants close to the ground, Delhi has experimented with alternating odd/even license plate restrictions on driving. There have also been calls to clean up India's air by minimizing reliance on cars. When wealthier automobile owners complained that a cheap alternative like the Nano would only make traffic jams worse by increasing the number of cars on the road, the Centre for Science and Environment (CSE) argued that the problem was not the Nano but automobiles as such. Even the small cars sold in Delhi needed twenty-three square meters to be "comfortably parked," in a city where entire families living in poverty had to crowd into a space of eighteen to twenty-five square meters ("Eye Openers" 2011:72). Automobiles are "dinosaurs" that cannot be part of "the solution to the pollution and climate mayhem," the CSE (2009) declared, inverting the social evolutionary narrative of national progress to mark the car as a relic of a bygone era.

Rhetorical moves to set modernity on its head in order to break affective attachments to the automobile can only go so far, however, especially in a country where people have associated a progression from bullock cart to two-wheeler (motorcycle) with upward mobility. The Indian government continues to subsidize automakers. Meanwhile, there are no corporate sponsors for billboards on the DND that would feature children with their arms wrapped around a city bus. Like so many other metropolises in the world, New Delhi has yet to develop a viscerally compelling narrative for public transport.

After Infinity: Crashing the Resource Limit

In 2011 Zhou Shengxian made a remarkable statement for an environmental minister from a country where economic development has dominated planning: "Natural resources are shrinking, degenerating, and drying up. Ecological and environmental decay has become a bottleneck and a serious obstacle to our economic and social development. If our homeland is destroyed and we lose our health, then what good does development do?" ("Beijing Warns on Pollution Threat" 2011:2).

The lyrics to the anthem of development are changing. For decades modernity rallied people to advance; precarity shrugs and says, "We cannot go back." But what does it mean to face "forward" with the precariousness of our ecological situation in view?

In the early stages, when the extent of the injury and the threat to life is unclear, amputation seems inconceivable. This way of formulating the situation—the CSE's way, perhaps, when it recommends a *future* path that requires giving up the car—departs from the presumption that a certain kind of amputation has not already occurred. Marshall McLuhan (1994) once applied the trope of amputation to the automobile to argue that technologies serve not only as prosthetic devices that extend the senses but also as media that can pull bodies back from sensory engagement. The same vehicle that hurtles people at unprecedented speeds through space has "amputated" wildlife corridors and landscapes made for walking, not to mention the time that could have been spent with loved ones who became fodder for the statistical rise in deaths on bad air quality days.

There is a clue here as to why the sense of a precarious hold of life on earth that arose with the debate on global warming has led to a project of reinscribing the present on some future, sustainably, while environmental conditions, by most measures, continue to deteriorate.[24] Amputative logics leave the terms of engagement in place. The salvific substitution promised by new automotive technologies and green consumerism may slow the destruction but can only defer it, because it entails no fundamental reorganization of business as usual, no critical perspective on the industrial strategy of profit-driven reinvention, or indeed any deep appreciation of the limits that business as usual has soldered into place.[25]

Over the course of several centuries, the sensory fabric of capitalism's affective relations has nurtured a reliance on infinity: Infinite resources. Infinite progress. Infinite growth. Political ecologies of the precarious raise the possibility, with some urgency, that there may be something after infinity. The limit of business as usual turns out not to lie in the dreamworld of the calculus, some boundary condition constantly approached but never reached. Organisms, ecologies, "resources"—all these have their limits. Things may run out—if not petrol or puffer fish, then perhaps that most ingenious of human inventions, time. In different sociocultural contexts with different histories, people may come at the boundary from different directions, but cross it they will.

The econometric propensity to turn the world into a collection of dead yet measurable and manipulated "resources" is itself symptomatic. By way of contrast, consider the affective stance available to people in some of the indigenous societies described in the introduction, where reeds for a living basket must be gathered in a certain way, where an animal conceived as a relative is not to be eaten out of season (and that by request). During Blessing Way ceremonies performed to reanimate kin ties in Dinétah (the Navajo homeland), sheep, a gift from the Holy People, would enter the hogan to receive their blessing alongside the humans. Many Diné recount the slaughter of their sheep by U.S. federal agencies during the 1930s not as the rational step toward rangeland management heralded by the government but as a traumatic event that resonated with their forced removal and the Long Walk toward incarceration at Fort Sumner back in the 1860s. Even by the government's own standards, this resource-driven policy of rangeland "conservation" proved disastrous, with weeds proliferating where sheep had once kept them in check (Weisiger 2009).

In a reanimated world inscribed by harsh histories such as these, the backstory to a bowl of lamb stew can never be properly recounted through some agricultural traceback project. Nonhuman people (to use a more indigenous vocabulary) or agents (to use the secularized language of the new materialities) would need to be consulted before bringing nuclear power plants online to "meet the world's energy needs." It would become clearer that acts of steely-eyed assessment like the ones that underwrite carbon credit schemes will never be sufficient to address climate change. Water forums that address scarcity, demand, and distribution would have to seek a less managerial register. A healthy respect for what Jane Bennett (2010) has called "thing power" would call attention to the visceral production of attachments and prevent worldly goods from being taken for goods without further inspection.

"Indigenous knowledge" is a catch phrase — oversimplified, no doubt — that gestures toward understandings of the world which are responsive and alive. Centuries of colonization and sovereignty struggles have reshaped the habitus of grasslands, trees, and beavers, right along with human communities. Elders will be the first to tell you that some of the older ways of moving through the world do not work as they once did, as climate change disrupts seasonal relationships with sea and land. Like any product of inquiry, indigenous knowledge changes. But unlike forms of knowledge more deeply indebted to the rise of capitalism, indigenous knowledge tends not to value change or originality for its own sake, the better to sell them on. It is possible to carry things forward in ways that accommodate whatever emerges by attending closely to the new without fetishizing it.

While gestures toward indigeneity might seem romanticized in an era when even tribal governments strike shady deals with corporations, indigenous ways of apprehending the world tend to sidestep the double binds that political ecologies of the precarious institute through assumptions about human exceptionalism. Sidestepping is not necessarily evading, however. The recent codification of "traditional ecological knowledge," complete with acronym (TEK), testifies to the pull of engagements with the practice of natural resource management, set over and against it as "NRM." Codification, like recourse to facile oppositions, has its perils, not least of which is the tendency to freeze-frame whatever it touches, abstracting practices from ever-shifting engagements with ever-shifting conditions. In joint ventures with the Australian state, indigenous groups have shared some of what they know about a kind of "ecological time" that correlates the position of a star constellation with emu egg laying and associates the flowering of a particular plant with the arrival of snapper in a harbor (Prober, O'Connor, and Walsh 2011). How compatible ecological time is with state-sponsored "resource"-oriented conservation schemes remains to be determined.

Codification aside, the wide range of practices grouped together under "TEK" find their inspiration in markedly different sensory mediations than the ones produced by industrialized forms of possessive individualism, where every instance of "toxic suffering" references an instance of chemical intoxication, some variation on that new car smell.[26] The classic Huron conception of a world in which things are renewed, destroyed, and remade, for instance, bears some affinity with the concept of recycling in its cyclicality, perhaps, but breaks the managerial frame by refusing to set people apart from a world of inert material resources, the better to recycle them (see Carpenter 2004).

Indigenous approaches are not the only alternatives, of course, but they offer a sense of where else a Chicagoan or a Delhiite who cares about the next turn of the wheel might look, if not to a greener automobile, if not to geoengineering. Cradle-to-cradle (C2C) or regenerative design, which attempts to fashion products that are recyclable in all their parts, could help salvage some of the alienated intimacies that chemical synthesis has fostered. So could biomimetic design, with its manufactured wetlands, light-sensitive clothing modeled on the layered skin of cuttlefish, and buildings that turn seawater into freshwater using architectural features inspired by fog-basking beetles.[27] The "tangle of potential connections" that Kathleen Stewart (2007:4) finds in "ordinary affects" can route themselves equally well through a high-tech biomimetic or C2C manufacturing process as through low-tech harvests of organically sourced materials, if conditions are right.

Conditions matter, because an idealist project that sets out merely to reconceive the world cannot dispel the anxieties about looming environmental threats that chemical synthesis has fostered.[28] There is simply too much sensory pull toward toxicity, and too many institutionalized mechanisms in place to replicate that pull. The farmers in Allahabad understood this when they decided to march. If minds were the only things that needed to change in order to help the Yamuna River, they would not have had to embark on a six-hundred-kilometer trek to appeal with arguments, invocations, *and* aching bones to India's highest court.

Acqua Alta, Rising: An Ethnographic Stopgap, Venice

Years ago in the breakfast room of a hotel near the Gran Teatro La Fenice in Venice, I awoke to share cappuccino with a couple of imperfect strangers. One was a schoolteacher from Australia, there to enjoy the fruits of her savings on a long-awaited holiday. The other turned out to be Malya Woolf, an actress who had married into the Bloomsbury crowd. Malya spent the morning telling stories about the dancer Isadora Duncan's time on the Lido, about wartime Italy, about the art exhibits currently on. In a few short hours, we would set out together to search for the building where Malya once lived. It was a "hail fellow travelers well met" moment, to be sure, but certainly not the scenario one would expect to pop up in a chapter in which the automobile is the protagonist. Venice, after all, is the rare city without cars.

Flash back, then, to the moment when the schoolteacher struggled to liberate a particularly delectable piece of pistachio biscotti from its wrapping. "Can someone help me?" she asked, pulling every which way in an attempt to get the transparent cover to release its prize. After Malya obliged with a knife, the schoolteacher savored a bite. "When I imagine what hell might be like," she observed, "I imagine it just like this. A place filled with lovely things wrapped in little plastic packages, where people have to spend their days trying to get the plastic off."

Even in this city without cars, the oil economy permeates everyday life, from the petrol required for coffee beans to reach its charming cafés, to the fuel required to transport all those tourists on whom the city now depends, to the petroleum-derived goods that beckon from the windows of shop after shop: Nylon woven into luxury fabrics. Polyester ribbons dangling from carnival masks. In other words, plastic.

These days Venice is famously engaged in a battle with climate change, the precariousness of its position evident each time the acqua alta, or peak tide, inundates entire sections of the city. Acqua alta floods have increased in frequency, in tandem with the documented rise in sea levels attributed to the heating of the earth's atmosphere. While there are other contributing factors that have caused subsidence, such as methane mining near the lagoon and the dredging of canals to accommodate larger ships, these, too, are linked to global commerce.

To combat acqua alta, stopgap measures have been implemented, including elevated walkways that allow people to pass as the waters rise. Officials have garnered support for dramatic interventions like the MOSE (Modulo Sperimentale Elettromeccanico) project, massive gates to protect the Venetian Lagoon from the Adriatic Sea. It would seem at a glance that people are facing the problems head-on. But here, too, hopes rest on supplements and substitutions, rather than a concerted attempt to reorganize a mode of production.

In a place such as Venice, most residents have a cognitive understanding of the dangers that climate change poses, as well as a tactile reminder, in the form of the recurrent acqua alta, of one of climate change's key effects. They have taken measures to counter the impact of environmental degradation, but the MOSE project, like automobile manufacturing, relies upon the kind of heavy resource extraction that helped get the world into this predicament in the first place. Their efforts are creative, flexible, and resilient in a way that Henry Ford and his successors could admire. But like the builders of a better vehicle, they have embraced the destruction in order to defer it. Too many of their efforts preserve the form of whatever is already in place, of which, when it comes to climate change, the buildings are the least of it.

Analysis is never supposed to culminate in some intermezzo. Even the most apocalyptic of narratives derives its power from the claim to know what happens in the end. For political ecologies of the precarious, however, interruption rather than crescendo may turn out to be the new motif. From Chicago to Delhi to Venice, people find themselves preoccupied, the hold of their species on this thing called "life" newly perceived as tenuous. They may even occasionally *feel* their impending displacement, which is to say, they may occasionally feel the gravity of their position. Yet, cognition and feeling aside, they are finding it difficult to reorganize their affective attachments, and with those attachments, the capital-intensive regimes of production designed to elicit them. Continuous sensory engagement with industrially sourced experiences of consumption discourages any meaningful reorganization of a system that represents immense short-term profitability for some. And for that very reason, unless we mobilize for a different sort of change, someday we—and I mean we—are likely to be all wrapped up in our projects and our plans for sustainability, immersed in what we believe to be another interlude on the way to pleasure or progress or the very next thing, when suddenly

NOTES

———

INTRODUCTION: ANIMATING INTIMACIES, REANIMATING A WORLD

1. Dreamworks can never be properly referenced, since they exceed the referential, but readers interested in pursuing some of these threads might start here: News coverage from *Indian Country Today* is available at http://indiancountrytodaymedianetwork .com/ and is highly recommended for anyone who presumes to think they know what it means to be "American" (accessed April 22, 2016). Coverage of the devastation caused by the mining of beaches and riverbeds for sand to mix into concrete can be found in P. Anand (2013); Babu (2013); Chakravarty (2014); HT Correspondent (2013d); Rajput (2013b); and Sinha (2013). For a timeless tale of another sort that plays with its historical setting, see the story about Victorian repression that opens Foucault's (1978) *The History of Sexuality*. I am grateful to Geeta Patel for making the connection.

2. I take my lead here from Harry Harootunian's (2000:33) account of the impossibly contradictory task embedded in the project of overcoming modernity and Shannon Lee Dawdy's (2010:762) observations on "the slow death of modernity as a temporal ideology."

3. By "futures past" I have in mind the ruins of a once forward-looking modernity so movingly portrayed in Tong Lam's (2013) photographs of "abandoned futures": the gutted concrete shell of an apartment block listing to one side, the rounded bodywork of an obsolete fire engine rusting in a field, the detached nose of a jetliner buffeted by the very air currents it once mastered.

4. My thanks to Rosalind Morris for articulating this question in a way that helped me in turn articulate my answer to it.

5. Even in the hands of theorists such as Elizabeth Povinelli (2006) and Ann Stoler (2006, 2010), who would be the first to acknowledge the importance of ecology for any analysis of empire, intimacy largely confines itself to human relationships (e.g., the ways that colonial rule enlisted intimacies associated with human kinship in the project of governance). Likewise for the intricately theorized, often counterintuitive accounts of intimacy offered by Lauren Berlant (2000), for Lisa Lowe's (2015) extension of intimacy to the reading practices that helped generate postcolonial critique, and for Nayan Shah's (2011) evocative use of the concept of "stranger intimacy" to examine sexual citizenship and racialization in North American immigration history.

6. For an argument that more recent speculative approaches to "nature" build upon, rather than supplant, earlier contemplative discourses, see Igoe (2013).

7. Some of the most sympathetic readings of indigenous eco-practices, such as Charles Menzies's (2006) *Traditional Ecological Knowledge and Natural Resource Management*, become oxymorons when viewed through this lens.

8. Like any illustrative list, this one could go on, adding, for example, Wendy Brown's (1995) cautionary tale about a politics of *ressentiment* that sorts people into neatly bounded constituencies of injuring and injured.

9. Note the allusion in the title of Herper's article to the feminist "know your body" manual, *Our Bodies, Ourselves*, periodically revised since the 1970s by the Boston Women's Health Book Collective (2005).

10. The editors make it clear that they mean to apply the term *organ* to the microbiome descriptively, not analogically: "It weighs as much as many organs (about a kilogram, or a bit more than two pounds). And although it is not a distinct structure in the way that a heart or a liver is distinct, an organ does not have to have form and shape to be real. The immune system, for example, consists of cells scattered all around the body but it has the salient feature of an organ, namely that it is an organised system of cells" ("Me, Myself, Us" 2012:69).

11. Knight (2015) and Spector (2015) offer pedagogical introductions to "our microbial guests" (or is it "our microbial components"?). For the microbiome to emerge, its constituents first had to take shape as a conceptually distinct entity ("the microbe"). Microbes occupy center stage in Bruno Latour's (1993) retelling of the story of pasteurization, serendipitously (for our purposes) becoming lead characters in Latour's attempt to work out how nonhuman entities might also become actants that exert a certain agency in the world.

12. For an introduction to the new materialisms, see Coole and Frost (2010) and Dolphijn and van der Tuin (2012).

13. There are exceptions, of course, most notably David Abram's embrace of animism in *The Spell of the Sensuous* (1997), but those exceptions tend to attribute a kind of subjectivity to objects that replicates some very humanist notions.

14. Bennett captures the flavor of the distinctions made in these debates in her *Eurozine* interview: "There is a difference between a human individual and a stone, but neither considered alone has real agency: the locus of agency is always a human-nonhuman collective" (Bennett and Loenhart 2011:6).

15. "Becoming-" in the technical sense formulated by Deleuze and Guattari indicates a process of change within the assemblage, in this case a becoming-animism that brings the old element "animism" into novel relationships that endow the assemblage with new and generative properties.

16. History, that is, conceived as more than contingency. For a related critique, see Ahmed (2008).

17. Of course, the status of the word vis-à-vis ontologically informed practice sets up its own tensions. On the ontological turn in anthropology, see also Henare, Holbraad, and Wastell (2007) and Jensen and Morita (2012). For an attempt to bring "local

knowledge" to bear in a way that becomes meaningful for ecological "management," see Cruikshank's *Do Glaciers Listen?* (2010).

18. To better locate the concept of perspective in its European Renaissance context, see James Elkins's *The Poetics of Perspective* (1996). For a nuanced consideration of *perspectivism* (not perspectivalism) as an attempt to grapple with the theoretical crisis of structuralism in Amazonian anthropology, see Turner (2009). Viveiros de Castro (2014:55) articulates the epistemological thrust of perspectivism concisely in his *Cannibal Metaphysics*, where he is at pains to distinguish perspectivism from relativism: "As various ethnographers have noted (unfortunately too often only in passing), virtually all peoples of the New World share a conception of the world as composed of a multiplicity of points of view. Every existent is a center of intentionality apprehending other existents according to their respective characteristics and powers." Or, as Harry Walker (2013:12) puts it, in the perspectivist formulation, "Animals are assumed [by Amazonians] to inhabit a cultural universe more or less shared by everyone: they may dwell in longhouses, drink manioc beer, have chiefs and shamans, marry exogamously, and so on. We do not see any of this under normal waking conditions, because of the limitations imposed by our own species-specific 'nature,' our (human) body with its unique capacities, affordances, and dispositions." Walker goes on to argue that some of the ideological emphases in perspectivist accounts—especially predation (the hungry jaguar again!)—do not really capture, as it were, the social life of Urarina and other Amazonian groups. More salient for the Urarina Walker got to know were sensation-saturated forms of companionship, of the sort that fabricate a self through participation in the lives of others (Walker 2013:14).

19. For an incisive take on personhood that treats enslavement, labor, and resistance as key to the emergence of specific forms of African American materialism, see Allewaert (2013), who traces the swish-crackle-fizz of boundary dissolution between persons and things back to eighteenth-century plantation economies.

20. And not just any garden, but gardens shaped by perspectival planning, as pioneered in quite different ways by André Le Nôtre at Versailles and Lancelot "Capability" Brown at various estates across England. Thomas Jefferson, the third president of the United States and an architect of landscapes in his own right, studied the designs of both men and emulated various features upon his return to North America.

21. See the October 24, 2011, entry in Mochizuki's blog, *Fukushima Diary*, "Breaking News: Uranium from Finger Nail of a Tokyo Citizen," at http://fukushima-diary .com/2011/10/breaking-news-uranium-from-nail-of-a-tokyo-citizen/ (accessed May 3, 2016).

CHAPTER 1: BIOSECURITY AND SURVEILLANCE IN THE FOOD CHAIN

1. Private initiatives that used electronic technologies to track children also began to appear around this time. One little-noticed yet historic example is Kidspotter, "the first Wi-Fi/RFID tracking network," installed at the Legoland theme park in Denmark. Rented RFID-chipped bands affixed to children's wrists alerted guardians via mobile

phone whenever a child strayed too far away. In response to an SMS sent by the adult to a Legoland server, RFID readers in the park could triangulate the child's position and have the server text the coordinates back to the guardian's phone (*Wired* 2004).

2. For illustrations of how this opposition threads its way through accounts of the local food movement in the United States, see Cobb (2011).

3. Patel has since developed her analysis of the techno-intimacy concept in her book, *Risky Bodies and Techno-Intimacies* (2016).

4. As well as a more generalized popular debate on the importance of sustaining face-to-face relations in an increasingly digitized world (e.g., Susan Pinker's [2014] *The Village Effect: How Face-to-Face Contact Can Make Us Healthier, Happier, and Smarter*).

5. Indeed, the capacity of face-to-face relations, including kinship relations, to foster fiduciary *irresponsibility* was recognized even in Renaissance times, when the Medici bank, which started as a family business, foundered in part due to the practice of branch managers "lending far too much of the bank's money to the people they wished to spend time with and resemble: kings, princes, dukes, lords, and cardinals" (Parks 2005: 171). For another version of the morality tale that privileges face-to-face relations in banking, see Hickman (2008). For face-to-face banking with a techno-intimacy twist, consider the ad campaign mounted by India's IndusInd Bank, whose flyers promised customers "face-to-face banking without going to your bank" using a "video branch" program activated by placing live video calls over the Internet (IndusInd Bank 2014).

6. Albeit, in the Japanese case, with an emphasis on reassuring consumers about food safety rather than providing stories of social or environmental accountability (Hall 2010).

7. See also Masco (2014), who examines preemption and other anticipatory temporalities associated with biosecurity projects in the larger context of security discourse and the emergence of supranational linkages between military and civilian emergency response.

8. Nor has the use of high-tech surveillance devices in wildlife biology been uncontroversial. For an overview of how aerial drones, PIT tags (passive integrated transponders), and the like are creating a "brave new habitat" for "wild" animals, see J. Robbins (2012).

9. For a discussion of what I have elsewhere called "metamateriality," in which metaphors and other forms of symbolic representation gain traction by being elaborated through specific forms of material substance, see Weston (2013).

10. For an explanation of some pragmatic advantages for the financial industry associated with nonprofit LEI standardization, see Tett (2014).

11. See the farm's website at http://www.boggycreekfarm.com/ (accessed January 12, 2012).

12. For salutary admonitions regarding the limitations of DNA testing and the erroneous conclusions fostered by "the allure of tenths-of-percentiles" in test results, see Marks (2002:30).

13. For a mid-century example, see Ruth Harrison's *Animal Machines: The New Factory Farming Industry* (1966), which called attention to a reorganization of food pro-

duction that, albeit not quite new at the time of the book's publication, had entered an aggressively expansionary phase.

14. A 2011 study, to take but one example, found that nearly half the retail meat tested in cities across the United States contained drug-resistant strains of *Staphylococcus aureus* (Cevallos 2011).

15. Although "commingling" in the North American context carries connotations of the illicit, in the film *Hollywood Homicide* (2003), Harrison Ford's character, Joe Gavilan, captures the impossibility of living in anything other than a way that is commingled when conditions are (anything but) right: "Commingled funds, huh? That's my crime, commingling? Guilty. My alimony number one comes from money commingled with my beer money. My refinanced car [is] commingled with the short-term loan to keep the second mortgage paid off, commingled with my alimony number three, commingled with every goddamn dime I've got tied up in my Mt. Olympus property. My whole life's commingled!" Special thanks to Linda Layne for leading me to this source.

16. Fences accomplished the work of English hedgerows in eastern regions of North America, supplemented by barbed wire in the west. On the history of inclusionary and exclusionary effects associated with the invention of barbed wire, see Razac (2002).

17. For a classic exposition of the polarization between city and country in literary sources, see Williams (1975).

18. Contrast the Oneida case with Robert Stolz's (2014:189) discussion of how the transformation of milk and butter into "just another commodity" in postwar Japan led to a failure by even ecologically minded dairy producers such as Snow Brand "to address the source of the environmental crisis—located in the specific moment of production, when labor transforms nature."

19. See the Oneida Nation's website at http://www.oneidanation.org/Tsyunhehkwa/ (accessed April 14, 2016).

20. For the text of the Final Rule as it appeared in the *Federal Register*, see USDA APHIS (2013).

CHAPTER 2: THE UNWANTED INTIMACY OF RADIATION EXPOSURE IN JAPAN

1. The Great Tōhoku Earthquake registered 7 in Miyagi on the Shindo intensity scale more widely used in Japan. Seven is the most intense rating on the scale, used to describe situations in which even earthquake-resistant buildings may fail.

2. See Ryan Sayre's (2011) perceptive essay, written shortly before 3.11, on the concealed landscape of disaster preparedness in Tokyo.

3. That wall of water turned out to be a mind-boggling 132.5 feet high at its maximum (Ryall 2011).

4. See the official report of the Fukushima Nuclear Accident Independent Investigation Commission (2012) established by the National Diet. The report called the accident "a manmade disaster" that should have been foreseen and prevented—effectively, that is, not an accident. For an outline of events at the plant after 3.11, see Tanaka (2012).

When ABP, a pension fund based in the Netherlands, decided to sell its 18 million Euro stake in TEPCO three years later, the fund cited the company's nonresponsiveness to mounting safety concerns: "we had no trust that the company was shoring up its practices" (McLannahan 2014).

5. Vulnerability to the disruption of electrical supply is a problem shared by militarized as well as peacetime uses for nuclear power, as Eric Schlosser (2013:25) documents in his investigation of accidents and a "near-miss" at a nuclear missile silo complex in the U.S. state of Arkansas.

6. Although then Prime Minister Kan has corroborated this account of events, Yoshizawa Atsufumi, one of the so-called Fukushima Fifty who worked tirelessly to cool nuclear materials at the plant after the tsunami, contends that the workers themselves did not intend to abandon their jobs: "At the time that rumour was circulating I was volunteering to go back" (McNeill 2013). The government's own official report on the disaster, however, included testimony by Yoshida Masao, manager of the Fukushima Daiichi plant at the time, that approximately 90 percent of plant workers resisted his order to remain and fled at least temporarily to the Daini facility some ten kilometers away (Fukushima Nuclear Accident Independent Investigation Commission 2012). And as an editorial in the *Asahi Shimbun* pointed out, regardless of what happened at the plant on 3.11, subsequent discussions of new regulatory standards for nuclear facilities in Japan did not even raise the issue of how to deal with a scenario in which workers leave their posts en masse ("Startling Fukushima Testimony" 2014).

7. The nationalist connotations of the mention of Mount Fuji in news accounts of tea contamination are not incidental. Green tea is, of course, not only a staple drink in Japan but a beverage symbolically identified with the country. Likewise, the fact that passengers traveling on that icon of the nation's technological prowess, the Shinkansen bullet train, were served meat that violated government radiation standards was a detail constantly reiterated in coverage of the radioactive beef scare.

8. MEXT stands for Ministry of Education, Culture, Sports, Science, and Technology, a rather large remit.

9. For more on fūhyōhigai, including the pre-3.11 history of the category and debates about whether such rumors constitute a "rational" response, see Matsuda (2011) and Takahashi (2011a, 2011b).

10. The video, originally titled うんち・おならで例える原発解説～「おなかがいたくなった原発くん」, was posted to YouTube by Onaradaijobu on March 15, 2011, just four days after the earthquake (http://www.youtube.com/ watch?v=ZUzBvxdnCFM), and reposted with English subtitles by Shibata Bread the following day (http://www.youtube.com/watch?v=5sakN2hSVxA). Both videos were accessed on July 1, 2014, by which time they had received 1,778,429 and 1,896,859 hits, respectively. A profile (in Japanese) of the video's creator, the media artist Hachiya Kazuhiko, can be found at http://trendy.nikkeibp.co.jp/article/column/20110404/1035108/?ST=life&P=1. For more on the video's international reception, see Jeffrey (2011), accessed May 3, 2016.

11. On the medical manifestations of internal radiation exposure in Japan following the Pacific War, see "Bomb Survivor Doctor" (2012) and Hida and Kamanaka (2005). Koide and Yagasaki (2011) draw upon this history to create a scientific cautionary tale

for 3.11. For a scientific comparison of radiotoxic effects and mutation accumulation in animals at the sites of the Chernobyl and Fukushima Daiichi meltdowns, see Møller et al. (2013).

12. For an anecdotal account that underscores many of Walker's points, see Kerr (2002).

13. In this chapter and throughout I follow the Japanese practice of listing Japanese surnames first, followed by personal names, except in reference citations of multiply authored articles where for consistency surnames may follow personal names. Mochizuki Iori, blog entry, "Breaking News: Uranium from Finger Nail of a Tokyo Citizen," *Fukushima Diary*, October 24, 2011, http://fukushima-diary.com/2011/10/breaking-news-uranium-from-nail-of-a-tokyo-citizen/.

14. For another allusion to the uninvited guest in commentary on the earthquake, see Murakami (2011): "You might say that we are living as uninvited guests on planet earth. If she shakes a little, we can't complain, because shaking from time to time is just one of the earth's natural behaviours. Whether we like it or not, we must live with nature."

15. On Japanese government withholding of meteorological data and predictions of the path taken by radioactive releases from the plant, see Onishi and Fackler (2011) and Witherspoon (2013). On some of the ways in which unreliable state and corporate data on radioactive emissions following 3.11 stoked public mistrust, see Lochbaum et al. (2014). Investigative journalism inside and outside Japan has repeatedly linked efforts by ordinary citizens to detect radioactivity to doubts about government assurances (e.g., Belson 2011).

16. Original Japanese headline: "劣化ウラン保管施設も延焼コスモ石油のガスタンク火災で" (http://www.asyura2.com/11/genpatu13/msg/715.html, accessed May 3, 2016).

17. In an important blog post on the recruitment of poor and homeless day laborers for nuclear maintenance and decontamination work, Nasubi (2012) reminds readers that this practice predates the 3.11 "accident." Nasubi notes that many local workers employed at Fukushima Daiichi would have migrated to cities seeking work as day laborers if not for the plant, and quotes Fujita Yuko, a physicist and historian of science, who has underscored the point that "no nuclear reactor can operate without radiation-exposed labor." One tangible product of this post-3.11 labor organizing was "The Manual for Radiation-Exposed Workers' Self-Protection." For a unique account of day-to-day life working to contain radiation at "Ichi-Ef" (1F, the local nickname for the plant), written under a pen name and illustrated in the form of a *manga* by a former laborer there, see Tatsuta (2014).

18. As Allison Alexy and Richard Ronald (2011:10) point out, the Japanese state had already undermined public confidence in its ability to handle disasters with its "poor institutional responses" to the 1995 Kobe earthquake and to the sarin gas attack in the Tokyo subway mounted by Aum Shinrikyō. Bestor (2013) links what he terms a clichéd "critique of the ineffectual government elite" to these disasters but also to perceptions that government could not extricate Japan from its economic "lost decade" in the 1990s. Allison (2013:13) sees the uncertainties attendant on 3.11 as exacerbating preexisting conditions of precarity in Japan, conditions fostered by market insecurity and accom-

panied by "an emerging and spreading skepticism—toward the government, its proclamations of safety and control, and social institutions that have been running on certain expectations and logics (hierarchy and dependency) that may no longer make sense."

19. For an investigative journalist's exposé of yakuza ties encountered while working undercover in the nuclear power industry, see Suzuki's (2011) ヤクザと原発 (*Yakuza to Genpatsu*).

20. For links to video footage of Kodama's testimony in the original Japanese and translations into English, French, and German, see http://ex-skf.blogspot.com/2011/07 /professor-kodamas-speech-in-four.html, accessed May 3, 2016.

21. Counts per minute (CPM) refers to the number of atoms in a radioactive material that a device such as a Geiger counter registers as having disintegrated during the time-span of one minute. See also Schwartz (2012), who analyzes the Geiger counter's beeps and clicks within a broader framework of musical activism among Rongelapese women who have to deal with bodies irretrievably altered by U.S. nuclear testing in the Pacific.

22. Posted on YouTube as "Summary of Shinkansen Radiation Nasu-Koriyama-Fukushima Max250CPM/2.5µSvh Low in Tunnels," http://www.youtube.com/watch ?v=XiSL2dEFRIE, accessed May 3, 2016.

23. Posted on YouTube as "Playground Radiation in Kashiwa Japan June 20, 2011," http://www.youtube.com/watch?v=BOIDFh3wPXY, accessed May 3, 2016.

24. Meanwhile, the intimate knowledge of design mastered by the workers who installed the controls and laid the pipe in Japan's nuclear plants remained uncelebrated and largely untapped by citizen groups, nuclear industry executives, and national government alike.

25. Groups such as the Tokyo-based Citizens' Nuclear Information Center (CNIC) helped broker these cooperative exchanges (see Burrett and Simons 2011).

26. Special thanks to Kavita Philip for calling this article to my attention.

27. For an early example of the international coverage that citizen scientists in Japan have received, particularly the ones involved in creating crowdsourced radiation maps, see Knox (2011).

28. For a sophisticated treatment of memory in relation to the wartime bombing, see Lisa Yoneyama's *Hiroshima Traces* (1999).

29. Hibakusha have endured both material and social consequences of uncontrolled exposure to radiation: not only illness and medicalization but also dislocation, dispossession, and discrimination in employment, housing, schooling, and marriage.

30. Roger Witherspoon (2013), an investigative journalist, has subsequently raised the possibility that "the discrete plume was a myth" that had ships like the USS *Ronald Reagan*, detailed to help with search and rescue, fruitlessly trying to evade what became, in effect, an enveloping environment of radioactive currents and steam.

31. At issue here is not so much the veracity of allegations of defective radiation detection equipment flooding the Japanese market post-3.11—that much has been established—but rather the political hay made out of the discovery of those defects. Rather than calling for bans on the sale of detection equipment, agencies could conceivably have taken steps to improve the reliability of equipment marketed as suitable for household use. For an English-language overview of the National Consumer Affairs

Center warning, see "Consumer Warning: Geiger Counters/Dosimeters That Do Not Work," http://www.japanprobe.com/2011/09/09/consumer-warning-geiger-counters-dosimeters-that-do-not-work/, accessed May 3, 2016.

32. For further reflections on the complicated, socially and politically negotiated matter of inferring danger from detectable radiation levels, see Weston (2014).

33. A copy of the press release (in Japanese) issued by the Akita prefectural government is archived at http://www.pref.akita.lg.jp/www/contents/1313541715957/files/kannri.pdf, accessed May 3, 2016.

34. This, in turn, undermined confidence in the old industry adage circulated by utility companies that proposed to green their operations without cutting into profits: "The solution to pollution is dilution." For coverage in the Japanese business press of the continuous discovery of new hot spots, see "Suupaa Hottosupotto" (2011). For an account that situates the hot spot in the wider context of the biopolitics of militarism and war, see Krupar (2013).

35. After 3.11 the central government raised the legal limit from 1 to 20 millisieverts/hour, eliciting a storm of protest and an international campaign to revert to the old figure.

36. For a historically contextualized discussion of other policy developments (and lack of developments) in the wake of 3.11, see Samuels (2013).

37. I am indebted to a conversation with Allison Alexy for pointing me in this direction.

38. For an example of a radiation dose neighborhood association formed to monitor postdecontamination radiation levels in Fukushima City, see "One Year On" (2012).

39. It is interesting to note, in the context of this critique, that in the iconography of media coverage of 3.11, it is very common for photographs to feature children as the ones undergoing body scans when the Geiger counters are in the hands of officials.

40. In this sense, the calls of antinuclear protestors who took to the streets of Japan in the name of children after 3.11 resonated in ways that went beyond the type of advocacy documented by Lisa Dodson (2009:174) in *The Moral Underground*. Dodson found that a shared concern for children supplied a common moral ground for middle-income people in North America to begin to break rules and find informal ways of challenging official pronouncements.

41. Personal communication, December 2011. The first character of the more specialized term 除染 for radioactive decontamination means to remove or exclude, while the second character in this context would mean a stain.

42. This is not, of course, to minimize material concerns, which were also compelling, as Winifred Bird (2012) explains in "Fukushima Nuclear Cleanup Could Create Its Own Environmental Disaster."

43. "A2" is the diagnostic category that marks the presence of thyroid cysts. Information on the documentary is available at http://www.a2documentary.com/, accessed May 3, 2016.

44. For an analysis of maternalist rhetoric in the context of environmental justice initiatives that targeted dioxin contamination at Love Canal in North America, see Blum (2011).

45. Mochizuki Iori posted and translated the leaflet on his blog, *Fukushima Diary*, on January 25, 2012, at http://fukushima-diary.com/2012/01/fukushima-gov-distributes -leaflet-to-stop-them-evacuate/, accessed May 3, 2016.

46. Sometimes also translated into English as "atomic divorce" (see, for example, Haworth 2013). A more literal translation would be "nuclear power divorce."

47. The radiation divorce, at the time of writing, was a new phenomenon awaiting its ethnographer, with little by way of scholarly documentation. For coverage in the English-language media, see "'Radiation Divorce' Enters Japanese Vernacular" (2012). On women's post-3.11 activism, sometimes with Geiger counters in tow, see Sanchanta (2011); Wilks (2011); and Yamaguchi (2011).

48. For a brief overview of the wedding and dating boom that followed 3.11, see Nakamoto (2011).

49. Taking its inspiration from phytoremediation efforts at Chernobyl, the Fuku-shima Sunflower-Parent Project (福島ひまわり里親プロジェクト) began distributing sunflower seeds to volunteers during the spring of 2011 and even sponsored a sunflower photo contest to publicize the project. One scheme proposed running cars with biofuel made from the oil of the seeds from the full-grown plants. (See the project's website at http://www.sunflower-fukushima.com/, accessed May 3, 2016.) A small-scale phyto-remediation experiment with sunflowers conducted by Ito Nobuyuki at Iitate farm found the plant's roots capable of absorbing approximately seven thousand becquerels of cesium per kilo (Quintana 2012a, 2012b).

50. On the dilemmas, uncertainties, and learning-by-doing that shaped the "cleanup" process in the aftermath of the meltdowns, see Mahr (2011); Quintana (2012a, 2012b); and Tabuchi (2012). For investigative journalism on the slapdash, even reckless, meth-ods employed by government decontamination subcontractors, contrary to the best practice recommendations of government scientists, see Aoki, Kihara, and Tada (2013); Aoki and Sato (2013); Kihara and Tada (2013); Tabuchi (2013); and Tada (2013).

CHAPTER 3: CLIMATE CHANGE, SLIPPERY ON THE SKIN

1. Ewen (1998) and Rampton and Stauber (2001) have written eloquently on the elit-ism that permeates technocratic and corporate public relations discourse. For a social history of the racialized imagery of American class politics that could easily extend to whitened media imagery of working-class climate change skeptics, see Wray (2006).

2. For an example of a government document that attempts to shape the latest re-search into a relatively accessible form of "actionable science" (albeit at a length of 841 pages!), see the 2014 U.S. National Climate Assessment (Melillo, Richmond, and Yohe 2014).

3. I have adopted the term *climate skepticism* throughout, rather than the arguably more precise term, *climate contrarianism*, in recognition of the degree to which *climate skepticism* has become common usage. My project here is to focus on the question of how empiricism shapes certain critiques, leaving to one side the hotly debated matter of whether those critiques meet the criteria for skepticism. For a sense of the contours of the latter debate, see Washington and Cook (2011).

4. Original tweet available in Japanese at https://twitter.com/yukioyamakawa/status /31493548703704678. Translated by Mochizuki Iori on March 24, 2013, on his blog, *Fukushima Diary* (http://fukushima-diary.com/2013/03/the-former-fuji-tv-announcer -yamakawa-home-grown-rice-and-vegetables-caused-me-health-problems/, accessed April 29, 2016). More conventional citizen science projects also emerged following the meltdowns. Scientists at the Woods Hole Oceanographic Institution, for example, invited "concerned citizens" to help them track the spread of radiation by taking samples (and raising money) at locations throughout the Pacific. See the website for the "How Radioactive Is Our Ocean?" project at http://ourradioactiveocean.org/, accessed April 29, 2016.

5. For more on contemporary self-experimentation, including the Spurlock and Hoffman cases, see Minkel (2008).

6. My thanks to Andrew Palmer for the suggestion to take a look at J. B. S. Haldane's ventures into self-experimentation.

7. Consider, for example, the title of the exhibit mounted at the Harvard Museum of Natural History, "Climate Change: Our Global Experiment" (http://hmnh.harvard .edu/climate-change-our-global-experiment, accessed April 29, 2016).

8. In *The Psychophysical Ear*, Alexandra Hui (2012) explores the synergy between scientific research into auditory sensation during this period and the experimental rhythms and harmonies in European classical music.

9. Beth Povinelli (2012) extends this view of the sensorially registering and interpreting body to disciplines such as anthropology, which she terms a "dwelling science," with reference to the ways that anthropologists rely upon modes of "dwelling in or with the otherwise" (aka Malinowskian-style fieldwork) that use the body to produce truth claims.

10. The other two were the National Coal Association and the Western Fuels Association. Excerpts from the Brier memo appear in Rampton and Stauber (2001:273); brief descriptions of ICE ads can be found in Ward (1991). For more on corporate sponsorship of climate change "denial campaigns," see Mooney (2005) and Oreskes and Conway (2010).

11. Figures are from the April 2016 quarterly market research report issued by Supplier Relations US (2016).

12. For an attempt to sketch the history of the circulation of the term *sound science* in the United States, see Mooney (2005:66).

13. There are also intermediary positions. Steven Pinker, a psychologist and proponent of evolution, has argued for a more nuanced view of creationist arguments, some of which he believes may not be antagonistic to science: "Instead of young-earth creationism, which can be laughed out of the room, intelligent design creationism has a few scientists who are not crackpots defending it" (Mooney 2005:171).

14. For a popular introduction (in German) to the phenomenon of *Bio-wetter* that includes coverage of medical meteorology and *Klimatherapie* ("climate therapy"), see Haltmeier (2002).

15. The backyard weather station has occupied center stage in the melodrama that sometimes passes for debate in the United States, with Anthony Watts, a former TV

weatherman, founding SurfaceStations.org, a website that urged people to post photographs of poorly sited stations in the U.S. Historical Climatology Network (USHCN) as a way of bolstering his contention that climate change models rely on erroneous data (see Revkin 2010). ("Poorly sited" in this context referred to temperature gauges located near air-conditioning units and the like.) The project received so much attention that scientists undertook their own studies of the USHCN to examine and ultimately refute these conclusions (Menne, Williams, and Palecki 2010).

16. My thanks to Andrew Palmer for pushing this point.

17. For an introduction to these and other U.S.-based citizen science projects, see Bowser and Shanley (2013).

18. I am grateful to Hugh Gusterson for calling attention to the relevance of Wynne's work to this argument.

19. As subsequently documented in publications such as Eileen Welsome's *The Plutonium Files: America's Secret Medical Experiments in the Cold War* (1999).

20. See Patrick Hill, "A Photography Based Proof Why We Most Definitely Did Land on the Moon," January 19, 2013, http://fstoppers.com/did-government-fake-landing -moon-photography-video-tricks, accessed April 29, 2016.

21. For two rather different ways of making an ethnographic case that ordinary people theorize every bit as much as experts, see Martin et al. (1997) and Weston (1996).

22. For an overview of ecologically oriented citizen science, see Dickinson et al. (2012).

23. This is not to say, of course, that efforts to communicate the results of the latest Big Science studies on climate change are not also critically important, even as they tend to be circumscribed by a politics of fear. Exemplary publications in this vein might include David Archer's *The Long Thaw: How Humans Are Changing the Next 100,000 Years of Earth's Climate* (2010), Michael E. Mann and Lee Kump's *Dire Predictions: Understanding Global Warming* (2008), and Fred Pearce's clear explanation of the particular threat posed by tipping points in *With Speed and Violence: Why Scientists Fear Tipping Points in Climate Change* (2008).

24. On the way that nuclear technologies work to estrange people from their own senses, see Masco (2006:28).

25. The campaign's website, since put into hibernation, was www.thesweatuation. com, accessed October 30, 2015.

26. For a description of Galaxy Zoo (and an invitation to participate in other Zooniverse projects), see the website at www.galaxyzoo.org, accessed April 29, 2016.

CHAPTER 4: THE GREATEST SHOW ON PARCHED EARTH

1. The India Meteorological Department maintains five years of district-level rainfall averages on its Customized Rainfall Information System website at http://hydro.imd .gov.in/hydrometweb/ (accessed April 30, 2016).

2. Originally called the Grand Venezia, the name became Anglicized en route to the Soft Launch, presumably for ease of apprehension in a country where familiarity with English readily trumps familiarity with Italian.

3. Here and throughout, unattributed promotional quotations come from the opening presentations at the Grand Venice Grand Preview Soft Launch.

4. With compliments and apologies to Shakespeare (*Henry V*).

5. The subsidiary centrally involved with this particular project, Bhasin Infotech & Infrastructure Pvt. Ltd., was registered in 2006. Its name has appeared on a succession of signs affixed to the site, the earliest bent and rusting after an apparent altercation with some form of mechanized transport. In 2011 the company listed two active directors: Satinder Singh Bhasin (appointed 2006) and Mohinder Singh Ahluwalia (appointed 2011).

6. As described on the now defunct developer's website at http://www.ecovillage4 .com/features.html (accessed December 22, 2014). Following an influx of feng shui manuals into India at the turn of the twenty-first century, it became popular to amalgamate elements of feng shui with *vaastu shastra*, guidelines for building layout and construction inspired by Vedic texts.

7. Shortly after the Soft Launch, for instance, in January 2015, the mall staged "A Gondola Date with Bollywood," a chance to sing along with the cast of *Tevar*, a film then on the verge of release.

8. Just two of many possible examples, in this case taken from advertisements in the entertainment section of the *Hindustan Times* on December 25, 2013.

9. TDS levels in various sectors of Noida registered from 700 to 2,200 mg/liter, with 500 mg/liter widely used globally as the upper limit for TDS in municipal water supplies (see Srivastava 2015).

10. View the summary of the TERI report, "Yamuna, the Poisoned River," January 31, 2012, http://www.teriin.org/index.php?option=com_ongoing&task=about_project &pcode=2008EE06 (accessed April 30, 2016).

11. Excerpt from the text of a quarter-page ad published in the *Hindustan Times*, August 20, 2013, 17.

12. See, for example, the op-ed in the *Financial Times* by Gurcharan Das (2014), who notes the Mars mission critics' call for "clean water and toilets," then goes on to argue that nation-building is not reducible to utilitarian project-building, however worthy.

13. That is to say, the first millennium BCE, when the philosophical debates in these Vedic texts were composed.

14. For a sense of how the world-traveling form of the shopping mall might shape up differently in another part of the Global South, even as it becomes inflected by boosterism, see Arlene Dávila's *El Mall* (2016).

15. Keeping in mind, as Paige West (2006:236–37) points out, that "to talk about anything through the language of scarcity is to bring it into a commoditized psychic landscape. If an object or thing is seen as less readily available, it will be put into equivalence with objects or things of great value."

16. The term *mafia* in the Indian context does not necessarily refer to organized crime as such, although it often applies to entities that enjoy a quasi-monopoly, which allows them to engage in activities that shade over into illegality or impropriety. A good example of the term's expansiveness, industry-specific character, and association

with unsavory activities would be its use in the following headline: "Liquor Mafia Use Temple's Loudspeaker to Announce Discount" (HT Correspondent 2014a).

17. Also sometimes rendered as Sidi Saiyyed, Sidi Saiyed, Sidi Sayed, or Sidi Sayeed.

18. Not incidentally, Davis's analysis builds upon Seibert's (1993) account of the abstraction of nature via televised images in nature shows. For an intriguing attempt to create a genealogy that pulls together the production of spectacle, on the one hand, and the production of Nature, on the other, see Igoe (2013). On the historical emergence of for-profit quasi-public amusements in a U.S. context, see Judith Adams (1991) and Nasaw (1993). On the extension of Disney-inspired theme park motifs to other forms of infrastructure and material culture such as malls, see Sorkin (1992).

19. For a closely observed account of the cultural productions and social struggles entailed in the establishment of a nature reserve, see Walley (2004).

20. For an example of alternative recommendations on Yamuna cleanup from the nonprofit sector, see Ciesielski (2012).

21. For astute critiques of the "Nature as service provider" framework in conservation ecology, see Büscher (2014); Igoe (2013); and Ashley Carse's (2014) analysis of representational politics at the Panama Canal, *Beyond the Big Ditch*.

22. For more vignettes of life along the Yamuna's banks, with comparative if somewhat impressionistic depictions of the colonial and postindependence periods, see Jain (2011).

23. Simply consider the chemical composition of the water used to cool the Fukushima reactors as described in chapter 2. The appearance and turbidity of the water has no bearing on the dangers its radioactivity may pose for organisms that ingest it. As Jennifer Beth Spiegel (2013) emphasizes in her study of water contamination in the aftermath of the Bhopal gas disaster, there is a politics to visibility.

CHAPTER 5: POLITICAL ECOLOGIES OF THE PRECARIOUS

1. A substantively different version of this chapter appeared in 2012 in *Anthropological Quarterly* 85 (2): 429–55.

2. Here I draw upon Seigworth and Gregg's (2010) conceptualization of affect as a phenomenon that traffics in something visceral, an embodied "pre-feeling" that both precedes and exceeds culturally configured emotions. This usage focuses attention on the traces that bodies and other forms of materiality leave upon bodies, in contradistinction to Eugenie Brinkema's (2014) intervention in *The Forms of the Affects*, which seeks to loosen or even dissolve the tethering of affect to embodiment.

3. See Masco's (2010) important argument that climate change has supplemented nuclear war as a category that makes it possible to conceptualize crisis on a planetary scale.

4. This affective dimension distinguishes the embrace of toxicity from the "ugly feelings" that Ngai (2007) associates with late modernity. The feelings Ngai explores— irritation, paranoia, and the like—discourage people from mobilizing politically in part because those feelings develop noncathartically, without attachment to an object, whereas the visceral embrace of toxicity has developed historically in and through its

objects, which include particular technologies such as the automobile but also extend to notional characters such as "the environment."

5. For an overview of the extensive literature on post-Fordism, including key points of contention, see Amin (1994). On the decline of manufacturing in what would come to be called postindustrial economies, it is worth reading Bluestone and Harrison's 1984 classic, *The Deindustrialization of America*, alongside later reflections on the significance of this trend, such as Adler (2001); Cowie and Heathcott (2003); Elam (1994); and High and Lewis (2007). Hothi's (2005) account of manufacturing decline in Britain uses the automotive industry as its test case.

6. For insightful discussions of how flexibility became a late twentieth-century watchword that permeated arenas as seemingly diverse as global trade, workplace discipline, and conceptions of bodily immunity, see Martin (1995) and Vallas (1999).

7. Some authors have emphasized continuities between Fordist and earlier forms of production (Norcliffe 1997, Wilson 1995), while others have argued that post-Fordism represents a kind of neo-Fordism because it is not sufficiently distinctive (Wood 1993) and questioned the coherence of the construct of Fordism altogether (Foster 1988). Peláez and Holloway (1990) see post-Fordist theory as a revival of earlier forms of technological determinism that leaves little place for social struggle.

8. See, for instance, the language of flexibility mechanisms in the 1997 Kyoto Protocol to the United Nations Framework Convention on Climate Change, http://unfccc .int/resource/docs/convkp/kpeng.html, accessed April 14, 2016. Flexibility also featured prominently in the Flexible Specialization (neo-Smithian) approach to theorizing post-Fordism, which identified a historical shift from mass production to flexible specialization that generated profits through customization rather than high-volume production of nearly identical goods (Vallas 1999).

9. For critical perspectives on apocalyptic thought, see Boyer (1992); O'Leary (1994); T. Robbins and Palmer (1997); and Stewart and Harding (1999). Morton (2013a:6–7) goes so far as to identify "the strongly held belief that the world is about to end 'unless we act now'" as "paradoxically one of the most powerful factors that inhibit a full engagement with our ecological coexistence here on Earth."

10. At the same time, this chapter bears on the problem of denial, insofar as an exploration of the relationship of affect and embodiment to relations of production shows why calls for "ecological revolution" (e.g., Foster, Clark, and York 2010) must confront more than ideologically framed "strategies of denial," however institutionalized those strategies might be.

11. "Mutant ecologies," again, is Joseph Masco's (2006) term to describe the broader ecological effects of aboveground atomic testing in particular and the knock-on effects of research into nuclear physics more generally.

12. As Foster (1988) and McIntosh (2006) have emphasized, Henry Ford's public relations triumphs should not be allowed to obscure the precarity of employment even during the heyday of Fordism. Ford himself fired thousands of workers in order to underwrite an offer of a "depression-beating wage" to his remaining employees. On Ford's labor politics and the introduction of the Five-Dollar Day, see his own account (Ford 1923), as well as May (1982); Meyer (1981); and S. Watts (2006).

13. For an example of this sort of exposé, see R. Smith and Lourie (2009).

14. Predictions also underscored the association of the automobile with futurity, from the once common anticipation that everyone would someday own a flying car, to ad campaigns like the one for the Cadillac XTS that proclaimed, "Predictions seem frivolous when you've ALREADY SEEN THE FUTURE" (as featured in the technology magazine *Wired* [2013]). See Nuttall (2011) and "What Happened to the Flying Car?" (2012).

15. Sperling and Gordon's (2009) notion of "driving toward sustainability" offers a case in point. On the viability of recycling carbon dioxide, a major greenhouse gas, back into liquid fuels, see Ampelli et al. (2011). For a policy-oriented overview of alternative automotive technologies, see Toro et al. (2010).

16. To characterize the automobile as a pedagogical device is to add another valence to the suggestive discussions in Lipset and Handler (2014) of how vehicles can become culturally/historically/metaphorically implicated in changing constructions of moral personhood. An understanding of the materiality through which such pedagogies have emerged historically in places such as the United States might also argue for extending Urry's (2004) politicized concept of *automobility* to embrace chemical synthesis.

17. For example, the Yogacara school within the Mahayana lineage.

18. For many, but not, significantly, for all. Despite the best efforts of carmakers to maintain sales, a generational shift may be emerging. Some young people in Japan, a country with extensive train networks, have come to feel that owning a car is "not cool" (Edahiro 2010). Their primary affective attachment to a technology is to the mobile phone, the one thing they cannot imagine giving up. With the rise of the sharing economy, young people in Europe and the United States have also begun to discuss the "art of living car-lessly" (Margolis 2016). Reasons advanced to explain the falloff in driving among the youngest eligible age cohort include busyness, Internet use, and concern for "the environment" (Sivak and Shoettle 2011).

19. For more on the (post)colonial politics of dirt, see Burke (1996) and McClintock (1995). While an analysis of the relationship between the postcolonial politics of dirt, on the one hand, and debates about pollution or environmental degradation in the postcolony, on the other, lies beyond the scope of this chapter, such a topic would clearly fall within the purview of political ecologies of the precarious as I elaborate the concept here.

20. The Noida Toll Bridge Company Ltd., which operates the flyway, lists shares on stock exchanges in Mumbai, Kanpur, and London. On the exponential growth of car ownership in Delhi, see Narain and Krupnick (2007:10).

21. On the historical reception of advertising billboards in India since the 1960s, when families made special trips to see them and advertisers yoked their products to nationalist dreams, see Patel (2012).

22. On the Singur struggle, see Majumder (2010).

23. For more background on the Nano and how it has figured in public debate, see HT Correspondent (2011); Plowright (2014); "Tata Nano's Nov. Sales" (2010); and Vats and Toms (2011).

24. Should the deterioration of ecosystems strike you as anything other than obvi-

ous, consider just two developments: (1) a 52 percent decline in wildlife populations in the exceedingly short span of four decades (World Wildlife Fund 2014), accompanied by (2) a precipitous rise in levels of atmospheric carbon dioxide that may indicate the biosphere has begun to reach its limits in terms of its ability to absorb emissions from burning fossil fuels through ocean acidification and other processes (World Meteorological Organization 2014).

25. For meditations on the question of whether capitalist growth can be sustained *as* growth and, depending on the answer, what would need to change, see Brennan (2002); Dale, Mathai, and Puppim de Oliveira (2016); Hawken, Lovins, and Lovins (2008); and Porritt (2007).

26. On the concept of toxic suffering, see Auyero and Swistun (2009). For a sense of the range of the growing literature on indigenous knowledge, particularly vis-à-vis environmentalism, see Aikenhead and Ogawa (2007); Alfred (2005); Cajete (1999); Dei, Rosenberg, and Hall (2000); Kimmerer (2013); Peat (2002); Prober, O'Connor, and Walsh (2011); and Wildcat (2009). Agrawal (2002) called attention, early on, to the political negotiations embedded in indigenous knowledge claims and the complexity of how these claims become authorized. Gordon and Krech (2014) insightfully approach the mapping of "indigenous" onto "knowledge" as the strategic product of a long history of colonization and resistance.

27. For more on these specific designs, see "Borrowing from Nature" (2007); Goldfarb (2014); and Mole (2014).

28. On the financialization of "nature" through chemical synthesis, see N. Smith (2006). On cradle-to-cradle (c2c) design, see McDonough and Braungart (2002).

REFERENCES

"1.1 Trillion Becquerels of Radioactivity Leak During Fukushima Cleanup." 2014. *Asahi Shimbun*, July 24.

Abraham, Itty. 2012. "Geopolitics and Biopolitics in India's High Natural Background Radiation Zone." *Science, Technology and Society* 17 (1): 105–22.

Abrams, David. 1997. *The Spell of the Sensuous: Perception and Language in a More-Than-Human World*. New York: Vintage.

Ackerman, Bryon. 2010. "Oneidas to End Cattle, Crops Farming." *Utica Observer-Dispatch*, November 11.

Adams, Jim. 2004. "Oneida Farm Fosters Culture and Profit." *Indian Country Today*, June 9, B1–B2.

Adams, Judith. 1991. *The American Amusement Park Industry: A History of Technology and Thrills*. Boston: Twayne.

Adler, William M. 2001. *Mollie's Job: A Story of Life and Work on the Global Assembly Line*. New York: Simon and Schuster.

Agarwal, Bina. 1992. "The Gender and Environment Debate: Lessons from India." *Feminist Studies* 18 (1): 119–58.

Agrawal, Arun. 2002. "Indigenous Knowledge and the Politics of Classification." *International Social Science Journal* 54 (173): 287–97.

———. 2005. *Environmentality: Technologies of Government and the Making of Subjects*. Durham, NC: Duke University Press.

Ahmed, Sara. 2008. "Imaginary Prohibitions: Some Preliminary Remarks on the Founding Gestures of the New Materialism." *European Journal of Women's Studies* 15:23–39.

Aikenhead, Glen S., and Masakata Ogawa. 2007. "Indigenous Knowledge and Science Revisited." *Cultural Studies of Science Education* 2:539–620.

Alexy, Allison, and Richard Ronald. 2011. "Introduction: Continuity and Change in Japanese Homes and Families." In *Home and Family in Japan: Continuity and Transformation*, edited by Allison Alexy and Richard Ronald, 1–24. London: Routledge.

Alfred, Taiaiake. 2005. *Wasáse: Indigenous Pathways of Action and Freedom*. Toronto: University of Toronto Press.

"Allahabad Farmers Take Out Rally to Spread River Pollution Awareness." 2011.

DailyIndia.com, April 2. Accessed February 21, 2012. http://www/dailyindia.com /show/432946.php.

Allewaert, Monique. 2013. *Ariel's Ecology: Plantations, Personhood, and Colonialism in the American Tropics*. Minneapolis: University of Minnesota Press.

Allison, Anne. 2006. *Millennial Monsters: Japanese Toys and the Global Imagination*. Berkeley: University of California Press.

———. 2013. *Precarious Japan*. Durham, NC: Duke University Press.

Altman, Lawrence K. 1987. *Who Goes First? The Story of Self-Experimentation in Medicine*. New York: Random House.

Amin, Ash, ed. 1994. *Post-Fordism: A Reader*. Hoboken, NJ: Blackwell.

Ampelli, Claudio, Rosalba Passalacqua, Chiara Genovese, Siglinda Perathoner, and Gabriele Centi. 2011. "A Novel Photo-electrochemical Approach for the Chemical Recycling of Carbon Dioxide to Fuels." *Chemical Engineering Transactions* 25: 683–88.

Anand, Nikhil. 2011. "Pressure: The PoliTechnics of Water Supply in Mumbai." *Cultural Anthropology* 26 (4): 542–64.

Anand, Panini. 2013. "A Few Rivers Dredged Dry: There's Gold in That Sand, Hence the Loot." *Outlook*, August 19, 28.

Ansell, Christopher, and David Vogel. 2006. *What's the Beef? The Contested Governance of European Food Safety*. Cambridge, MA: MIT Press.

Anzaldúa, Gloria. 2012. *Borderlands/La Frontera: The New Mestiza*. 4th ed. San Francisco: Aunt Lute Books.

Aoki, Miki, Tamiyuki Kihara, and Toshio Tada. 2013. "Crooked Cleanup (1): Radioactive Waste Dumped into Rivers during Decontamination Work in Fukushima." *Asahi Shimbun*, January 4.

Aoki, Miki, and Jun Sato. 2013. "Crooked Cleanup (2): Some Decontamination Workers Sorry for Following Orders." *Asahi Shimbun*, January 4.

Archer, David. 2010. *The Long Thaw: How Humans Are Changing the Next 100,000 Years of Earth's Climate*. Princeton, NJ: Princeton University Press.

Armstrong, Fanny. 2009. *The Age of Stupid*. London: Spanner Films.

Asai, Fumikazu. 2012. "Tests Show Normal Rate of Thyroid Cysts in Fukushima Children." *Asahi Shimbun*, December 1.

Ashenburg, Katherine. 2008. *The Dirt on Clean: An Unsanitized History*. New York: North Point Press.

Auyero, Javier, and Débora Alejandra Swistun. 2009. *Flammable: Environmental Suffering in an Argentine Shantytown*. New York: Oxford University Press.

Babu, Ramesh. 2013. "'Kerala Durga' Wages a Lonely Battle against Sand Mafia." *Hindustan Times*, August 9, 13.

Bahadur, Sanjay. 2008. *The Sound of Water*. New Delhi: IndiaInk/Roli Books.

Bakhtin, Mikhail. 1984. *Rabelais and His World*. Translated by Hélène Iswolsky. Bloomington: Indiana University Press.

Balmaseda, Magdalena A., Kevin E. Trenberth, and Erland Källén. 2013. "Distinctive Climate Signals in Reanalysis of Global Ocean Heat Content." *Geophysical Research Letters* 40:1–6.

Beck, Ulrich. 1992. *Risk Society: Towards a New Modernity*. Thousand Oaks, CA: Sage.

"Beijing Warns on Pollution Threat." 2011. *Financial Times*, March 1, 2.

Belson, Ken. 2011. "Japanese Find Radioactivity on Their Own." *New York Times*, July 31.

Benjamin, Walter. 2003. "On Some Motifs in Baudelaire." In *Walter Benjamin: Selected Writings*, vol. 4, 313–55. Cambridge, MA: Harvard University Press.

Bennett, Jane. 2010. *Vibrant Matter: A Political Ecology of Things*. Durham, NC: Duke University Press.

Bennett, Jane, and Klaus K. Loenhart. 2011. "Vibrant Matter, Zero Landscape: An Interview with Jane Bennett." *Eurozine*, October 19, 1–7.

Berkes, Fikret. 2012. *Sacred Ecology*. 3rd ed. New York: Routledge.

Berlant, Lauren, ed. 2000. *Intimacy*. Chicago: University of Chicago Press.

———. 2007. "Nearly Utopian, Nearly Normal: Post-Fordist Affect in *La Promesse* and *Rosetta*." *Public Culture* 19 (2): 272–301.

———. 2016. "Living in Ellipsis: On Biopolitics and the Attachment to Life." Talk delivered as part of The Intimacy Lectures series at the University of Virginia, Charlottesville, VA, January 28.

Bestor, Theodore C. 2013. "Disasters, Natural and Unnatural: Reflections on March 11, 2011, and Its Aftermath." *Journal of Asian Studies* 72 (4): 763–82.

Bhabha, Homi K. 1994. *The Location of Culture*. New York: Routledge.

Bhadra, Monamie. 2013. "Disaster Scripting in India's Nuclear Energy Landscape." Unpublished manuscript circulated at the STS Forum on the 2011 Fukushima/East Japan Disaster, University of California at Berkeley, May 11–14.

Bird, Winifred. 2012. "Fukushima Nuclear Cleanup Could Create Its Own Environmental Disaster." *Guardian*, January 9.

———. 2013. "Fukushima Radiation Threatens to Wreak Woodland Havoc." *Japan Times*, February 17.

Birmingham, Lucy, and David McNeill. 2012. *Strong in the Rain: Surviving Japan's Earthquake, Tsunami, and Fukushima Nuclear Disaster*. New York: Palgrave Macmillan.

Bluestone, Barry, and Bennett Harrison. 1984. *The Deindustrialization of America: Plant Closings, Community Abandonment, and the Dismantling of Basic Industry*. New York: Basic Books.

Blum, Elizabeth D. 2011. *Love Canal Revisited: Race, Class, and Gender in Environmental Activism*. Lawrence: University Press of Kansas.

"Bomb Survivor Doctor Continues to Speak Up about Significance of Internal Exposure." 2012. *Mainichi Daily News*, January 23.

"Borrowing from Nature." 2007. *Economist, Technology Quarterly*, September 8, 30–32.

Bosker, Bianca. 2013. *Original Copies: Architectural Mimicry in Contemporary China*. Honolulu: University of Hawaii Press.

Boston Women's Health Book Collective. 2005. *Our Bodies, Ourselves: A New Edition for a New Era*. New York: Touchstone Books.

Bowser, Anne, and Lea Shanley. 2013. *New Visions in Citizen Science*. Case Study Series 3. Washington, DC: Woodrow Wilson Center.

Boyer, Paul S. 1992. *When Time Shall Be No More: Prophecy Belief in Modern American Culture*. Cambridge, MA: Harvard University Press.

Brahinsky, Josh. 2012. "Pentecostal Body Logics: Cultivating a Modern Sensorium." *Cultural Anthropology* 27 (2): 215–38.

Brennan, Teresa. 2002. *Globalization and Its Terrors*. New York: Routledge.

Brinkema, Eugenie. 2014. *The Forms of the Affects*. Durham, NC: Duke University Press.

Brown, Jane. 2011. *Lancelot "Capability" Brown: The Omnipotent Magician, 1716–1783*. London: Random House UK.

Brown, Wendy. 1995. *States of Injury: Power and Freedom in Late Modernity*. Princeton, NJ: Princeton University Press.

Brownlee, Christen. 2004. "DNA Bar Codes: Life under the Scanner." *Science News* 166 (23): 360–61.

Brulle, Robert J. 2013. "Institutionalizing Delay: Foundation Funding and the Creation of U.S. Climate Change Counter-Movement Organizations." *Climatic Change* 122 (4): 681–94. doi: 10.1007/s10584-013-1018-7.

"The Bubble Car Is Back." 2010. *Economist*, September 30, 86–87.

Bullard, Robert D. 2005. *The Quest for Environmental Justice: Human Rights and the Politics of Pollution*. San Francisco: Sierra Books.

Burke, Timothy. 1996. *Lifebuoy Men, Lux Women: Commodification, Consumption, and Cleanliness in Modern Zimbabwe*. Durham, NC: Duke University Press.

Burrett, Tina, and Christopher Simons. 2011. "Nuclear Debate Intensifies Post-Fukushima." *New Internationalist* 442 (May): 12–13.

Busch, Akiko. 2013. *The Incidental Steward: Reflections on Citizen Science*. New Haven, CT: Yale University Press.

Büscher, Bram E. 2014. "Nature on the Move I: The Value and Circulation of Liquid Nature and the Emergence of Fictitious Conservation." In *Nature™ Inc.: Environmental Conservation in the Neoliberal Age*, edited by Bram E. Büscher, Wolfram Dressler, and Robert Fletcher, 183–201. Tucson: University of Arizona Press.

Cajete, Gregory. 1999. *Native Science: Natural Laws of Interdependence*. Santa Fe, NM: Clear Light Publishers.

Callison, Candis. 2014. *How Climate Change Comes to Matter: The Communal Life of Facts*. Durham, NC: Duke University Press.

Carpenter, Roger M. 2004. *The Renewed, the Destroyed, and the Remade: The Three Thought Worlds of the Huron and the Iroquois, 1609–1650*. East Lansing: Michigan State University Press.

Carse, Ashley. 2014. *Beyond the Big Ditch: Politics, Ecology, and Infrastructure at the Panama Canal*. Cambridge, MA: MIT Press.

Casacuberta, N., P. Masqué, J. Garcia-Orellana, R. Garcia-Tenorio, and K. O. Buesseler. 2013. "90Sr and 89Sr in Seawater Off Japan as a Consequence of the Fukushima Dai-ichi Nuclear Accident." *Biogeosciences Discuss* 10:2039–67.

Cattelino, Jessica R. 2008. *High Stakes: Florida Seminole Gaming and Sovereignty.* Durham, NC: Duke University Press.

Ceballos, Gerardo, Paul R. Ehrlich, Anthony D. Barnosky, Andrés García, Robert M. Pringle, and Todd M. Palmer. 2015. "Accelerated Modern Human-Induced Species Losses: Entering the Sixth Mass Extinction." *Science Advances* 1 (5). doi: 10.1126/sciadv.1400253.

Centre for Science and Environment (CSE). 2005. *A Wastewater Recycling Manual for Urban Areas with Case Studies.* New Delhi: Centre for Science and Environment.

———. 2009. "Why CSE Says 'No' to Cars." Centre for Science and Environment, March 13. Accessed May 3, 2016. www.cseindia.org/node/85.

Cevallos, Marissa. 2011. "Meat Contaminated with Resistant Bacteria." *Los Angeles Times*, April 15.

Chakravartty, Anupam. 2014. "Beachside Troubles." *Down to Earth*, February 28, 16–17.

Chatterjee, Partha. 1993. *Nationalist Thought and the Colonial World: A Derivative Discourse.* Minneapolis: University of Minnesota Press.

Chen, Mel Y. 2012. *Animacies: Biopolitics, Racial Mattering, and Queer Affect.* Durham, NC: Duke University Press.

"Chipped Kids." 2005. PC *Magazine*, April 12, 20.

Ciesielski, Linda. 2012. "The Yamuna River Basin: An Alternative Action Plan." MIT MISTI-India Program/PEACE Institute Charitable Trust. http://www.peaceinst.org/publication/reports/iedp%20final%20report/Yamuna%20River%20Basin%20-%20An%20Alternative%20Action%20Plan.pdf.

Cobb, Tanya Denckla. 2011. *Reclaiming Our Food: How the Grassroots Food Movement Is Changing the Way We Eat.* North Adams, MA: Storey.

Coole, Diana, and Samantha Frost, eds. 2010. *New Materialisms: Ontology, Agency, and Politics.* Durham, NC: Duke University Press.

Cooper, Chris, and Kiyotaka Matsuda. 2013. "Tokyo Prepares for a Once-in-200-Year Flood to Top Sandy." *Bloomberg*, May 31.

Corburn, Jason. 2005. *Street Science: Community Knowledge and Environmental Health Justice.* Cambridge, MA: MIT Press.

Counihan, Carole M. 1999. *The Anthropology of Food and Body: Gender, Meaning, and Power.* New York: Routledge.

Counihan, Carole, and Penny van Esterik, eds. 2007. *Food and Culture: A Reader.* New York: Routledge.

Cowie, Jefferson, and Joseph Heathcott, eds. 2003. *Beyond the Ruins: The Meanings of Deindustrialization.* Ithaca, NY: ILR Press.

Cruikshank, Julie. 2010. *Do Glaciers Listen? Local Knowledge, Colonial Encounters, and Social Imagination.* Vancouver: University of British Columbia Press.

Curie, Marie. 1923. *Pierre Curie.* Translated by Charlotte and Vernon Kellogg. New York: Macmillan.

Dale, Gareth, Manu V. Mathai, and Jose A. Puppim de Oliveira, eds. 2016. *Green Growth: Ideology, Political Economy, and the Alternatives.* London: Zed Books.

Das, Gurcharan. 2014. "The Mars Mission Benefits India as Much as Clean Water." *Financial Times*, September 28.

Das, Veena. 1995. *Critical Events: An Anthropological Perspective on Contemporary India*. Delhi: Oxford University Press.

Dávila, Arlene. 2016. *El Mall: The Spatial and Class Politics of Shopping Malls in Latin America*. Berkeley: University of California Press.

Davis, Susan G. 1997. *Spectacular Nature: Corporate Culture and the Sea World Experience*. Berkeley: University of California Press.

Dawdy, Shannon Lee. 2010. "Clockpunk Anthropology and the Ruins of Modernity." *Current Anthropology* 51 (6): 761–93.

Debord, Guy. 1995. *The Society of the Spectacle*. New York: Zone Books.

Dei, George J. Sefa, Dorothy Goldin Rosenberg, and Budd L. Hall, eds. 2000. *Indigenous Knowledge in Global Contexts: Multiple Readings of Our Worlds*. Toronto: University of Toronto Press.

Descola, Philippe. 2013. *The Ecology of Others*. Translated by Geneviève Godbout and Benjamin P. Luley. Chicago: Prickly Paradigm Press.

DesMarais, Christina. 2013. "US Judge Rules for Texas School District in RFID Tracking Case." *PC World*, January 13.

Dickens, Charles. 1839. *The Life and Adventures of Nicholas Nickleby*. London: Chapman and Hall.

———. 1854. *Hard Times: A Novel*. New York: Harper and Brothers.

Dickinson, Janis L., Jennifer Shirk, David Bonter, Rick Bonney, Rhiannon L. Crain, Jason Martin, Tina Phillips, and Karen Purcell. 2012. "The Current State of Citizen Science as a Tool for Ecological Research and Public Engagement." *Frontiers in Ecology and the Environment* 10 (6): 291–97.

Dodson, Lisa. 2009. *The Moral Underground: How Ordinary Americans Subvert an Unfair Economy*. New York: New Press.

Doherty, Peter. 2013. *Their Fate Is Our Fate: How Birds Foretell Threats to Our Health and Our World*. New York: The Experiment.

Dolphijn, Rick, and Iris van der Tuin. 2012. *New Materialism: Interviews and Cartographies*. Ann Arbor: Open Humanities Press.

Dupont, Daniel G. 2003. "Food Fears: The Threat of Agricultural Terrorism Spurs Calls for More Vigilance." *Scientific American* 289 (4): 20–22.

Edahiro, Junko. 2010. "Letter from Japan." *Resurgence* 262:16–17.

Edmond, Gary, and David Mercer. 1998. "Trashing 'Junk Science.'" *Stanford Technology Law Review* 3:1–31.

Elam, Mark. 1994. "Puzzling Out the Post-Fordist Debate." In *Post-Fordism: A Reader*, edited by Ash Amin, 43–70. Cambridge, MA: Blackwell.

Elkins, James. 1996. *The Poetics of Perspective*. Ithaca, NY: Cornell University Press.

Emery, Theo. 2006. "Plan for Tracking Animals Meets Farmers' Resistance." *New York Times*, December 13.

Engels, Friedrich. 1892. *The Condition of the Working Class in England in 1844*. London: Swan Sonnenschein.

Ewen, Stuart. 1998. *PR! A Social History of Spin*. New York: Basic Books.

"Eye Openers." 2011. *Down to Earth*, October 1–15, 72.

Fackler, Martin. 2005. "Japan Partly Lifts Ban on Imports of U.S. Beef, Easing Trade Dispute." *New York Times*, December 12.

Fedoruk, Marion J., and Brent D. Kerger. 2003. "Measurement of Volatile Organic Compounds inside Automobiles." *Journal of Exposure Analysis and Environmental Epidemiology* 13:31–41.

Ferry, Elizabeth Emma, and Mandana E. Limbert. 2006. *Timely Assets: The Politics of Resources and Their Temporalities*. Santa Fe, NM: School for Advanced Research Press.

Finan, Timothy. 2009. "Storm Warnings: The Role of Anthropology in Adapting to Sea-Level Rise in Southwestern Bangladesh." In *Anthropology and Climate Change: From Encounters to Actions*, edited by Susan A. Crate and Mark Nuttall, 175–85. New York: Routledge.

Ford, Henry. 1923. *My Life and Work*, with Samuel Crowther. London: Heinemann.

"Ford Motor Company's River Rouge Truck Plant." 2010. *Greenroofs*. http://www .greenroofs.com/projects/pview.php?id=12.

Fortun, Kim. 2012. "Ethnography in Late Industrialism." *Cultural Anthropology* 27 (3): 446–64.

Foster, John Bellamy. 1988. "The Fetish of Fordism." *Monthly Review* 39 (10): 14–33.

Foster, John Bellamy, Brett Clark, and Richard York. 2010. *The Ecological Rift: Capitalism's War on the Earth*. New York: Monthly Review Press.

Foucault, Michel. 1978. *The History of Sexuality*. Vol. 1. Translated by Robert Hurley. New York: Random House.

Fujioka, Chisa. 2011. "Japan Priest Speaks Out on Spiritual Toll of Nuclear Crisis." *Reuters*, June 9.

Fukushima Nuclear Accident Independent Investigation Commission. 2012. *The Official Report of the Fukushima Nuclear Accident Independent Investigation Commission*. Tokyo: The National Diet of Japan. https://www.nirs.org/fukushima/naiic _report.pdf.

"Fukushima Plant 'Set to Collapse' from Another Quake or Tsunami." 2013. *The Australian*, March 9.

Gabrys, Jennifer, Gay Hawkins, and Mike Michael, eds. 2013. *Accumulation: The Material Politics of Plastic*. New York: Routledge.

Gal, Ofer, and Raz Chen-Morris. 2010. "Empiricism without the Senses: How the Instrument Replaced the Eye." In *The Body as Object and Instrument of Knowledge: Embodied Empiricism in Early Modern Science*, edited by Charles T. Wolfe and Ofer Gal, 121–48. London: Springer.

Gambino, Megan. 2009. "Cracking the Code: Every Form of Life Has a Unique DNA Barcode. The Trick Is Finding It." *Smithsonian*, August, 23.

Gates, Sara. 2013. "Passwords in Tattoos and Pills? Motorola Announces Plans for Wearable Tech." *Huffington Post*, June 3.

Ghertner, D. Asher. 2011. "Green Evictions: Environmental Discourses of a 'Slum-Free' Delhi." In *Global Political Ecology*, edited by Richard Peet, Paul Robbins, and Michael Watts, 145–65. New York: Routledge.

Goldfarb, Ben. 2014. "The Biomimicrist: Bruce Kania Thinks He Can Save Our Water with Artificial Wetlands." *High Country News*, November 24, 7–9.

Gordon, David M., and Shepard Krech III, eds. 2014. *Indigenous Knowledge and the Environment in Africa and North America*. Athens: Ohio University Press.

Greenough, Paul. 2012. "Bio-Ironies of the Fractured Forest: India's Tiger Reserves." In *India's Environmental History: From Ancient Times to the Colonial Period*, vol. 2, edited by Mahesh Rangarajan and K. Sivaramakrishnan, 316–56. New Delhi: Permanent Black.

Grossman, Wendy M. 2004. "Missing Movement: Mad Cow Reveals the Limits of Animal Tracing." *Scientific American*, April, 26–27.

Guerrera, Francesco. 2009. "Old Bank Axioms Gain New Currency." *Financial Times*, July 7, 10.

Haggerty, Kevin D., and Richard V. Ericson. 2006. *The New Politics of Surveillance and Visibility*. Toronto: University of Toronto Press.

Haldane, J. B. S. 1928. *Possible Worlds and Other Papers*. New York: Harper and Brothers.

Hall, Derek. 2010. "Food with a Visible Face: Traceability and the Public Promotion of Private Governance in the Japanese Food System." *Geoforum* 41 (5): 826–35.

Haltmeier, Hans. 2002. "Frontalangriff auf Leib und Seele: Medizin-Meteorologen erforschen die Abhängigkeit des Menschen von den himmlischen Kräften." *Focus* 47:113–24.

Hansen, James. 2009. *Storms of My Grandchildren: The Truth about the Coming Climate Catastrophe and Our Last Chance to Save Humanity*. New York: Bloomsbury.

Haraway, Donna. 1991. "A Cyborg Manifesto: Science, Technology, and Socialist-Feminism in the Late Twentieth Century." In *Simians, Cyborgs, and Women: The Reinvention of Nature*, 149–81. New York: Routledge.

Harootunian, Harry. 2000. *Overcome by Modernity: History, Culture, and Community in Interwar Japan*. Princeton, NJ: Princeton University Press.

Harrison, Ruth. 1966. *Animal Machines: The New Factory Farming Industry*. New York: Ballantine.

Hawken, Paul, Amory Lovins, and L. Hunter Lovins. 2008. *Natural Capitalism: Creating the Next Industrial Revolution*. Boston: Back Bay Books.

Haworth, Abigail. 2013. "After Fukushima: Families on the Edge of Meltdown." *Guardian*, February 23.

"Heard around the West." 2008. *High Country News*, December 22, 32.

Henare, Amiria, Martin Holbraad, and Sari Wastell. 2007. *Thinking through Things: Theorising Artefacts Ethnographically*. New York: Routledge.

Herper, Matthew. 2009. "Our Germs, Ourselves." *Forbes*, March 30, 70–71.

Herzog, Karen. 2009. "Oneidas Return to Roots in Food Production." *Indian Country Today*, December 9, 8–9.

Hickman, Kent. 2008. "There's Nothing Wonderful about the Nation's Mortgage Crisis." *Seattle Times*, October 10.

Hida, Shuntarō, and Hitomi Kamanaka. 2005. 内部被爆盧の脅威：原爆から劣化ウ

ラン弾まで [*Naibu Hibaku no Kyōi: Genbaku Kara Rekka Urandan Made*]. Tokyo: Chikuma Shobō.

High, Steven, and David W. Lewis. 2007. *Corporate Wasteland: The Landscape and Memory of Deindustrialization*. Ithaca, NY: ILR Press.

Hoeppe, Götz. 2007. *Conversations on the Beach: Fishermen's Knowledge, Metaphor, and Environmental Change in South India*. New York: Berghahn.

Hothi, Nicola R. 2005. *Globalisation and Manufacturing Decline: Aspects of British Industry*. Bury St. Edmonds, UK: Arena Books.

Hounshell, David. 1985. *From the American System to Mass Production, 1800–1932: The Development of Manufacturing Technology in the United States*. Baltimore: Johns Hopkins University Press.

HT Correspondent. 2011. "Tata to Replace Starter in Nanos." *Hindustan Times*, December 27, 1, 21.

———. 2012. "We Missed Opportunity on Nano: Tata." *Hindustan Times*, January 6, 1, 6.

———. 2013a. "Rain Chokes Noida's Drainage System." *Hindustan Times*, August 11, 9.

———. 2013b. "Roads Crumble like Cookies." *Hindustan Times*, July 22, 3.

———. 2013c. "Same Old Rain Story: Waterlogging, Jams." *Hindustan Times*, July 28, 3.

———. 2013d. "Sand Mining Rampant: Government Panel." *Hindustan Times*, August 11, 3.

———. 2013e. "'Separate Potable Water Supply': Checking Misuse." *Hindustan Times*, July 13, 8.

———. 2013f. "Water Refuses to Go Down the Drain." *Hindustan Times*, July 22, 9.

———. 2014a. "Liquor Mafia Use Temple's Loudspeaker to Announce Discount." *Hindustan Times*, December 22, 8.

———. 2014b. "New Year Gift: 100% Ganga Supply in Noida." *Hindustan Times*, December 16, 8.

———. 2014c. "Rain Exposes Ghaziabad Civic Body's Lack of Preparedness." *Hindustan Times*, May 27, 8.

———. 2014d. "₹25,000 Crore to Revive Yamuna, Connect More Areas with Sewer Network." *Hindustan Times*, June 25, 3.

"Huge Leak of Tritium Feared in Fukushima." *Japan Times*, August 3.

Hui, Alexandra. 2012. *The Psychophysical Ear: Musical Experiments, Experimental Sounds, 1840–1910*. Cambridge, MA: MIT Press.

Huizinga, Johan. 1971. *Homo Ludens: A Study of the Play Element in Culture*. Boston: Beacon.

Hulme, Mike. 2009. *Why We Disagree about Climate Change: Understanding Controversy, Inaction, and Opportunity*. Cambridge: Cambridge University Press.

Hutner, Heidi. 2012. "In Japan, a Mothers' Movement against Nuclear Power." *Yes! Magazine*, April 25.

Igoe, Jim. 2013. "Nature on the Move II: Contemplation Becomes Speculation." *New Proposals: Journal of Marxism and Interdisciplinary Inquiry* 6 (1–2): 37–49.

"In Court: Mad Cow Blame." 2005. *Down to Earth* (May 15): 12.

IndusInd Bank. 2014. "Experience Face-to-Face Banking without Going to Your Bank." Mumbai: IndusInd Bank.

Ingold, Tim. 2000. *The Perception of the Environment: Essays on Livelihood, Dwelling, and Skill.* New York: Routledge.

Jain, Sarandha. 2011. *In Search of Yamuna: Reflections on a River Lost.* New Delhi: Vitasta.

Jamieson, Dale. 2014. *Reason in a Dark Time: Why the Struggle against Climate Change Failed—And What It Means for Our Future.* New York: Oxford University Press.

"Japan Nuclear Crisis: Radiation Spike Report 'Mistaken.'" 2011. BBC *News,* March 27.

Jeffrey, Simon. 2011. "Nuclear Boy: Explaining Fukushima with a Cartoon." *Japan Disaster* (blog), *Guardian,* March 24. Accessed May 3, 2016. http://m.guardian .co.uk/world/blog/2011/mar/24/nuclear-boy-fukushima-cartoon?cat=world &type=article.

Jenkins, McKay. 2011. *What's Gotten into Us? Staying Healthy in a Toxic World.* New York: Random House.

Jensen, Casper Brunn, and Atsuro Morita. 2012. "Anthropology as Critique of Reality." HAU: *Journal of Ethnographic Theory* 2 (2): 358–70.

Johnson, T. 2004. "First U.S. Mad-Cow Scare Left Bad Taste in East Asia." *Detroit Free Press,* November 19.

Jones, Jeffrey M. 2010. "In U.S. Many Environmental Issues at 20-Year-Low Concern." *Gallup News,* March 16.

Jopson, Barney. 2014. "First-Moover Advantage in Methane Fight." *Financial Times,* April 9, 1.

Kazin, Michael. 1995. *The Populist Persuasion: An American History.* Ithaca, NY: Cornell University Press.

Kazmin, Amy. 2010. "UN Scientist Hits at 'Skulduggery.'" *Financial Times,* February 4, 6.

Kerr, Alex. 2002. *Dogs and Demons: Tales from the Dark Side of Japan.* New York: Hill and Wang.

Kershaw, Sarah, and Bernard Simon. 2004. "What's a Canadian Cow? Trade Blurred Distinctions." *New York Times,* January 6.

Kihara, Tamiyuki, and Toshio Tada. 2013. "Crooked Cleanup: Decontamination Workers Say Cutting Corners Came Naturally." *Asahi Shimbun,* January 9.

Kimmerer, Robin Wall. 2013. *Braiding Sweetgrass: Indigenous Wisdom, Scientific Knowledge, and the Teachings of Plants.* Minneapolis: Milkweed Editions.

Kittredge, Jack. 2007. "The Truth about the Animal ID Plan." *Mother Earth News,* June/July, 87–93.

Klein, Naomi. 2014. *This Changes Everything: Capitalism vs. the Climate.* New York: Simon and Schuster.

Klinenberg, Eric. 2003. *Heat Wave: A Social Autopsy of Disaster in Chicago.* Chicago: University of Chicago Press.

Knight, Rob. 2015. *Follow Your Gut: The Enormous Impact of Tiny Microbes*. New York: Simon and Schuster.

Knox, Richard. 2011. "'Citizen Scientists' Crowdsource Radiation Measurements in Japan." *Shots* (blog), *National Public Radio*, March 24. http://m.npr.org/story /134823329?url=/blogs/health/2011/03/24/citizen-scientists-crowdsource -radiation-measurements-in-japan.

Kohn, Eduardo. 2013. *How Forests Think: Toward an Anthropology Beyond the Human*. Berkeley: University of California Press.

Koide, Hiroaki, and Yagasaki. 2011. 3・11原発事故を語る [*3.11 Genpatsu Jiko o Kataru*]. Tokyo: Hon no Izumisha.

Kolbert, Elizabeth. 2006. *Field Notes from a Catastrophe: Man, Nature, and Climate Change*. New York: Bloomsbury.

Krauss, Clifford. 2004. "Trade Issues Sour U.S.-Canadian Friendships." *New York Times*, November 14.

Krupar, Shiloh R. 2013. *Hot Spotter's Report: Military Fables of Toxic Waste*. Minneapolis: University of Minnesota Press.

Kuklick, Henrika. 2008. "Fieldworkers and Physiologists." In *Cambridge and the Torres Strait: Centenary Essays on the 1898 Anthropological Expedition*, edited by Anita Herle and Sandra Rouse, 158–80. New York: Cambridge University Press.

Kurtenbach, Elaine. 2014. "Fukushima Farmers Appeal to Tokyo with Live Bull." AP, June 20.

Laclau, Ernesto. 2007. *On Populist Reason*. London: Verso.

Lam, Tong. 2013. *Abandoned Futures: A Journey to the Posthuman World*. Darlington, UK: Carpet Bombing Culture.

Landrigan, Philip J., Babasaheb Sonawane, Donald Mattison, Michael McCally, and Anjali Garg. 2002. "Chemical Contaminants in Breast Milk and Their Impacts on Children's Health: An Overview." *Environmental Health Perspectives* 110 (6): 313–15.

Lane, Carrie. 2011. *A Company of One: Insecurity, Independence, and the New World of White-Collar Unemployment*. Ithaca, NY: ILR Press.

Lansing, J. Stephen. 2007. *Priests and Programmers: Technologies of Power in the Engineered Landscape of Bali*. Princeton, NJ: Princeton University Press.

Latour, Bruno. 1988. *Science in Action: How to Follow Scientists and Engineers through Society*. Cambridge, MA: Harvard University Press.

———. 1993. *The Pasteurization of France*. Translated by Alan Sheridan and John Law. Cambridge, MA: Harvard University Press.

———. 2010. *On the Modern Cult of the Factish Gods*. Durham, NC: Duke University Press.

Lavin, Chad. 2013. *Eating Anxiety: The Perils of Food Politics*. Minneapolis: University of Minnesota Press.

Lemay, Konnie. 2013. "The Water Walkers: Healing the Mighty Mississippi with a Bucket of Water." *Indian Country Today*, June 19, 30–31.

Lemos, Robert. 2004. "RFID Tags Become Hacker Target." CNET, July 29.

Lindsey, Daryl. 2001. "Will Mad Cows Kill the Big Mac?" *Salon*, August 12.

Lipset, David, and Richard Handler, eds. 2014. *Vehicles: Cars, Canoes, and Other Metaphors of Moral Imagination*. New York: Berghahn.

Lochbaum, David, Edwin Lyman, Susan Q. Stranahan, and the Union of Concerned Scientists. 2014. *Fukushima: The Story of a Nuclear Disaster*. New York: New Press.

Lovelock, James. 2006. *The Revenge of Gaia: Earth's Climate Crisis and the Fate of Humanity*. New York: Basic Books.

Lowe, Lisa. 2015. *The Intimacies of Four Continents*. Durham, NC: Duke University Press.

Loy, David. 2010. "Healing Ecology." *Journal of Buddhist Ethics* 17:253–67.

Lucas, Greg. 2005a. "Pupil Radio-Signal Test Stopped, School District Halts Program as Parents Protest Badges." *San Francisco Chronicle*, February 17.

———. 2005b. "Students Kept under Surveillance at School, Some Parents Angry over Radio Device." *San Francisco Chronicle*, February 10.

Luce, Edward. 2015. "The Jesters Shaping American Politics." *Financial Times*, February 9, 7.

Lundstrom, Marjie. 2005. "Electronic Badges for Students Put Parents, Privacy Groups on Edge." *Sacramento Bee*, February 10.

Lutz, Catherine. 2014. "The U.S. Car Colossus." *American Ethnologist* 41 (2): 232–45.

Lyon, David. 2001. *Surveillance Society: Monitoring Everyday Life*. New York: Open University Press.

———, ed. 2006. *Theorizing Surveillance: The Panopticon and Beyond*. Devon, UK: Willan.

Lytton, Timothy D. 2013. *Kosher: Private Regulation in the Age of Industrial Food*. Cambridge, MA: Harvard University Press.

Madrigal, Alexis. 2011. *Powering the Dream: The History and Promise of Green Technology*. Cambridge, MA: Da Capo Press.

Mahr, Kristen. 2011. "In Fukushima City, Decontamination Begins: But What to Do with the Radioactive Waste?" *Time*, August 9.

Majumder, Sarasij. 2010. "The Nano Controversy: Peasant Identities, the Land Question, and Neoliberal Industrialization in Marxist West Bengal, India." *Journal of Emerging Knowledge on Emerging Markets* 2 (1): 41–66.

Malaby, Thomas M. 2009. "Anthropology and Play: The Contours of Playful Experience." *New Literary History* 40:205–18.

Mann, Michael E. 2012. *The Hockey Stick and the Climate Wars: Dispatches from the Front Lines*. New York: Columbia University Press.

Mann, Michael E., and Lee R. Kump. 2008. *Dire Predictions: Understanding Global Warming*. New York: DK.

Manning, Richard. 2014. "Idaho's Sewer System: As Big Ag Flourishes, the Snake River Suffers." *High Country News*, August 4, 10–17.

Marcus, George E., ed. 1999. *Paranoia within Reason: A Casebook on Conspiracy as Explanation*. Chicago: University of Chicago Press.

Margolis, Jonathan. 2016. "Art of Living Car-lessly in the City." *Financial Times*, February 7, 12.

Marks, Jonathan. 2002. *What It Means to Be 98% Chimpanzee: Apes, People, and Their Genes*. Berkeley: University of California Press.

Marres, Noortje. 2012. *Material Participation: Technology, the Environment, and Everyday Publics*. New York: Palgrave Macmillan.

Martin, Emily. 1995. *Flexible Bodies: The Role of Immunity in American Culture from the Days of Polio to the Age of* AIDS. Boston: Beacon.

Martin, Emily, Laury Oaks, Karen-Sue Taussig, and Ariana van der Straten. 1997. "AIDS, Knowledge, and Discrimination in the Inner City: An Anthropological Analysis of the Experiences of Injection Drug Users." In *Cyborgs and Citadels: Anthropological Interventions in Emerging Science and Technologies*, edited by Gary Lee Downey and Joseph Dumit, 49–66. Santa Fe, NM: School for Advanced Research Press.

Marx, Leo. 2000. *The Machine in the Garden: Technology and the Pastoral Ideal in America*. New York: Oxford University Press.

Masco, Joseph. 2006. *The Nuclear Borderlands: The Manhattan Project in Post-Cold War New Mexico*. Princeton, NJ: Princeton University Press.

———. 2010. "Bad Weather: On Planetary Crisis." *Social Studies of Science* 40 (1): 7–40.

———. 2014. "Pre-empting Biosecurity: Threats, Fantasies, Futures." In *Biosecurity and Vulnerability*, edited by Nancy N. Chen and Lesley A. Sharp, 5–24. Santa Fe, NM: School for Advanced Research Press.

Massumi, Brian, ed. 1993. *The Politics of Everyday Fear*. Minneapolis: University of Minnesota Press.

Masters, Brooke. 2012. "Plan for Global Register of All Financial Companies." *Financial Times*, June 9–10, 8.

Matsuda, Misa. 2011. "Rumors and 'Fuhyo Higai (Harmful Rumors)' during the Ongoing Disaster (2)." *ChuoOnline*, June 27.

May, Martha. 1982. "The Historical Problem of the Family Wage: The Ford Motor Company and the Five Dollar Day." *Feminist Studies* 8 (2): 399–424.

Mazzarella, William. 2008. "Affect: What Is It Good For?" In *Enchantments of Modernity: Empire, Nation, Globalization*, edited by Saurabh Dube, 291–309. New York: Routledge.

McClintock, Anne. 1995. *Imperial Leather: Race, Gender, and Sexuality in the Colonial Contest*. New York: Routledge.

McDonough, William, and Michael Braungart. 2002. *Cradle to Cradle: Remaking the Way We Make Things*. New York: North Point Press/Farrar, Straus and Giroux.

McIntosh, Ian. 2006. "'It Was Worse Than Alcatraz': Working for Ford at Trafford Park." In *The Fordism of Ford and Modern Management*, edited by Huw Beynon and Theo Nichols, 169–79. Northampton, MA: Edward Elgar.

McLannahan, Ben. 2014. "ABP Dumps €18m Tepco Stake after Unsettled Safety Concerns." *Financial Times*, January 9, 20.

McLuhan, Marshall. 1994. *Understanding Media: The Extensions of Man*. Cambridge, MA: MIT Press.

McNally, David. 2012. *Monsters of the Market: Zombies, Vampires, and Global Capitalism*. Chicago: Haymarket.

McNeil, Donald G., Jr. 2006. "Mad Cow Disease Is Confirmed in Alabama." *New York Times*, March 14.

McNeill, David. 2013. "'I Am One of the Fukushima Fifty': One of the Men Who Risked Their Lives to Prevent a Catastrophe Shares His Story." *Independent*, March 2.

McWilliams, Carey. [1939] 1999. *Factories in the Field: The Story of Migratory Farm Labor in California*. Berkeley: University of California Press.

"Me, Myself, Us." 2012. *Economist*, August 18, 69–71.

Mehra, Akhil. 2009. "Politics of Participation: Walter Reed's Yellow-Fever Experiments." *History of Medicine* 11 (4): 326–30.

Melillo, Jerry M., Terese (T. C.) Richmond, and Gary W. Yohe, eds. 2014. *Climate Change Impacts in the United States: The Third National Climate Assessment*. U.S. Global Change Research Program. doi:10.7930/J0Z31WJ2.

Menne, Matthew J., Claude Williams Jr., and Michael A. Palecki. 2010. "On the Reliability of the U.S. Surface Temperature Record." *Journal of Geophysical Research* 115 (D11108): 1–9.

Menzies, Charles R. 2006. *Traditional Ecological Knowledge and Natural Resource Management*. Omaha: University of Nebraska Press.

Merleau-Ponty, Maurice. 2012. *Phenomenology of Perception*. New York: Routledge.

Meyer, Stephen, III. 1981. *The Five Dollar Day*. Albany: State University of New York Press.

"Microbes Maketh Man." 2012. *Economist*, August 18, 9.

Minkel, J. R. 2008. "Self-Experimenters Step Up for Science." *Scientific American*, March 10.

Mole, Beth. 2014. "Nature-Inspired Camouflage." *Science News*, October 4, 5.

Møller, Anders Pape, Isao Nishiumi, Hiroyoshi Suzuki, Keisuke Ueda, and Timothy A. Mousseau. 2013. "Difference in Effects of Radiation on Abundance of Animals in Fukushima and Chernobyl." *Ecological Indicators* 24:75–81.

Mooney, Chris. 2005. *The Republican War on Science*. New York: Basic Books.

Morton, Timothy. 2007. *Ecology without Nature: Rethinking Environmental Aesthetics*. Cambridge, MA: Harvard University Press.

———. 2013a. *Hyperobjects: Philosophy and Ecology after the End of the World*. Minneapolis: University of Minnesota Press.

———. 2013b. *Realist Magic: Objects, Ontology, Causality*. Ann Arbor: University of Michigan Press.

Mould, R. F. 2007. "Pierre Curie, 1859–1906." *Current Oncology* 14 (2): 74–82.

Moynihan, Elizabeth B. 1979. *Paradise as a Garden in Persia and Mughal India*. New York: George Braziller.

Muehlebach, Andrea, and Nitzan Shoshan. 2012. Introduction. *Anthropological Quarterly* 85 (2): 317–44.

Muehlmann, Shaylih. 2013. *Where the River Ends: Contested Indigeneity in the Mexican Colorado Delta*. Durham, NC: Duke University Press.

Murakami, Haruki. 2011. Acceptance speech for the Cataluña International Prize, Barcelona, June 10. English translation at http://www.senrinomichi.com/?p=2728.

Nakamoto, Michiyo. 2011. "Japan Disaster Sparks Rush to the Altar." *Financial Times*, June 7, 6.

Nancy, Jean-Luc. 2015. *After Fukushima: The Equivalence of Catastrophes*. Translated by Charlotte Mandell. New York: Fordham University Press.

Nash, Linda. 2006. *Inescapable Ecologies: A History of Environment, Disease, and Knowledge*. Berkeley: University of California Press.

Narain, Urvashi, and Alan Krupnick. 2007. "The Impact of Delhi's CNG Program on Air Quality." Discussion Paper, RFF DP 07-06. Washington, DC: Resources for the Future.

Nasaw, David. 1993. *Going Out: The Rise and Fall of Public Amusements*. New York: Basic Books.

Nasubi. 2012. "Challenging the Issues around the Radiation-Exposed Labor That Connects San'ya and Fukushima: Toward a Revival of the Underclass Workers' Movement." *Japan—Fissures in the Planetary Apparatus*, August 31.

Nayak, Nalini. 2009. "Development for Some Is Violence for Others." In *Eco-Sufficiency and Global Justice: Women Write Political Ecology*, edited by Ariel Salleh, 109–20. New York: Pluto Press.

Newport, Frank. 2012. "In U.S., 46% Hold Creationist View of Human Origins." *Gallup News*, June 1.

Ngai, Sianne. 2007. *Ugly Feelings*. Cambridge, MA: Harvard University Press.

Nixon, Rob. 2011. *Slow Violence and the Environmentalism of the Poor*. Cambridge, MA: Harvard University Press.

"No Mandatory NAIS in Arizona." 2007. *Mother Earth News*, August/September, 22.

Norcliffe, Glen. 1997. "Popeism and Fordism: Examining the Roots of Mass Production." *Regional Studies* 31 (3): 267–80.

Nuttall, Chris. 2011. "A Road Trip into the Future." *Financial Times*, January 14, 10.

O'Harrow, Robert, Jr. 2005. *No Place to Hide*. New York: Free Press.

O'Leary, Stephen. 1994. *Arguing the Apocalypse: A Theory of Millennial Rhetoric*. New York: Oxford University Press.

Olsson, Karen. 2006. "Welcome to the Jungle: Does Upton Sinclair's Famous Novel Hold Up?" *Slate*, July 10.

"One Year On, Fukushima Still Fights Uphill Battle to Decontaminate Farming District." 2012. *Mainichi*, October 18.

Onishi, Norimitsu, and Martin Fackler. 2011. "Japan Held Nuclear Data, Leaving Evacuees in Peril." *New York Times*, August 8.

Onozawa, Katsuno. 2013. "Government's Lethargic Response Stresses Fukushima Mothers." *Asahi Shimbun*, April 30.

Oreskes, Naomi, and Erik M. Conway. 2010. *Merchants of Doubt: How a Handful of Scientists Obscured the Truth on Issues from Tobacco Smoke to Global Warming*. New York: Bloomsbury.

Orlove, Ben. 2002. *Lines in the Water: Nature and Culture at Lake Titicaca*. Berkeley: University of California Press.

Ostherr, Kirsten. 2005. *Cinematic Prophylaxis: Globalization and Contagion in the Discourse of World Health*. Durham, NC: Duke University Press.

Otake, Tomoko. 2011. "Experts Urge Great Caution Over Radiation Risks." *Japan Times*, June 26.

"Overcoming Hang-Ups: Mobile Operators Have More High-Speed Networks Than They Know What to Do With." 2007. *Economist*, April 28, 6–9.

Pallavi, Aparna. 2009. "Nature's Forecasters." *Down to Earth*, July 31, 30.

Parenti, Christian. 2003. *The Soft Cage: Surveillance in America from Slavery to the War on Terror*. New York: Basic Books.

Parks, Tim. 2005. *Medici Money: Banking, Metaphysics, and Art in Fifteenth-Century Florence*. London: Profile Books.

Patel, Geeta. 2002. "Diasporas and Sexuality." Talk delivered at the Diasporas, Transnationality and Global Conflict workshop, Harvard Academy for International and Area Studies, Cambridge, MA, March 16.

———. 2007. "Imagining Risk, Care, and Security: Insurance and Fantasy." *Anthropological Theory* 7 (1): 99–118.

———. 2012. "Advertisements, Proprietary Heterosexuality, and Hundis: Post-Colonial Finance, Nation-State Formations, and the New Idealized Family." *Rethinking Marxism* 24 (4): 516–35.

———. 2016. *Risky Bodies and Techno-Intimacy*. New Delhi: Women Unlimited.

Pearce, Fred. 2008. *With Speed and Violence: Why Scientists Fear Tipping Points in Climate Change*. Boston: Beacon.

Peat, F. David. 2002. *Blackfoot Physics*. Boston: Red Wheel/Weiser.

Peláez, Eloína, and John Holloway. 1990. "Learning to Bow: Post-Fordism and Technological Determinism." *Science as Culture* 8:15–26.

Peña, Devon. 2013. "Restoring Heritage Cuisines and Indigenous Agroecosystems." *Indian Country Today*, March 6, 8–9.

Pennisi, Elizabeth. 2010. "Body's Hardworking Microbes Get Some Overdue Respect." *Science* 330:1619.

Pepper, Daniel. 2007. "India's Rivers Are Drowning in Pollution." *Fortune*, June 4.

Peterson, Thomas C., Peter A. Stott, and Stephanie Herring. 2012. "Explaining Extreme Events of 2011 from a Climate Perspective." *Bulletin of the American Meteorological Society* 93 (7): 1041–67.

Petryna, Adriana. 2002. *Life Exposed: Biological Citizens after Chernobyl*. Princeton, NJ: Princeton University Press.

Pico della Mirandola, Giovanni. 2012. *Oration on the Dignity of Man: A New Translation and Commentary*. Edited by Francesco Borghesi, Michael Papio, and Massimo Riva. Cambridge: Cambridge University Press.

Pilkey, Orrin H., and Keith C. Pilkey. 2011. *Global Climate Change: A Primer*. Durham, NC: Duke University Press.

Pinker, Susan. 2014. *The Village Effect: How Face-to-Face Contact Can Make Us Healthier, Happier and Smarter*. New York: Spiegel and Grau.

Plowright, Adam. 2014. "Tata Nano, Other Indian Cars Fail Crash Tests." AFP, January 31.

Pollan, Michael. 2006. *The Omnivore's Dilemma: The Search for a Perfect Meal in a Fast-Food World.* London: Bloomsbury.

———. 2013. "Some of My Best Friends Are Germs." *New York Times Magazine,* May 15.

Porritt, Jonathan. 2007. *Capitalism as if the World Matters.* London: Earthscan.

Povinelli, Elizabeth A. 2006. *The Empire of Love: Toward a Theory of Intimacy, Genealogy, and Carnality.* Durham, NC: Duke University Press.

———. 2012. "The Dwelling Science." Talk delivered at the Department of Anthropology Senior Seminar, Cambridge University, Cambridge, UK, March 2.

Prabhu, Anjali. 2007. *Hybridity: Limits, Transformations, Prospects.* Albany: State University of New York Press.

Prober, Suzanne M., Michael H. O'Connor, and Fiona J. Walsh. 2011. "Australian Aboriginal Peoples' Seasonal Knowledge: A Potential Basis for Shared Understanding in Environmental Management." *Ecology and Society* 16 (2): 12.

Quaid, Libby. 2006. "US Safeguards against Mad Cow Disease Called Inadequate: Strict Regulations on Cattle Feed Are Needed, Critics Say." *Boston Globe,* January 5.

Quintana, Miguel. 2012a. "At Edge of Japan's Nuclear Zone, Residents Face an Uncertain Future." *Time,* March 12.

———. 2012b. "Radiation Decontamination in Fukushima: A Critical Perspective from the Ground." *Asia-Pacific Journal* 10 (13): 3.

"'Radiation Divorce' Enters Japanese Vernacular." 2012. *Japan Today,* January 23.

Radjou, Navi, Jaideep Prabhu, and Simone Ahuja. 2012. *Jugaad Innovation: Think Frugal, Be Flexible, Generate Breakthrough Growth.* San Francisco: Wiley/Jossey-Bass.

Rajput, Vinod. 2013a. "Admin to Plant Trees along Drain to Get Rid of Stench." *Hindustan Times,* July 17, 8.

———. 2013b. "CM Pulls Up Babus for Failure to Curb Mining." *Hindustan Times,* August 13, 9.

———. 2013c. "Illegal Housing Takes Sheen Off Noida, G Noida; Turns Them into Urban Slums." *Hindustan Times,* August 11, 8.

———. 2014a. "100% Ganga Water Supply by Mid-July." *Hindustan Times,* May 27, 9.

———. 2014b. "Identify Erring Realtors Near Okhla Park, Says Green Body." *Hindustan Times,* February 26, 8.

———. 2014c. "Realty Boom in Noida Has Led to Groundwater Depletion." *Hindustan Times,* June 27, 6.

———. 2014d. "Warrant against Officials over Dadri Wetland." *Hindustan Times,* March 25, 9.

Raloff, Janet. 2006. "Prions' Dirty Little Secret." *Science News* 169 (6): 93–94.

———. 2012. "Studies Start Linking Climate Change to Current Events." *Science News* 182 (10): 22–26.

Ramnani, Vandana. 2014. "Against Nature and Man." *Hindustan Times,* June 28, 1.

Rampton, Sheldon, and John Stauber. 2001. *Trust Us, We're Experts! How Industry Manipulates Science and Gambles with Your Future.* New York: Penguin.

———. 2003. *Mad Cow U.S.A.* Monroe, ME: Common Courage Press.

Razac, Olivier. 2002. *Barbed Wire: A Political History*. New York: New Press.

Repeta, Lawrence. 2014. "Japan's 2013 State Secrecy Act: The Abe Administration's Threat to News Reporting." *Asia-Pacific Journal* 12 (10): 1.

Revkin, Andrew C. 2010. "On Weather Stations and Climate Trends." *Dot Earth* (blog), *New York Times*, January 28. http://dotearth.blogs.nytimes.com/2010/01/28/on-weather-stations-and-climate-trends/.

Ritter, Steve. 2002. "New Car Smell." *Chemical and Engineering News* 80 (20): 45.

Robbins, Jim. 2012. "Wildlife Biology Goes High-Tech." *High Country News*, December 10, 12–19.

Robbins, Thomas, and Susan J. Palmer, eds. 1997. *Millennium, Messiahs, and Mayhem: Contemporary Apocalyptic Movements*. New York: Routledge.

Rodríguez, Sylvia. 2006. *Acequia: Water Sharing, Sanctity, and Place*. Santa Fe, NM: School for Advanced Research Press.

Rose, Deborah Bird. 2011. *Wild Dog Dreaming: Death and Extinction*. Charlottesville: University of Virginia Press.

Ross, Andrew. 1991. *Strange Weather: Culture, Science, and Technology in the Age of Limits*. New York: Verso.

Ross, Douglas S. 2002. "Nonpalpable Thyroid Nodules—Managing an Epidemic." *Journal of Clinical Endocrinology and Metabolism* 87 (5): 1938–40.

Rudolf, John Collins. 2010. "New Car Smell Blamed in Hit-and-Run." *Green* (blog), *New York Times*, December 15. http://green.blogs.nytimes.com/2010/12/15/new-car-smell-blamed-in-hit-and-run/.

Ruhl, Onno. 2014. "A Cleaner Ganga." *Hindustan Times*, December 19, 8.

Ryall, Julian. 2011. "Japanese Tsunami Stood at 132.5 Feet." *The Telegraph*, July 18. Accessed May 3, 2016. http://www.telegraph.co.uk/news/worldnews/asia/japan/8645094/Japanese-tsunami-stood-at-132.5ft.html.

Rybczynski, Natalia, John C. Gosse, Richard Harington, Roy A. Wogelius, Alan J. Hidy, and Mike Buckley. 2013. "Mid-Pliocene Warm-Period Deposits in the High Arctic Yield Insight into Camel Evolution." *Nature Communications* 4. doi: 10.1038/ncomms2516.

Sachan, Dinsa. 2011. "Monsoon Dates to Be Revised." *Down to Earth*, October 29, 13.

Sachs, Wolfgang. 1999. *Planet Dialectics: Explorations in Environment and Development*. New York: Zed Books.

Samuels, Richard J. 2013. *3.11: Disaster and Change in Japan*. Ithaca, NY: Cornell University Press.

Sanchanta, Mariko. 2011. "The Geiger Counter Club: Mothers Bust Silent Radiation Consensus." *Japan Real Time* (blog), *Wall Street Journal*, June 17. http://blogs.wsj.com/japanrealtime/2011/06/17/the-geiger-club-mothers-bust-silent-radiation-consensus/.

Sanon, Malika. 2014. "Rainwater Harvesting a Dream in Noida." *Hindustan Times*, June 28, 8.

Sarris, Greg. 1992. "'What I'm Talking about When I'm Talking about My Baskets': Conversations with Mabel McKay." In *De/Colonizing the Subject: The Politics of*

Gender in Women's Autobiography, edited by Sidonie Smith and Julia Watson, 20–33. Minneapolis: University of Minnesota Press.

Sato, Jun, Chiaki Fujimori, Miki Aoki, Tamiyuki Kihara, and Takayuki Kihara. 2012. "TEPCO Subcontractor Used Lead to Fake Dosimeter Readings at Fukushima Plant." *Asahi Shimbun*, July 21.

Sato, Sachiko. 2011. "Testimony of a Fukushima Mother." Translated by Kaori Izumi. *Counterpunch*, May 31.

Sato, Shigeru, Sachiko Sakamaki, and Tsuyoshi Inajima. 2011. "Japan's Radiation Sleuths Toil with Borrowed Geiger Counters." *Bloomberg*, June 13.

Sayre, Ryan. 2011. "The Un-Thought of Preparedness: Concealments of Disaster Preparedness in Tokyo's Everyday." *Anthropology and Humanism* 36 (2): 215–24.

Schapiro, Mark. 2007. *Exposed: The Toxic Chemistry of Everyday Products and What's at Stake for American Power*. White River Junction, VT: Chelsea Green.

Schlosser, Eric. 2013. *Command and Control: Nuclear Weapons, the Damascus Accident, and the Illusion of Safety*. New York: Penguin.

Schubert, G. 2007. "Uncle Sam Plays Big Brother." *Mother Earth*, October/November, 14.

Schwantes, Carlos A. 2009. *Just One Restless Rider: Reflections on Trains and Travel*. Columbia: University of Missouri Press.

Schwartz, Jessica A. 2012. "A 'Voice to Sing': Rongelapese Musical Activism and the Production of Nuclear Knowledge." *Music and Politics* 6 (1): 1–21.

Screech, Timon. 2002. *The Lens within the Heart: The Western Scientific Gaze and Popular Imagery in Later Edo Japan*. Honolulu: University of Hawaii Press.

Seibert, Charles. 1993. "The Artifice of the Natural: How TV's Nature Shows Make All the Earth a Stage." *Harper's*, February, 43–51.

Seigworth, Gregory J., and Melissa Gregg. 2010. "An Inventory of Shimmers." In *The Affect Theory Reader*, edited by Gregory J. Seigworth and Melissa Gregg, 1–25. Durham, NC: Duke University Press.

Sender, Henny. 2015. "If You Build It, Can They Come?" *Financial Times*, June 25, 9.

Seth, Bharat Lal. 2013. "Sewage Stink." *Down to Earth*, September 15, 16.

Seth, Bharat Lal, and S. V. Suresh Babu. 2007. *Sewage Canal: How to Clean the Yamuna*. New Delhi: Centre for Science and Environment.

Shah, Nayan. 2011. *Stranger Intimacy: Contesting Race, Sexuality, and the Law in the North American West*. Berkeley: University of California Press.

Sharpsteen, Bill. 2010. *Dirty Water: One Man's Fight to Clean Up One of the World's Most Polluted Bays*. Berkeley: University of California Press.

Shepard, Paul. 1996. *The Others: How Animals Made Us Human*. Washington, DC: Island Press.

Shi, David E. 1995. *Facing Facts: Realism in American Thought and Culture*. New York: Oxford University Press.

Sicart, Miguel. 2014. *Play Matters*. Cambridge, MA: MIT Press.

Sieberg, Daniel. 2006. "Is RFID Tracking You?" *CNN*, October 23.

Sinclair, Upton. [1906] 2004. *The Jungle*. New York: Pocket Books.

Singh, Abhay Kumar, B. K. Tewary, and A. Sinha. 2011. "Hydrochemistry and Quality

Assessment of Groundwater in Part of NOIDA Metropolitan City, Uttar Pradesh." *Journal of the Geological Society of India* 78:523–40.

Singh, Darpan. 2013. "Yamuna Belongs to Nobody." *Hindustan Times*, July 14, 3.

———. 2014a. "Green Notice to Govt on Toxic Yamuna Veggies." *Hindustan Times*, July 5, 2.

———. 2014b. "Yamuna: Biggest Water Source Is Now a Drain." *Hindustan Times*, June 27, 6.

Sinha, Bhadra. 2013. "Won't Interfere with Green Court's Order: SC." *Hindustan Times*, August 17, 4.

Sivak, Michael, and Brandon Schoettle. 2011. "Recent Changes in the Age Composition of U.S. Drivers: Implications for the Extent, Safety, and Environmental Consequences of Personal Transportation." Report no. UMTRI-2011-23, June. University of Michigan Transportation Institute, Ann Arbor. Accessed May 3, 2016. http://deepblue.lib.umich.edu/bitstream/handle/2027.42/85149/102751.pdf.

Smith, Gary. 2010. "7 Days in the Life of a Catastrophe." *Sports Illustrated*, July 5, 68–74.

Smith, Neil. 1990. *Uneven Development: Nature, Capital, and the Production of Space.* Oxford: Basil Blackwell.

———. 2006. "Nature as Accumulation Strategy." In *Coming to Terms with Nature,* edited by Leo Panitch and Colin Leys, 16–36. New York: Monthly Review Press.

Smith, Rick, and Bruce Lourie. 2009. *Slow Death by Rubber Duck: The Secret Danger of Everyday Things.* With Sarah Dopp. Berkeley, CA: Counterpoint.

Soble, Jonathan. 2016. "Fukushima Keeps Fighting Radioactive Tide 5 Years After Disaster." *New York Times*, March 10.

Solomon, Harris. 2016. *Metabolic Living: Food, Fat, and the Absorption of Illness in India.* Durham, NC: Duke University Press.

Sorkin, Michael, ed. 1992. *Variations on a Theme Park: The New American City and the End of Public Space.* New York: Hill and Wang.

Spector, Tim. 2015. *The Diet Myth: The Real Science behind What We Eat.* London: Weidenfeld and Nicolson.

Sperling, Daniel, and Deborah Gordon. 2009. *Two Billion Cars: Driving Toward Sustainability.* New York: Oxford University Press.

Sperry, Rod Meade. 2013. "Ruin, Beasties, and Constant Craving." *Shambhala Sun,* March, 60–69.

Spiegel, Jennifer Beth. 2013. "Subterranean Flows: Water Contamination and the Politics of Visibility after the Bhopal Disaster." In *Thinking with Water,* edited by Cecilia Chen, Janine MacLeod, and Astrida Neimanis, 84–103. Montreal: McGill-Queen's University Press.

Srivastava, Gautami. 2015. "Noida Water Unfit for Drinking, Cooking: Residents." *Hindustan Times*, January 5, 8.

Staff Reports. 2004. "USDA Awards Animal ID Funds: Tribal Projects to Receive $250,000." *Indian Country Today*, September 1, C1–C2.

Standing, Guy. 2014. *The Precariat: The New Dangerous Class.* London: Bloomsbury.

"Startling Fukushima Testimony Raises Grave Questions." 2014. *Asahi Shimbun*, May 21.

Steady, Filomina Chioma. 2009. *Environmental Justice in the New Millennium: Global Perspectives on Race, Ethnicity, and Human Rights*. New York: Palgrave Macmillan.

Stein, Rachel, ed. 2004. *New Perspectives on Environmental Justice: Gender, Sexuality, and Activism*. New Brunswick, NJ: Rutgers University Press.

Stewart, Kathleen. 2007. *Ordinary Affects*. Durham, NC: Duke University Press.

———. 2012. "Precarity's Forms." *Cultural Anthropology* 27 (3): 518–25.

Stewart, Kathleen, and Susan Harding. 1999. "Bad Endings: American Apocalypse." *Annual Review of Anthropology* 28:285–310.

Stoler, Ann, ed. 2006. *Haunted by Empire: Geographies of Intimacy in North American History*. Durham, NC: Duke University Press.

———. 2010. *Carnal Knowledge and Imperial Power: Race and the Intimate in Colonial Rule*. 2nd ed. Berkeley: University of California Press.

Stolz, Robert. 2014. *Bad Water: Nature, Pollution, and Politics in Japan, 1870–1950*. Durham, NC: Duke University Press.

Stone, Allucquère. 1995. *The War of Technology and Desire at the Close of the Mechanical Age*. Cambridge, MA: MIT Press.

Strang, Veronica. 2013. *Gardening the World: Agency, Identity, and the Ownership of Water*. New York: Berghahn.

Strathern, Marilyn. 2012. "Response: A Comment on 'the Ontological Turn' in Japanese Anthropology." HAU: *Journal of Ethnographic Theory* 2 (2): 402–5.

Striffler, Steve. 2005. *Chicken: The Dangerous Transformation of America's Favorite Food*. New Haven, CT: Yale University Press.

Subramanian, Ajantha. 2009. *Shorelines: Space and Rights in South India*. Stanford, CA: Stanford University Press.

Suchman, Lucy. 2006. *Human-Machine Reconfigurations: Plans and Situated Actions*. 2nd ed. Cambridge: Cambridge University Press.

Suess, Oliver. 2012. "North America Has Biggest Rise in Weather Catastrophes." *Bloomberg*, October 17.

Sullivan, Sian. 2009. "Green Capitalism and the Cultural Poverty of Constructing Nature as Service Provider." *Radical Anthropology* 3:18–27.

———. 2013. "Nature on the Move III: (Re)countenancing an Animate Nature." *New Proposals: Journal of Marxism and Interdisciplinary Inquiry* 6 (1–2): 50–71.

Sumner, Thomas. 2015. "Global Warming 'Hiatus' an Artifact." *Science News* 187 (13): 6.

Supplier Relations US. 2016. *Alkalies and Chlorine Manufacturing Industry in the U.S. and Its International Trade*. Accessed April 29, 2016. http://www.supplierrelations us.com/reports/alkalies-and-chlorine-manufacturing-industry-us.

Sutton, David E. 2001. *Remembrance of Repasts: An Anthropology of Food and Memory*. New York: Berg.

"Suupaa Hottosupotto o Tsugi-tsugi Hakken" (スーパーホットスポットを次々発見, Super-Hotspots Discovered One after Another). 2011. 現代　ビジネス (*Gendai Bijinesu*), July 14. http://gendai.ismedia.jp/articles/print/11933.

Suzuki, Tomohiko (鈴木智彦). 2011. ヤクザと原発：福島第一潜入記 (*Yakuza to Genpatsu: Fukushima Daiichi Sennyūki*). Tokyo: Bungei Shunjū.

Swyngedouw, Erik. 2004. *Social Power and the Urbanization of Water*. New York: Oxford University Press.

Tabuchi, Hiroko. 2006. "Japanese Stores Pull U.S. Beef off Shelves." AP, January 21.

———. 2012. "A Confused Nuclear Cleanup." *New York Times*, February 10.

———. 2013. "In Japan, a Painfully Slow Sweep." *New York Times*, January 7.

Tada, Toshio. 2013. "Crooked Cleanup: Photos, Videos Show Contractors Lied in Decontamination Reports." *Asahi Shimbun*, January 17.

Takahashi, Satsuki. 2011a. "Fourfold Disaster: Renovation and Restoration in Post-Tsunami Coastal Japan." *Anthropology News* 52 (7): 5, 11.

———. 2011b. "Nuclear Fisheries: From Industrial Modernity to Risk Society." Unpublished manuscript.

Tanaka, Shun-ichi. 2012. "Accident at the Fukushima Dai-ichi Nuclear Power Stations of TEPCO: Outline and Lessons Learned." *Proceedings of the Japanese Academy*, series B, 88 (9): 471–84.

Tankha, Rajkumari. 2013a. "Danger to Life in Area around Transformers." *Hindustan Times*, August 9, 1.

———. 2013b. "Demand for Water Harvesting Pits." *Hindustan Times*, August 9, 1.

"Tata Nano's Nov. Sales One-Sixth of Oct. Figures." 2010. *Economic Times*, December 1.

Tatsuta, Kazuto. 2014. いちえふ：福島第一原子力発電所労働記 (*Ichi-Ef: Fukushima Daiichi Nuclear Power Station Labor Record*). Vol. 1. Tokyo: Kodansha.

TEPCO. 2011. "Detection of Radioactive Material in the Soil in Fukushima Daiichi Nuclear Power Station," March 28. Accessed May 3, 2016. http://www.tepco.co.jp/en/press/corp-com/release/11032812-e.html.

Tett, Gillian. 2014. "A Bubblegum Fix for Banks Will Make Finance Safer." *Financial Times*, August 1, 7.

Thompson, Damian. 2008. *Counterknowledge: How We Surrendered to Conspiracy Theories, Quack Medicine, Bogus Science, and Fake History*. New York: W. W. Norton.

Thornton, Frank. 2007. *How to Cheat at Deploying and Securing RFID*. Rockland, MA: Syngress.

Thorsheim, Peter. 2006. *Inventing Pollution: Coal, Smoke, and Culture in Britain since 1800*. Athens: Ohio University Press.

Toro, Felipe Andrés, Sulabh Jain, Felix Reitze, Amela Ajanovic, Reinhard Haas, Sandro Furlan, and Hein de Wilde, eds. 2010. "State of the Art for Alternative Fuels and Alternative Automotive Technologies." Institute of Resource Efficiency and Energy Strategies (IREES). Karlsruhe: Alter-Motive Consortium.

Trautmann, Thomas R. 2015. *Elephants and Kings: An Environmental History*. New Delhi: Permanent Black.

Tudge, Colin. 2006. *The Tree: A Natural History of What Trees Are, How They Live, and Why They Matter*. New York: Crown.

Turner, Terry S. 1980. "The Social Skin." In *Not Work Alone*, edited by Jeremy Cherfas and Roger Lewin, 111–40. London: Temple Smith.

———. 2009. "The Crisis of Late Structuralism: Perspectivism and Animism: Rethinking Culture, Nature, Spirit, and Bodiliness." *Tipiti: Journal of the Society for the Anthropology of Lowland South America* 7 (1): 1.

Tylor, Edward B. 1871. *Primitive Culture: Researches into the Development of Mythology, Philosophy, Religion, Art, and Custom*. London: J. Murray.

Ufkes, Frances M. 1995. "Lean and Mean: US Meat-Packing in an Era of Agro-Industrial Restructuring." *Environment and Planning D: Society and Space* 13: 683–705.

Union of Concerned Scientists. 2013. "It's Cold and My Car Is Buried in Snow: Is Global Warming Really Happening?" February 8. Accessed May 3, 2016. http://www.ucsusa.org/global_warming/science_and_impacts/science/cold-snow-climate-change.html.

United States Department of Agriculture (USDA). 2004. "Transcript of Remarks by Bill Hawks, Under Secretary for Marketing and Regulatory Programs at a Press Briefing Regarding the Animal I.D. Plan." Release no. 0171.04, April 27. Accessed May 3, 2016. http://www.usda.gov/wps/portal/usda/usdahome?contentid=2004/04/0171.html.

United States Department of Agriculture, Animal and Plant Health Inspection Service (USDA APHIS). 2004a. "APHIS' BSE Surveillance Program." Accessed May 3, 2016. http://www.aphis.usda.gov/lpa/pubs/fsheet_faq_notice/faq_ahbsesurv.html.

———. 2004b. *The National Animal Identification System (NAIS): Why Animal Identification? Why Now? What First?* Program Aid no. 1797. Washington, DC: United States Department of Agriculture.

———. 2004c. *Premises Identification: The First Step toward a National Animal Identification System*. Program Aid no. 1800. Washington, DC: United States Department of Agriculture.

———. 2004d. "Transcript of Public Comments Received during the National Animal ID Program Listening Session, Fayetteville, North Carolina." June 14.

———. 2005. "National Animal Identification System: Notice of Availability of a Draft Strategic Plan and Draft Program Standards." Docket No. 05-015-1. *Federal Register* 70 (87): 23961–62.

———. 2013. "Traceability for Livestock Moving Interstate; Final Rule." *Federal Register* 78 (6): 2040–75.

USDA APHIS Veterinary Services. 2005. "The Evolution of the National Animal Identification System in the United States." Accessed May 3, 2016. http://brahman journal.com/brahman/wp-content/media/Art_1.pdf.

———. 2006. "National Animal Identification System: Animal Identification Number (AIN) Tags." Accessed May 3, 2016. http://www.ok-safe.com/files/documents/1/Official_Animal_Identification_Numbering_System_Fact_Sheet.pdf.

Urry, John. 2004. "The 'System' of Automobility." *Theory, Culture, and Society* 21 (4/5): 25–39.

"US Beef Ban Lifted." 2006. *Down to Earth*, February 15, 18.

U.S. Census Bureau. 2012. "Table 1377. Meat Consumption by Type and Country: 2009 and 2010." Accessed May 3, 2016. http://eaza.portal.isis.org/activities/sustainability/Documents/meat%20consumption%20worldwide.pdf.

Vallas, Steven P. 1999. "Rethinking Post-Fordism: The Meaning of Workplace Flexibility." *Sociological Theory* 17 (1): 68–101.

Vasagar, Jeevan. 2014. "Bayer Eyes Consumer Healthcare Push." *Financial Times*, November 25, 17.

Vashishtha, Akash. 2012. "Builders Will Leave Noida Dry, Say Environment Experts." *Mail Today*, July 20.

Vats, Rachit, and Manu P. Toms. 2011. "Tata Motors Scans Bharat for Nano Sales Points." *Hindustan Times*, December 8, 21.

Villar, Ruairidh, and Yuriko Nakao. 2012. "Japan Priest Fights Invisible Demon: Radiation." *Reuters*, February 10.

Viveiros de Castro, Eduardo. 1998. "Cosmological Deixis and Amerindian Perspectivism." *Journal of the Royal Anthropological Institute* 4 (3): 469–88.

———. 2014. *Cannibal Metaphysics*. Translated by Peter Skafish. Minneapolis: Univocal.

Walker, Brett L. 2010. *Toxic Archipelago: A History of Industrial Disease in Japan.* Seattle: University of Washington Press.

Walker, Harry. 2013. *Under a Watchful Eye: Self, Power, and Intimacy in Amazonia.* Berkeley: University of California Press.

Wallace, Rick. 2011. "Discrimination Increases Torment of Fukushima." *Australian*, June 11.

Walley, Christine J. 2004. *Rough Waters: Nature and Development in an East African Marine Park*. Princeton, NJ: Princeton University Press.

Ward, Matthew L. 1991. "Pro-Coal Ad Campaign Disputes Warming Idea." *New York Times*, July 8.

Washington, Haydn, and John Cook. 2011. *Climate Change Denial: Heads in the Sand.* New York: Earthscan.

Watts, Jonathan. 2011. "Fukushima Parents Dish the Dirt in Protest over Radiation Levels." *Guardian*, May 2.

Watts, Steven. 2006. *The People's Tycoon: Henry Ford and the American Century*. New York: Vintage.

"Wee-Fi: The Legoland Tracking System." 2004. *Wired*, September 1, 50.

Weisiger, Marsha. 2009. *Dreaming of Sheep in Navajo Country*. Seattle: University of Washington Press.

Weissert, Will. 2004. "Microchips Implanted in Mexican Officials: Attorney General, Prosecutors Carry Security Pass under Their Skin." MSNBC, July 14.

Welsome, Eileen. 1999. *The Plutonium Files: America's Secret Medical Experiments in the Cold War*. New York: Dial Press.

West, Paige. 2006. *Conservation Is Our Government Now: The Politics of Ecology in Papua New Guinea*. Durham, NC: Duke University Press.

Weston, Kath. 1996. "Theory, Theory, Who's Got the Theory? Or, Why I'm Tired of That Tired Debate." GLQ: *A Journal of Lesbian and Gay Studies* 2:347–49.

————. 2013. "Lifeblood, Liquidity, and Cash Transfusions: Beyond Metaphor in the Cultural Study of Finance." *Journal of the Royal Anthropological Institute* 19:S24-S41.

————. 2014. "Detectable/検出可能." In *To See Once More the Stars: Living in a Post-Fukushima World*, edited by Daisuke Naito, Ryan Sayre, Heather Swanson, and Satsuki Takahashi, 8–11. Santa Cruz, CA: New Pacific Press.

"What Happened to the Flying Car?" 2012. *Economist Technology Quarterly* (March 3): 3–4.

Whitaker, Reginald. 1999. *The End of Privacy: How Total Surveillance Is Becoming a Reality*. New York: New Press.

"Why *Gobar Times*?" 2013. *Gobar Times* (*Down to Earth* supplement), July 1–15, 61.

Wildcat, Daniel R. 2009. *Red Alert! Saving the Planet with Indigenous Knowledge*. Golden, CO: Fulcrum.

Wilks, Jon. 2011. "Yokohama Mums against Radiation: The Fight to Remove Contaminated Food from the School Menu." *TimeOut Tokyo*, August 29.

Williams, Raymond. 1975. *The Country and the City*. New York: Oxford University Press.

Wilson, James M. 1995. "Henry Ford's Just-in-Time System." *International Journal of Operations and Production Management* 15 (12): 59–75.

Witherspoon, Roger. 2013. "A Lasting Legacy of the Fukushima Rescue Mission, Part 3: Cat and Mouse with a Nuclear Ghost." March 3. http://spoonsenergy matters.wordpress.com/2013/03/03/404/.

Wolfe, Charles T., and Ofer Gal, eds. 2010. *The Body as Object and Instrument of Knowledge: Embodied Empiricism in Early Modern Science*. London: Springer.

Wood, Stephen. 1993. "The Japanization of Fordism." *Economic and Industrial Democracy* 14:535–55.

Woodard, Stephanie. 2013. "Spiritual Listening: Alaska Natives Tackle Youth Suicide with Lessons from the Land." *High Country News*, March 6, 34–37.

World Meteorological Organization. 2014. WMO *Greenhouse Gas Bulletin* 10 (September 9). https://www.wmo.int/pages/mediacentre/press_releases/documents/1002 _GHG_Bulletin.pdf.

World Wildlife Fund. 2014. *Living Planet Report 2014: Species and Spaces, People and Places*. Edited by Richard McLellan, Leena Iyengar, Barney Jeffries, and Natasja Oerlemans. Gland, Switzerland: World Wide Fund for Nature.

Wray, Matt. 2006. *Not Quite White: White Trash and the Boundaries of Whiteness*. Durham, NC: Duke University Press.

Wynne, Brian. 1996. "May the Sheep Safely Graze? A Reflexive View of the Expert-Lay Knowledge Divide." In *Risk, Environment, and Modernity: Towards a New Ecology*, edited by Scott Lash, Bronislaw Szerszynski, and Brian Wynne, 44–83. London: Sage.

Yamaguchi, Mari. 2011. "Can Web-Savvy Activist Moms Change Japan?" *Times of India*, December 29.

"Yamuna Reduced to Sewer Canal Again." 2014. *Times of India*, October 13.

Yang, Manuel. 2011. "People Who Transcend Catastrophe: Connecting the Radiation-

Measuring Movement to People's Movements around the World." *Japan—Fissures in the Planetary Apparatus*, November 21.

Yoneyama, Lisa. 1999. *Hiroshima Traces: Time, Space, and the Dialectics of Memory.* Berkeley: University of California Press.

Young, Zoe. 2004. "Painful Entry for Poland into the EU: Zoe Young Travels through Poland to Find That Its Farmers Dread Integration with the EU." *Down to Earth*, February 29, 49–52.

Zhang, J. 2005. "FDA Proposes Wider Feed Ban to Bolster Mad-Cow Defenses." *Wall Street Journal*, October 5, D13.

INDEX

Conway, Erik, 117, 118
Cornelius, Vickie, 65
corporeal intimacy, 7, 22, 106, 112, 114, 129, 178, 182
cradle-to-cradle (c2c) design, 196
creationism, 118, 209n13
Cree hunters, 9, 79
Critical Events (Das), 76
culture/nature divide, 9, 10
Curie, Marie, 108
Curie, Pierre, 108

"damage by rumor," 77, 83, 204n9
Das, Veena, 7, 76
Davis, Susan, 162, 212n18
Debord, Guy, 162
"Deep Food," 66
Deepwater Horizon spill, 16, 17
Descola, Philippe, 9, 13, 32
Dickens, Charles, 183, 184
Dinétah, 194, 195
dirt, 189
disinformation campaigns, 115–19
DNA barcoding, 45, 46, 202n12
Dodson, Lisa, 207n40
Doherty, Peter, 107
dreams, 1–3, 5, 11, 188, 194, 199nn1,2

"eco" building projects, 139, 140, 207n34
"eco-functional nature," 8
eco-intimacies, 17–20, 32, 33; Grand Venice, 165; varieties of, 19–24
ecological damage, 3, 6, 8, 11, 214n24; automobiles and, 182, 185–89, 192, 193; bio-intimacy and, 79, 80; citizen science, 84–94; Deepwater Horizon spill, 16, 17; economic precarity, 178, 179; environmental justice movement, 14–16, 33, 207n44; Fukushima Daiichi nuclear power plant, 21, 33, 75–78, 81–83, 128, 204n11, 212n23; as global self-experiment, 111; Grand Venice, 174; industrial chemical pollutants, 152, 169, 170, 182, 183; interior/exterior divide, 31; international protocols, 180, 181; intimate engagement with, 178; maternalist rhetoric, 99, 100, 207n44; postcolonial discourse and, 189, 214n19; quest narratives, 186, 187; sixth mass extinction, 178; smoke, as sym-

bol, 183, 184; stopgaps, 178; toxic exposure, 78–81, 86–95; water, 151, 152, 168–70, 212n23
ecological intimacy, 4, 10
Edison Electrical Institute (EEI), 115
Edmond, Gary, 117
Electric Networked Vehicles, 186
Elkins, James, 201n18
embodied empiricism, 22; bio-intimacy and, 119; body as sensory apparatus, 105–15, 123–28, 209n9; citizen science, 120–32; climate skepticism, 22, 114, 115, 120–31; corporate spin and, 115–20
embodied intimacy, 4, 5, 10, 11, 23, 31
embodied process, 187–89
"Empiricism without the Senses: How the Instrument Replaced the Eye" (Gal and Chen-Morris), 112, 113
Engels, Friedrich, 183
Environmentality: Technologies of Government and the Making of Subjects (Agrawal), 13
environmental justice movement, 14–16, 33, 207n44
Exposed: The Toxic Chemistry of Everyday Products (Schapiro), 80

"factish," 82
Factories in the Field (McWilliams), 61
factory farms, 20, 61
Federation of Noida Residents Welfare Association (FONRWA), 151
Ferry, Elizabeth Emma, 6, 10
Finan, Timothy, 129
folly, 137
food chain, 20, 40–67, 202n13
food safety, 44–46, 203n14, 204n7; alphanumeric identification markers, 55–58; "Deep Food," 66; nationality of animals, 51–53; Oneida Indian Nation, 64–67, 203n18; poultry, 47, 59; routes of transmission, 49, 52; "storied food," 40, 41; unique individual identifier, 51–64; warranting, 49–60. *See also* bovine spongiform encephalopathy; National Animal Identification System
Ford, Bill, 189
Ford, Henry, 179, 184–88, 198, 213n12
Fordism, 178, 184, 213n7, 213n12
foreshadowing, 3, 4, 177, 178, 199n3

Igoe, Jim, 8
The Incidental Steward: Reflections on Citizen Science (Busch), 123
Indian Country Today (periodical), 3, 199n1
indigenous knowledge, 8, 9, 64–67, 194–96, 215n26
industrial capitalism, 8, 10, 179, 186, 213n6
industrial chemicals, 152, 169, 170, 182–85
Inescapable Ecologies: A History of Environment, Disease, and Knowledge (Nash), 78
Information Council on the Environment (ICE), 115–18, 209n10
Ingold, Tim, 8, 9, 29–31
In Search of Yamuna: Reflections on a River Lost (Jain), 165, 168
interspecies accommodation, 30, 31
Intertribal Bison Cooperative, 66
intimacy, 7–10; banking and, 42, 202n5; corporeal, 7, 106, 112, 114, 122, 129, 178, 182; ecological, 4, 10; embodied, 4, 5, 10, 11, 23, 31; worldly, 3, 4. *See also* affective intimacy
intimate animacy, 16
intimate engagement, 14, 15, 72, 106, 178
"Italy in India," 140–48, 160

Jain, Sarandha, 165, 168
jali screen, 137, 142, 160, 161
James, William, 29
Jefferson, Thomas, 123, 201n20
The Jungle (Sinclair), 61
"junk science," 105, 117

Kazin, Michael, 125
Kepler, Johannes, 113, 114
Kidspotter, 201n1
Kodama, Tatsuhiko, 84
Kohn, Eduardo, 28, 29
kore (life force), 8
Kosako, Toshiso, 89

labor market insecurity, 179, 180, 205n17
Laclau, Ernesto, 125
Lam, Tong, 199
Lane, Carrie, 179
Lansing, J. Stephen, 155
Last Man question, 177
Las Vegas, 32, 138, 160
Latour, Bruno, 13, 82, 200n11

Lavin, Chad, 41
Legoland, 201n1
Le Nôtre, André, 201n20
Limbert, Mandana, 6, 10
Lines in the Water (Orlove), 155
Lionnet, Françoise, 13
livestock tracking. *See* National Animal Identification System; RFID
Lovelock, James, 122, 171
Lowe, Lisa, 199n5
Loy, David, 15

Macau, 138, 160
Madrigal, Alexis, 111
Malaby, Thomas, 166
Mann, Michael, 114, 120, 121
Marcus, George, 126
Marres, Noortje, 25
Marshall, Barry, 109
Martin, Emily, 15
Marx, Leo, 31
Masco, Joseph, 81, 202n7, 210n24, 212n3, 213n11
Massumi, Brian, 44
"May the Sheep Safely Graze?" (Wynne), 124
Mazzarella, William, 185
McKay, Mabel, 24–29
McLuhan, Marshall, 194
McNeill, David, 88, 89
McWilliams, Carey, 61
Mehra, Akhil, 108
MeineKleineFarm.org, 40, 41
Menzies, Charles, 200n7
Mercer, David, 117
merchants of doubt, 117, 126, 132
Merleau-Ponty, Maurice, 120
metamateriality, 202n9
MEXT, 76, 99
microbiome, 15–17, 200nn10,11
Miyazaki, Hayao, 89
Mochizuki, Iori, 33, 79
monsoon season, 122, 137, 153, 155, 166, 173
Mooney, Chris, 118
The Moral Underground (Dodson), 207n40
Morton, Timothy, 15, 26, 130
Muehlmann, Shaylih, 155
Murakami, Haruki, 84, 205n14
mutant ecologies, 81, 183, 213n11

technostruggle (*continued*)
  crowd-sourced radiation maps, 92, 93;
    post-3.11, 94, 95; sovereignty and, 94–97;
    supply chain and, 91, 92
Thames Barrier, 163, 164
theme-parked nature, 162, 163, 212n18
Thompson, Damian, 118
thyroid cysts, 98
Tokyo Electric Power Company (TEPCO),
    73–83, 92, 203n4
Tokyo Hackerspace, 85, 86
Tönnies, Ferdinand, 43
toxic exposure, 78–81, 84–95, 204n7, 204n11
traditional ecological knowledge (TEC), 195,
    196
*Traditional Ecological Knowledge and Natural
    Resource Management* (Menzies), 200n7
Trust Us, We're Experts! (Rampton and Stau-
    ber), 125, 126
Tudge, Collin, 27
Turner, Terry, 119, 201n18
Tylor, Edward, 4, 26, 27

Union of Concerned Scientists, 129, 130
unique individual identifier, 51–64
United Nations Intergovernmental Panel on
    Climate Change (IPCC), 117
USDA: animal identification, 43, 55–66; bio-
    security, 44–48; campaigns, 48, 59, 60;
    commingling, 63

Venice, replicas of, 137, 138, 160. *See also*
    Grand Venice
Vibrant Matter (Bennett), 26
Viveiros de Castro, Eduardo, 28, 29, 201n18
volatile organic compounds (VOCS), 182, 185

Walker, Harry, 201
Walkoff, Friedrich, 108
warranting, 49–60; embodiment, 49, 50, 202;
    Oneida Indian Nation, 64–66
water: *acequias*, 165, 166; carnivalesque and,

168–74; citizen science, 151; class and, 172–
74; culture and, 155; deserts, 32, 138; Fukushima Daiichi reactors, 212n23; Grand
Venice and, 148–51, 153–56; hydraulic citizenship, 158; industrial chemical pollutants, 152, 169, 170, 190; knowledge of, 18;
monsoon season, 122, 137, 153, 155, 166, 173;
as motif, 162, 163; National Capital Region,
137, 152, 153; Noida water supply, 135, 151–53,
211n9; oasis, 159; play and, 137, 150, 155,
159, 163–66, 172–74; politics of, 137, 153–56,
158; pollution, 152, 169, 170, 190; sewage
treatment, 75, 152, 153, 158, 159, 169–72; as
spectacle, 31, 32, 135, 136, 155–74; Thames
barrier, 163, 164. *See also* Grand Venice;
Yamuna River
weather and climate, 120, 121, 129
West, Michael, 64
West, Paige, 8, 13, 211n15
"What I'm Talking about When I'm Talking
    about My Baskets" (Sarris), 24
*What's Gotten into Us? Staying Healthy in a
    Toxic World* (Jenkins), 80
Where the River Ends (Muehlmann), 155
Who Goes First? (Altman), 109
Witherspoon, Roger, 206n30
Wolfe, Charles, 114
Woolf, Malya, 197
Wynne, Brian, 124

Xie, Shang-Ping, 121

Yamakawa, Yukio, 109, 110, 209
Yamuna River, 32, 138, 140, 151, 174, 195, 197;
    pollution of, 137, 152, 168–72, 190, 192, 212;
    *In Search of Yamuna: Reflections on a River
    Lost*, 165, 168
Yang, Manuel, 87, 88
yes-and thinking, 155–59, 163

Zhou, Shengxian, 193